Vladimir Medinskiy

MYTHS ABOUT RUSSIA

AD VERBUM

Published with the support of the Institute
for Literary Translation, Russia

Glagoslav Publications

Myths about Russia
by Vladimir Medinskiy

© 2011, Vladimir Medinskiy

Translated by Christopher Culver

Edited by Camilla Stein

© 2015, Glagoslav Publications, United Kingdom

Glagoslav Publications Ltd
88-90 Hatton Garden
EC1N 8PN London
United Kingdom

www.glagoslav.com

ISBN: 978-1-78267-087-2

This book is in copyright. No part of this publication
may be reproduced, stored in a retrieval system or transmitted
in any form or by any means without the prior permission
in writing of the publisher, nor be otherwise circulated
in any form of binding or cover other than that in which
it is published without a similar condition,
including this condition, being imposed
on the subsequent purchaser.

In writing this book, I am indebted to my editor, the scholar and professor Dr. Andrei Mikhailovich Burovsky and my technical Gennady Vladimirovich Potapov, as well as the journalist Andrei Nazarov.

CONTENTS

CHAPTER 1. Foreword 7

CHAPTER 2. Myth 1: On criminality, the merchant's word and official corruption 11
   The roots of the myth 11
   The merchants and soldiers of Ancient Rus'................. 16
      Merchantry... 16
      Seafarers and jus litoris.................................. 19
      Oral agreements 22
   Locks and keys 27
   The aristocracy 30
   Officialdom — a striking trend 34

CHAPTER 3. Myth 2: On widespread dirtiness 41
   The roots of the myth 41
   Characteristics of Russian plumbing 42
      Bathing customs 42
   The Slavic god Bannik 47
   The holiday of Ivan Kupala 49
   City life 51
      From antiquity to the present day 51
      Cities in Rus' 55
      Epidemics 57
      Dramatic population growth 60

CHAPTER 4. Myth 3: A tradition of serfdom and lack of democracy 63
   The roots of the myth 63
   Was ancient Rus' a democracy? 67
      The beginning of the Eastern Slavs' statehood 67
      The rule of law 72
      When did the popular assembly come to an end? 74
   Democracy in Russia under Muscovy 75
      Local democracy 76
      Free peasants and serfdom 78

The serfs of Muscovy	79
Free peasants in Muscovy	83
Moscow bureaucrats and the "staff elevator"	85
Assemblies of the lands — the Russian parliament of the 16th century	87
Electing of tsars	89
Democracy in the Russian Empire	92
An attempt at an aristocratic constitution	93
The 1734 project of emancipating the serfs	96
Social welfare	112

CHAPTER 5. Myth 4: Russia as a prison for peoples 116

The roots of the myth	117
The road to an empire	121
The ruler of the world	121
The Sepoy Mutiny and the Fate of Shamil	122
Nationality means nothing	126
The Russian Empire	130
How it conquered its territories	130

CHAPTER 6. Myth 5: Russia as a threat 169

The roots of the myth	170
No such myth in the days of Rus'	172
Rus': aggressor or victim?	172
An important rule of Russian history	179
The rule of writing history	180
The birth and death of the myth	181
"Orsha propaganda"	181
Cold War myths	222
What does one's historical memory say?	222

NOTES 231

CHAPTER I
Foreword

> There is no people about which so many lies, absurdities and slander have been made up as the Russian people.
>
> — *Catherine the Great, née German princess Sophie Friederike Auguste von Anhalt-Zerbst-Dornburg*

A great many books have been published in the West, with various degrees of impartiality and historical credibility that look at not only the history of Russia but also what has been called the Russians' "national character". Unfortunately, in such literature one can hardly hear the side of the Russians themselves. It is precisely for that reason that we have decided to offer the English-speaking reader an overview of the opinions — that have developed over the centuries — about the Russians, their strong points and their flaws, an overview made, as it were, "in the first person".

Every country has a certain image in the eyes of its citizens and of foreigners. Swedes call themselves a calm, reasonable people for whom democratic values, social equality, and nature are foremost. The English are convinced that their nation is one of the most civilized, if one is speaking of good manners and knowing how to carry oneself in society. They consider themselves to be law-abiding, polite, magnanimous and gentlemanly, steadfast and just. They are also extremely proud of their self-deprecating sense of humor, holding it to be unquestionable proof of their magnanimity.

The Germans consider themselves to be a humble, simple and honest people. They are to some degree Romantics, to some degree philosophers, and they are undoubtedly a highly educated nation.

Also Russians have an image of themselves. Russians consider themselves to be a proud and hard-working people with a sense of *joie de vivre*, able to survive in difficult circumstances, and they are also complicated, spiritual, and creative.

Unfortunately, as can be seen in practice, a people's self-identification sometimes has nothing to do with how those in neighboring countries perceive them. Just think of how many myths have arisen about Russia and the Russian people! Among these myths, some are fairly reflective of reality, while others are silly, uninformed, or even completely ridiculous. For a long time, especially during the Cold War, stereotypes about Russia came down to bears, vodka, ballet, and icons. Today these myths have slightly changed, and now Russia is seen as a country ruled by the mafia, where crime and criminals flourish, and drunkenness is widespread. If one trusts the results of studies carried out by the North Sweden European Office under the title of *Våga satsa på Ryssland!* (Don't Be Afraid to Do Business in Russia), a Russian person's working day begins as follows: they wake up in the morning, play the accordion, drink a glass of vodka, eat porridge, and head off to work. There is still another cliché, that Russia is cold and terribly dirty.

According to sociologists, a myth is a firm idea arising in the depths of individual or mass consciousness and making one's own desires true or making the impossible possible. A myth is the self-delusion of a person or a nation, a freely-held individual or collective illusion. In a practical sense myths, or rather stereotypes, are supposed to lessen one's discomfort in encountering a foreign culture, they describe people's expectations and the rituals they perform that allow them to relate to what is "foreign". However, myths also prevent us from looking impartially at how things really are; myths lead to mistakes and sometimes to tragic consequences.

The publicist and social activist Ivan Solonevich wrote in his book *National Monarchy* (1991) about how German "Soviet experts" looked at the USSR before the Second World War: "The background of all foreign understanding about Russia has been set by Russian literature, such as Oblomov and Manilov, useless people, poor people, idiots and barefoot people... Against this background emigration has left its own mark, first the pre-World War I revolutionary emigration and then the post-war counter-revolutionary emigration. They both told lies. The pre-World War I emigrants went on about Asiatic despotism, which reduced the nation to miserable slavery, the post-war emigration went about an Asiatic barbarity among the people who tore down their aristocratic estates, which were the only toehold of European culture on the vastness of the Tartar steppes." By depicting Russia as a "giant with feet of clay", Hitler made the same mistake that Napoleon did, with the same predictable result.

The history of Russia is inseparable from the history of Europe. Therefore, in considering various events that lay the foundation for the emergence of a myth, we could not help but trace historical parallels, we could not help but show how similar events served as a source of pride to one nation and shame to another. However, this book is not historical research, especially since, as one man quipped, "History is sometimes what never happened, written by people who were never there", and historical evidence tends to be highly contradictory.

Let's leave history to historians. This doesn't mean that I as an author don't care about historical accuracy, but *Myths about Russia* is historical journalism. In this book I have relied on famous works by Russian historians as well as the testimony of foreign observers, but the facts described in these sources have been chosen according to a certain sequence and from a certain point of view.

Alexandre Dumas wrote that for him, history is only a nail that he hung his paintings on. I will carry this idea further: for me history is only the frame for the painting. The main events in my book are not happening in the distant past but right now, in our own minds, and beyond them in the social consciousness of Russia and the world.

Let's try to figure out what the origins are of myths about Russia, let's try to evaluate the facts with the impartial view of an interested and curious reader. I would be happy to hear what you think on the forum at the address: forum.medinskiy.ru

Vladimir Medinskiy

CHAPTER 2
Myth 1: On criminality, the merchant's word and official corruption

> Criminality in earlier times meant any illegal action: arson, pimping, forgery of documents, crimes against the state, etc.
>
> —*Brockhaus and Efron Encyclopedic, 1892*

It is often thought that a general criminality, corruption and bribery has distinguished the Russians since the formation of the Moscow state in the 15th century, and that no one in the country has ever challenged this. The fact that Russia hasn't been completely ransacked means only one thing: it's too rich a country. Any outbreak of corruption is nothing new, only the continuation of a venerable national tradition. But is this really true?

The roots of the myth

As in practically every case, the genesis of this myth goes back to the accounts of foreigners who visited Russia in the 16th to the 18th centuries. "They have a strong tendency to do evil, they readily lie and steal," claims Barberini. [1] "They are distinguished by a deceitful character. Muscovites are considered more sneaky and deceitful than all the other Russians," Siegmund Freiherr von Herberstein was convinced. [2] Naturally there's no sense in asking who exactly "considered" them more sneaky and deceitful than other Russians.

Some certainty was brought to this matter by the German adventurer Heinrich von Staden [3], who had become an officer of the Tsar's political police. Staden assumed that the merchants and businessmen of Muscovy "lie constantly and readily cheat people," that one should not loan them money as they will not repay it, and any valuables which one leaves unattended for even a second will be immediately stolen. But as the Russian saying goes, "The good deeds a man does are not talked about while his bad deeds become widely known," and the myth about the ineradicable criminality of the Russians came to be repeated again and again, without caring about the grounds for it. We recall however that Siegmund Freiherr von Herberstein wrote his *Notes on Muscovite Affairs* after he had spent a total of nine months in the country as part of a diplomatic mission, acting as an intermediary in peace negotiations between Moscow and the Grand Duchy of Lithuania, in 1517 and 1526, and both times his efforts proved unsuccessful. As far as Heinrich von Staden is concerned, he came to Muscovy and talked a lot of rubbish to the local officials about his own war exploits and his great political importance at the finest courts of Europe. Staden left Muscovy with several business partners' shares, which he shamelessly admits in his writings. In his assessment of Staden's work, the Russian historian Vladimir Korbin notes that "The author of this account is so devoid of morality that he feels no shame about his most depraved deeds." Meanwhile, there are completely opposed accounts by other foreigners on the moral qualities of the Russians — nothing even slightly resembling the stream of hostility and accusations of criminality that arose after the 18th century.

CHAPTER 2

Scandinavians visiting the old state of Rus' spoke highly of certain qualities of the Russians that, in their view, they themselves lacked. Russians are depicted as honest and reliable people, who can be taken at their word, whom one could entrust with large amounts of money and who know how to do business — on a large scale and sensibly. [4] Muslim accounts also say this about Russians. [5]

The 17th century was the height of the glorious age of discovery, a transition from the Middle Ages to the modern era, when European countries established their influence over other continents. By this time the New World, India and China, Australia and New Zealand had been discovered by Europeans. Following on Portugal, France, England and, slightly later, Holland became colonial empires too. There was a marked increase in the flow of gold and precious metals brought to metropolitan centers. During this time, there was not so great an increase in the production of goods. In the 18th century European society underwent a crisis that affected the majority of countries on the continent and impacted the economies of many of them.

A revolutionary overthrow of feudal states and the development of a capitalist manufacturing began in Western Europe. At the same time as the English bourgeois revolution, revolutionary movements arose in France, Germany, Italy, Russia, Poland, and other countries. However, feudalism remained on the European continent. For an entire century the rulers of these states would continue to apply a feudalistic policy of "stabilization". Nearly everywhere throughout Europe feudal or absolute monarchies were preserved, and the aristocracy remained the dominant class of society.

Absolute monarchy was strengthened also in Russia. At the same time, Russia in the 17th century continued to conquer the vast spaces of Eastern Europe and Siberia. The 1654 union of Ukraine with Russia dates from this era. The political position of Russia became stronger. In the 17th century Russia rose up in international relations as a great power, extending from the Dnieper in the west to the Pacific Ocean in the east. The powerful Russian state turned into a serious competitor in trade as well, as a result of which the great tradition arose of complaining about the difficulty of doing business in Russia. As usual, the myth was not without foundation, but the reality was distorted like in a funhouse mirror, taking on a truly epic character. There was a basis for the myth: together with the strengthening of absolute rule, the positions of state officials were also strengthened, which led to more abuse of power.

Alas, the myth about every Russian being a criminal emerged not without some help from Russian writers. Russian classics are full of stories about money-grubbing, thievery, and embezzlement. Let's take, for example, the novels of Leo Tolstoy: the criminality of his characters is depicted as something commonplace, as a matter of course. In the *Sevastopol Sketches* many places are simply frightening to read. While some Russians heroically defend Sebastopol during the Crimean War, spilling their blood on the ramparts, others calmly embezzle funds meant for the army to buy food, clothing and weapons. They steal to such an unbelievable degree that it just takes one's breath away.

Also Stepan Oblonsky in Tolstoy's *Anna Karenina* was hired on one condition, that he would not steal much. Such a man was sought after — he may know nothing of the workings of the railway, for as long as he did not have a habit of stealing.

In Alexander Ostrovsky's *A Profitable Position* the whole plot turns on the fact that the main character, full of lofty ideals, doesn't want to accept bribes, and the people around him think him an idiot. They put pressure on him, and when his beloved wife threatens to leave him, he gives up and goes to his father-in-law, asking him to find him a "cushy place". [6] However, by that time his father-in-law gets caught in the act and is disgraced.

In Ostrovsky's works all the wealth of the merchants is either obtained by taking some off the top, or through other dishonest means. His characters declare fictional bankruptcies, marry women from wealthy families, expropriate orphans' funds, or make shop clerks cheat their employers. In works of this great

CHAPTER 2

Russian dramatist there's not a single honest entrepreneur who would make money in an honest way. For Ostrovsky, a merchant is a *zhulik*, a swindler.

There's no need to prove something that's obvious, so I won't try to convince the reader that hard work is the basis for every single fortune created out of nothing, whether large or small. That said, if the estates of Ryabushinksky, Morozov, Mamontov, and Tretyakov had been built up solely through scheming and cheating, there would not have been such a huge development in the Russian economy in the second half of the 19th century. But it is as if the classic Russian authors made an agreement: if someone is at the court, he's embezzling from the treasury; if someone is a public servant, he's taking bribes; and if someone is a merchant, he's a swindler and thief. If we take this position found in Russian literature seriously, we end up concluding that "they steal" is really the most honest, picture-perfect definition of the essence of Russian life. But as we all know, the task of literature is to "lance the boils of society". As the noted Russian poet Yevgeny Yevtushenko said, "A poet in Russia is more than just a poet." The poet (and the writer, we might add) in Russia is the foremost of all a citizen.

A poet in Russia is more than just a poet.
[Only those have been destined to be born poets in Russia
in whom a proud spirit of citizenship wanders
and does not find comfort or rest.]

In this way the myth was formed about the extraordinary perennial criminality of the Russians, and about the fact that among the people themselves there has never been a distinction between an honest, hard-working man and a thief.

But let us look at Russian history impartially, let us look at how Russians use to live, and we will see that Russians have a lot to learn from their forefathers about simple honesty.

The merchants and soldiers of Ancient Rus'

> In Novgorod, like everywhere in Russia, one can safely leave their gold or other valuables outside or in a tavern.
>
> — *Adam of Bremen, German chronicler*

Merchantry

It was the old Russian city of Novgorod that traded the most with the cities of Europe. The people of Novgorod not only invited merchants to them, but they regularly sailed the sea themselves to Denmark, Lübeck, and Schleswig and founded a colony of their own on the Swedish island of Gotland.

It was not just Novgorod, however. Many lands and towns of Rus' carried out a lively trade with Europe. As late as the Mongol invasion of the 12th century, trade agreements were signed between Smolensk and the German cities of Bremen, Dortmund, Groningen, Münster, Lübeck, and Riga. Trade with Germany went through Bohemia and Poland, through Galich and Lviv. [7]

The chronicle writer Thietmar von Merseburg (975–1018) emphasized the wealth of Rus' and its large turnover. He considered Russians to be decent people and reliable business partners.

The chronicler Adam of Bremen in his *History of the Archbishops of Hamburg–Bremen* called Kiev the rival of Constantinople and the glory of Christendom. He described Kiev as a city where the inhabitants behaved righteously and did not violate the Ten Commandments — even the pagan population there did not steal or assault people.

The *Annals* of Lambert of Hersfeld were written around 1077. They contain many details about Rus' and speak of it only in glowing terms. The Russians are considered to be a highly upright people and what they say can be relied on. It is said that this is what distinguishes the Russians from the Scandinavian pagans and the peoples of the south of Europe. [8]

German traders often visited Smolensk, and some of them lived there on a long-term basis. They even had their own church there.

In 1187 the emperor Fredrick I of the German-dominated Holy Roman Empire gave the Russians and Dutch special rights to trade in Lübeck. By doing this he favored Russian merchants over those from other German cities and the Flemish and Danes. Why was this? It was because "the Russians can be trusted due to their exceptional honesty and goodness."

In the 13th century the free cities of northern Europe founded the Hanseatic League (from the Middle German word *Hanse* 'association') for defending trade and traders from feudal regimes and piracy. At the end of the 14th century the Hanseatic League included over a hundred cities and controlled the majority of trade on a European scale. The trade and financial operations of the Hanseatic League were based at its centers in Bruges (Flanders), London, Bergen (Norway), Venice and, Novgorod. The capital of the Hanseatic League was Lübeck, which was the primary point of loading and unloading on the overland routes and waterways from the Baltic to the North Sea. Novgorod was located at the beginning of the trade routes that connected the Baltic with the Black Sea and the Caspian, and Eastern Europe with Western Europe.

It was the Hanseatic League who determined the flow of goods and raw materials across the whole of Europe, acting as a middleman for all the centers of craftsmen and traders.

From Italy came silk and woven fabrics; from Flanders, England, and northern Germany textiles, from southern Germany, England, and Scandinavia metals; from Northern Germany and western France salt; from Sweden honey; from Norway fish. From the countries of Eastern Europe merchants brought wax, honey, and furs.

The German cities were the center of the Hanseatic League, and German merchants were the major players, the middlemen.

Not everyone who wanted to trade with other countries was able to, only those who received special permission, the privileges of a city or guild. The Hanseatic League's policy in every country was a simple one: a German monopoly, a system of permissions and restrictions. The Hanseatic League put strong pressure on English, Flemish, and Dutch merchants. Was this simply fear of competition? It wasn't just that: the Hanseatic League believed for some reason that the English and Dutch didn't know how to take their partners' interests into account, they didn't closely collaborate but instead thought only about themselves.

During this time the Hanseatic League had a monopoly on trade with Novgorod. Only members of the League had the right to learn Russian, trade with the Russians and — most importantly — loan the Russians money or merchandise. Why was this? It turns out that the Russians were very reliable partners, they always repaid loans with interest. It was considered a lucrative enterprise to loan Russians money.

The Hanseatic League passed a law that visiting Russian traders could not be arrested in any town of the League. This might seem strange. Really, why was this? The Middle Ages were a harsh era. If a court found that a merchant could not repay his debts, the sentence could even be the death penalty, torture with red-hot irons, or cutting off an arm or leg. Debtors' prison was a stone enclosure or a pit dug into the earth, where the debtor was doomed to rot. These are by far not the worst things that could happen under the medieval justice system dealing with debt collection. [9]

Only the small-scale Russian merchants went without punishment or torture. They would send them home, to Novgorod, so that they could start up some enterprise and over time repay the debt.

This rule in the Hanseatic League did not apply to anyone else, neither the Germans, nor the English, Swedes, Dutch, or Flemish. It was only a Russian privilege.

There is one more important fact. The trading posts of the

Hanseatic League were based in different cities, among them Bergen in Norway and Novgorod. The senior merchants at the trading posts kept careful watch over the behavior of their employees. It was of great importance that adult males never kindle a romance with the local girls. Why this was the case is not clear to us today, but it was strictly enforced.

In city of Bergen, the second-largest city in Norway after Oslo, there is a famous Hanseatic wharf. It has been recognized as a UNESCO World Heritage Site. On this waterfront a building has been preserved that served as the trading post of the Hanseatic League, and a room where German clerks would have slept. The clerks' beds were of very peculiar design. Resembling a trough or coffin, they were specially made so that no matter how much one wished it, it was impossible to get another person into the bed.

Only in one city were the beds for Hanseatic League clerks made differently, i.e. normally, and this was in Novgorod. It was thought that it was impossible to bed Novgorodian maidens without marrying them first.

Seafarers and jus litoris

In the history of various peoples there are quite numerous examples of what today would be considered robbery or raiding being something commonplace. The heroes of the Homeric epics, brave Greek seafarers, sailed the whole world of their era, whether to trade or raid other ships on the open sea or seaside towns. Almost every seafarer of the Middle Ages did the same. Merchants knew how to fight with swords in order to fend off robbers and savage tribes. They readily drew their swords if they saw an opportunity to easily seize someone else's goods.

> That sea raiding (and robbery in general) was a common occurrence may be shown by one of the stories of the origin of the so-called Sigtuna Gate at Novgorod's St. Sophia Cathedral. This was named

after the town of Sigtuna in Sweden, an important trade center, where merchants came from even as far as Novgorod. Even in Sigtuna the gate had arrived through robbery. They were made in the 12th century by German craftsmen from Magdeburg (it is for this reason that the gate is also called the Magdeburg Gate) for the Cathedral of the Blessed Virgin Mary in Płock. The men of Sigtuna took hold of this gate, however, and in 1187 during a sea campaign the gate was seized by the Novgorodians and the town burned to the ground.

According to a different version of the story, Sigtuna was captured and destroyed by either the Karelians or the Estonians, and the gate appeared in Novgorod in the 14th century. According to Vasily Tatishchev, in 1336 in the Cathedral of St. Sophia a copper gate was erected, which the archbishop Vasily had "brought from Germany after buying at great price".

But one thing commonplace in Europe, even during an age of cruel customs, was seen as unacceptable for Russian merchants. We are talking here about the so-called "right of shore", the *jus litoris*.

The concept of the *jus litoris* arose in the mists of history and, with the development of seafaring, spread over many coastal areas. An official rule was established that people living on the coast could take anything growing along their shore, as well as whatever remained of ships that ran aground, their cargo, and generally anything that the waves cast up on the beach. From the time that this rule was founded, the lives of sailors and passengers and the safety of the cargo was threatened not only by the raging elements, but also by any shore they turned to for safety. Even people who were rescued — the passengers, sailors and their captain — could theoretically become the property of the lord of the land. He had the right to kill them, enslave them, or hold them for ransom.

With the rise of the Roman Empire this right passed to the state authorities, and after the fall of the Roman Empire it passed to the feudal lords of coastal regions. In the Middle

Ages the feudal authorities and even powerful monarchs felt no shame in considering the fruits of *jus litoris* a source of income. According to the maritime law declared in 1681 by Louis XIV of France, all property rescued from shipwreck passed into the royal treasury. A feudal lord on the coast gave up this "legal right" only if the sailors paid him a determined sum.

In the 12th century the navy of King Richard the Lionheart set off on a crusade, but part of his fleet was swept off towards Cyprus by a storm. According to the general *jus litoris* custom then in force throughout Europe, the English navy that had landed on the coast of Cyprus seeking rescue, was confiscated and used for the locals' own purposes. The knights on board were arrested and a ransom was demanded for their release. The concept of *jus litoris* was abolished in Italy only in the 12th century, while in England and Flanders it was abolished only a century later. And this was only in some cases, i.e. for the ships of the rich and powerful Hanseatic League. This was done, I presume, not as much for humane reasons as to guarantee their own safety: it was dangerous to raid the Hanseatic League, their cargo and passengers, as the cities of the League could put their resources together and raise a formidable army.

> The *jus litoris* reached its height in the Middle Ages. The desire for easy takings pushed people to all manner of evildoing and plotting. Robbers destroyed lighthouses and navigational markers, set up fake lighthouses in places treacherous for ships to pass, and bribed pilots to lead ships to shallow waters or places where it would be hard for the crew to defend themselves from attack. It sometimes happened that marauders on dark nights would light a torch, hang it around a horse's neck, and tie the horse's legs so that it would limp about. Sailors on board a passing ship would think that this was the light of another passing and thus they would run aground on the rocks. The waves would faithfully conceal any traces of the tragedy and the criminals would get away scot-free. As the best time for such undertakings was on pitch-black nights, robbers considered the moon their greatest

energy. This is why people engaged in this enterprise were called moon-haters, hobblers, beach-combers, and other derogatory names.

With the further development of trade many countries enacted laws that would outlaw such crimes and oblige one to save people and cargo from foundered ships. However, cases of piracy along the coasts continued until the mid 19th century. After the opening of the Suez Canal in 1869, the expansion of ship traffic along the eastern coast of Africa and the Somalian littoral led to an increase in shipwrecks. These disasters often ended in the complete looting of the ships and the slaughter of the crew and passengers. The merchant fleet of Great Britain suffered the worst. To end this barbarity, the English were forced to make an agreement with the leadership of the country and pay fifteen thousand pounds annually as "compensation".

The history of sailing has shown an opposing tendency to this day. In the age when *jus litoris* had spread over many settlements along the coasts and rivers, the Russians, and the Slavs in general, never engaged in such affairs. This is attested by the Rus' — Byzantine Treaty of 911, the first of its kind, and also the agreements that Novgorod made with Riga and the Baltic coast in the 12th and 13th centuries. According to these agreements, the local inhabitants should "protect ships and their cargo, send them back to their Christian lands, and accompany them through any dangerous passages until they reach a safe place." Any abuse of foreign sailors was treated as a great crime. In the time of Peter the Great, laws were enacted according to which any cargo and ship property, whether Russian or foreign, rescued within the boundaries of the Russian Empire, would fall under the "protection of his imperial majesty" and could not be touched.

Oral agreements

The honest word of a merchant... It's a national trait that speaks to Russian businessmen, as well the character of the Russian people. If one searches for a "typical Russian", someone embodying the soul of the nation, it would be those making oral agreements without insisting on the payment of security, those who settle contracts for large amounts with only a handshake. In Russia since the 17th century, merchants who knew how to bring their capital together would found associations by issuing shares. Such associations, in which everyone's share was taken into account and everyone drew dividends according to their shares, differed from Europe's joint-stock companies only in one way: they were less formal.

In the 17th century the following businessmen made huge amounts through joint-stock companies in the salt and fish industries: Grigori Nikitnikov, Yaroslav Patokin, Danila Pankratyev, Nadeya Sveteshnikov, Vasili Shorin, Ostafi Filatyev, and many others under them.

In the 17th century any free man could become a merchant, and they formed over half of the population.

Russian serfs in the 17th century "could do whatever they wished with their plots of land: sell them, pawn them, give them away as gifts, present them as a dowry, and hand them down to their heirs, whether in whole or in part."

Here too this peasant capitalism extended so far that a kind of joint-stock company would emerge, where every man had a share and could do with it what he wished: sell it, rent it out, buy up the shares of other members, or cash out his shares.

At this time in Europe entrepreneurs would register a new company as a legal person, write down the minutes of meetings and issue shares. They would hire lawyer's offices to draw up and safeguard their documents, stock traders would follow the company's fortunes closely, seeing how the company's shares went up or down, how this or that merchandise was selling.

Generally speaking, from a present-day perspective this seems to us rather modern and methodological, but the fact that they would run their affairs under such detailed regulation means, perhaps, only one thing: was this all just protection from being swindled? Let us admit, hand on heart, what do we need all those legal formalities for today in our modern age? Why do we need a vast army of notaries and lawyers, who needs tons of paper contracts, signatures, and seals? Of course, on one hand this is done in order to not forget what one has agreed to, to clearly put down what was promised by each side. But this is not the most important thing. If we were talking only about people's tendency to forget things, 99% of contracts would be written down in simple language — and then millions of lawyers around the world would go starving.

Alas, all the complicated legalese in our time has never eradicated fraud.

On the other hand, the merchants of old Russia rather bothered with writing the minutes of meetings and other hassles of legal formalities surrounding deals. They had no idea of procedures for issuing shares or how the stock market worked. Nevertheless, things worked for them! Oral agreements made between merchants proved sufficient for founding associations and productively managing them.

One of the writer Ivan Bunin's characters, living in the Russian countryside, describes merchants with heartwarming simplicity:

What do we need promissory notes for! That's not a Russian thing. We didn't have them in olden times, a businessman would just write down who owed him what just like that, on a board with a simple piece of chalk. If the debtor missed a payment once, the businessman would kindly remind him about it. The second time he would warn him, "Hey there, look, don't forget again, if you forget a third time I'll wipe out a previous payment. That would bring you great shame!" [10]

Merchants would usually not meet at each other's homes. That is, they would visit each other, have a quiet chat and sometimes befriend each other's families, but they would do their business and make deals in public houses. Generally alcohol was not sold in these particular public houses for the greater part of Russian history. They would down glasses of booze in other establishments. The public houses they would meet at were places for having a meal and drinking tea. Nor is this something unique: the international system of insurance began with deals made in the Lloyd's café of London. The major deals of the 19th century American trade barons were sealed in cafés and restaurants on Wall Street. Thus the way of reaching agreements over tea was the same for Russians and entrepreneurs in the West. But the Russians trusted each other more.

> A merchant in Moscow "bought" a bell tower. How did he do this? It's very simple. He had come from Samara and was walking through Moscow. His gaze fell on the bell tower. The merchant walked around, thinking about how he could buy it. A man came up to him, saying "What is it, merchant? Do you like this tower?" They talked and the merchant's new friend said, "That's my tower, but I don't really need it, so I can sell it to you."
>
> In a nearby public house they agreed on a price, and the merchant became the "happy owner" of the Ivan the Great Bell Tower in the Kremlin. Sealing deals in public houses, making oral agreements for large amounts of money was a normal affair. In place of a notary they used stamped paper. The most expensive cost 10 rubles a sheet. The paper was beautiful, with bright, snow-white watermarks, a crimson governmental seal and a gold border.
>
> It was the custom to close deals for whatever amount on this paper – they were all considered legally binding. Naturally they didn't use any seal. What would they need that for? This wasn't simple paper, it had an official stamp. They would drink to seal the deal. How would one not eat and drink on such an occasion? It was all good fun.
>
> On the next day, when the happy "owner" of the bell tower claimed his right to the bell tower, there was a lot of merriment and laughter. The merchant himself of course had no reason to smile. The merchant's name was Akinfiev or maybe Anufriev, accounts differ. The same goes for the city that he was from, as well as the price that he paid for the bell tower, with some saying five thousand rubles, others ten and some even twenty thousand.
>
> The most unbelievable thing about this story is that everything in it is the simple truth.

There are many stories about the exceptional credulity of Russian merchants. Journalists wrote many accounts, true or made up, about con artists selling state buildings to naive merchants. They even "sold" the Field of Mars in Saint Petersburg, as well as the governor-general's house in Moscow (today the office of the mayor of Moscow at 13 Tverskaya Street). It's strange that they never sold the Winter Palace or the Moscow Kremlin. The Ivan the Great Bell Tower was bought by Anufriev from Samara and the Field of Mars by Akinfiev from Arzamas.

The governor-general's house was bought by a certain Frolov from Yekaterinburg, a merchant of the second guild even! He was an entrepreneur with a turnover of many thousands of rubles.

What is surprising is that all these buyers never even suspected that their new friend was simply a con artist. If a person calls himself a businessman, then he's a businessman. If he says that he owns a building and crosses himself, then he's the owner. After a person had been swindled, the poor guy just couldn't understand how it happened. It seemed incredible that a grown man, with an elegant appearance, an Orthodox believer and from the capital city, could lie just like that in broad daylight.

There is only one conclusion: these people didn't cheat and didn't expect anyone to cheat them, and that's why the tricks in these stories were played on them.

It's not insignificant that never in the entire history of Europe did someone manage to palm off to a trader from rural Norfolk Westminster Abbey, the London Bridge, or the Tower of London. Nor in France has it ever been recorded that some provincial trader from Brittany bought at a cheap price Tuileries or the Petit Trianon in Versailles. Nor in the United States did it ever happen that some fool from Oregon or Kentucky was sold Capitol Hill and its buildings or the east wing of the White House.

CHAPTER 2

Locks and keys

The roots of psychological stereotypes, approaches, trust in or wariness of other people lie at the very heart of the life of a people, its existence through time. Until recently, 80–90%, and in ancient times 99% of the Russian people were peasants.

Peasants worked long and hard, and for that reason they treated what little they had with reverence. Sometimes they would even be miserly, again because of their poverty and the fact that everything they owned was got with such toil.

But we won't get into here people's natural greed and avarice or, on the contrary, the joy of Russian peasants or how they held on to their property; whether they were constantly afraid of thieves, in constant trepidation about their possessions, like the image of the American colonist with a Winchester rifle in his hand and the constant risk that he would have to defend his home and possessions.

It would be pointless to discuss all that. First of all, every human being was and is different. Even peasants were all different and, I think, colonists and pioneers were too. They had different circumstances, lived at different times, had different customs.

Secondly, discussing such things would inevitably lead us to political and even philosophical generalizations, to drawing historical analogies, to starting to compare things like the common good and the sacred right to private property. Russians have a patriarchal system, "autocratic, Orthodox and collectivist", and they've got the "second amendment to the American Constitution".

There's an amusing detail here, one little known for most Russians. Everyone knows that the American Constitution, written by the Founding Fathers over 200 years ago, has never changed. Only a few times have important amendments been made to it, among which is the First Amendment, guaranteeing the right to free speech. But why don't we Russians ever talk about the Second Amendment, second both in the order in which it was adopted and in its importance, which deals with the right of citizens to bear arms?

It's that way all over the world: as soon as the concept of private property emerged, they invented locks and keys. Archeologists say that the oldest key in the world was discovered in the tomb of the pharaoh Ramses II (13th century BCE). It was made of wood and very simple in design, with teeth fitting a cylinder lock.

The Egyptian pharaoh was, of course, a monarch, and like every absolute ruler, he had a lot of things to lock up. But the very same locks and keys are found in archaeological layers of many ancient cities and even the smallest settlements dating back two or three thousand years, from the shores of China to the Atlantic Ocean. To protect their property, people invented locks with various designs, from different kinds of reeds, fibers, wood, or metal. Locks and keys are even attested in Babylon and Egypt and in the Old Testament.

For example, already in Ancient Rome they used padlocks with a spring mechanism similar to ours today, which snapped shut and could be opened by turning a key. Furthermore, the Romans refined the lock mechanism: inside they set parts of different heights so that someone else's key could not turn the lock.

The first locks made entirely from metal were created by English craftsmen sometime when Rurik ruled in Rus' (one must not forget to mention that when it comes to these kinds of mechanisms, the British vastly outperformed the Slavs.

Later European craftsmen developed locks for gates, doors, chests and cupboards. In paintings by the old masters, the classic depiction of the lady of a house is a woman standing with a key in her hand.

And the locks on the front doors! These were simply masterpieces, not only made beautiful with ornamentation and carvings, but also very reliable. Imagine, already in the

17th century in Europe there were combination locks. Our modern locks on bank vaults are their direct descendants.

But in Rus' there was never such a variety of locks. For example, Arab travelers wrote of the ancient Slavs, "They don't have locks or bars on their doors."

The old Slavic locks and keys found in archaeological digs of Russian cities, were very simple, even primitive.

And they have not been found everywhere. Many are found in Pskov [11] and Novgorod, but as scholars say, "Novgorod is the most European of Russian cities, while Pskov is the most Russian city of Europe." [12]

In Russian cities further to the east and south, which were less European, one finds even fewer locks and keys. Even in the 16th and 17th centuries (a time when, as mentioned above, the combination lock was being invented in Europe) in Muscovy locks and keys on doors and gates were still just for the sake of appearances. These simple keys resembled more the keys of little boxes or chests than the keys of padlocks. There were, in fact, no professional locksmiths in Rus' at all. [13]. How did the old Russians manage without locks? An old tradition was to shove a stick under the door after stepping out. Anyone who into the front yard would see that the door was blocked and would immediately understand that the master of the house had gone out. Even in the beginning of the 20th century the majority of Russian villagers and residents of small towns did not lock their doors at all.

People in the cities still locked their doors, but only with simple locks resembling those of little boxes. Even if they locked their doors, they would put the key under the doormat or into the postbox. After World War II life began to change quickly, and when it came to general safety, it changed for the worst (why this was, is a topic for a different discussion, but it is a curious thing that it was at that time that the problem of widespread alcoholism first arose). Law enforcement bodies began to write desperate entreaties to people who had always done things "the old way": don't make extra work for the police, don't put the key somewhere others can see it. To get people to follow this advice, both police and burglars applied great effort.

Russians today, especially those in the big cities, in the last two decades have gone crazy with locks and strong doors. The trade in installing steel doors, covered with wood or faux leather, has flourished in all the major cities of Russia. But one has to remember that this appeared only with the beginning of perestroika and the outbreak of uncontrolled crime, especially burglaries. Before that time, no one thought much about the sturdiness of their front doors, or how fancy their lock was.

The aristocracy

> Take care of your clothes from the moment you buy them and protect your honor from your very youth.
>
> —*Russian proverb*

Aristocrats considered themselves the most honest and conscientious people of the land. Alexander Pushkin claimed that the essence of the aristocracy lied precisely in this: being the most refined, educated, and decent people in Russia.

For that reason they were given privileges that set them apart from the common people and estates that they could live on, without having to worry about having something to eat.

At the same time it should be noted that, although Russia after Peter III had exempted the aristocracy from state and military service, the majority of them could choose to live an easy life on the rents on their estates, but practically none did so. It wasn't accepted. So what if you don't have to work? Even if you were a huge millionaire or oligarch, like the prince Andrei Bolkonsky or the count Leo Tolstoy, you were obliged all the same to do something of service. This was your duty to your country, to your tsar. That was the custom.

CHAPTER 2

A good example of this can be seen in a dialogue that the British officer James Edward Alexander wrote in his travelogue.

The Russians do not understand what a mere gentleman means; and a person who refuse to state his rank or profession is looked on with suspicion. I head a friend of mine cross-questioned at Cronstadt as to what he was.

"I'm an English gentleman," he replied.

"What *chin* (rank) have you?" said the police officer.

"None."

"What is your profession?"

"I'm of no profession."

"How so?"

"Because I'm a private gentleman."

"But you must have had rank some time or other; and you must have been in some business?"

"I live on my property."

"But that won't do, sir. In God's name, what are you?"

"Well, then, I'm a magistrate of a county, and a deputy-lieutenant."

"Well, well, that will do: why did you not say so at first?"

So, that's how Russian aristocrats did not understand, at least at this stage, when a person simply lived off his own money and did not do any work or government service.

Of course, the aristocracy rarely produced prominent individuals; the majority of aristocrats were ordinary men and women who did nothing exceptional. There was a code of honor, however. Aristocrats could not do many things permitted to the common people.

How cruel this code of honor could be is illustrated by *The Captain's Daughter* by the great Russian poet Alexander Pushkin. Pushkin based this on a true story: in the time of the pretender to the throne Pugachev, over 300 aristocratic men and women were hanged for refusing to swear an oath to Pugachev, "the emperor Peter III who had miraculously escaped", just like the novel's characters Captain Mironovy and his wife. Pugachev's followers lined aristocratic families up in front of the gallows and executed one member of a family after another, including women and children. Aristocrats did not swear an oath to that impostor, with the exception of one case.

At this time, ordinary soldiers from a peasant background, recognized Pugachev as the true tsar. But what's surprising is that they later, after the uprising had been suppressed, went back "into government service" just as simple as that, and they were accepted! So what if they had lapsed and broken their oath? Peasants had no concept of honor anyway. From among the aristocracy, only one person gave in and chose to serve with Pugachev. After the impostor had been defeated, the traitor tried to save himself, as he wasn't an ideological opponent of Catherine the Great. At first he was afraid that he had betrayed his country, and later he had no choice. His last name, Shvanvich, has come down to us. In Pushkin's novel he was called Shvabrin, and everyone at the time knew right away who was being talked about.

Incidentally, in *The Captain's Daughter* Pushkin wasn't inventing the story of Shvabrin's duel: in real life exactly the same breach of the law concerning duels occurred, though not by Shvanvich but by his father. This was even widely talked about at the time. Shvanvich's father scarred the cheek of Aleksei Orlov, whom Catherine the Great favoured, when he heard someone calling him and looked to the side.

For the rest of his life, Aleksei Orlov's cheek was marked by a terrible scar extending from his ear to the corner of his mouth. People who didn't know him well would withdraw in horror at his smile. The elder Shvanvich was forgiven: he managed to convince society that it was not his intention, that he had not meant to take advantage of his opponent's inattention, but Orlov had just happened to look away at the same time.

When the younger Shvanvich was tried, the sin of his father was brought up. And this time they didn't forgive him. Things allowed to the common folk were not allowed or forgiven to aristocrats under any circumstances.

CHAPTER 2

It is difficult to fully describe how much the aristocratic society of his time despised Shvanvich. He was a political nonentity. When they led him in chains to his trial, women avoided touching him even with the hem of their skirts. No one except the court officials spoke to him or answered his words.

They did not execute him, for he remained an aristocrat, but he was sentenced to exile in Turukhansky District [14] for the rest of his life. Catherine the Great died, Paul I became emperor and was assassinated, then Alexander I ascended to the throne and the Napoleonic Wars broke out. Shvanvich was still alive during all of this.

None of the later tsars, regardless of the age-old tradition of pardoning political prisoners upon a new ruler's ascension to the throne, pardoned this one. The doomed man rotted away on the bank of the Yenisei River, in the tundra, a good forty years after his exile.

The Russian aristocrats, including the highest-ranking, guarded their family's honor. Indeed, they were not selfless, they worked to get somewhere, such as a political appointment, land holdings, grants and other rewards. They wanted to "build a career" and, of course, by far not all of them used only honest means in doing so.

They toiled for their seniors, kowtowed to their superiors, married wealthy brides, and played tricks of various kinds. But when it came to stealing, taking what belonged to someone else, or money from the state treasury... According to the French diplomat Talleyrand, Russian courtiers were "strange people" because, among other reasons, they weren't "on the take". The Prussian king Frederick the Great observed the same "strange" habits of the Russians, as did Lestocq, the French adventurer who played a major role in the conspiracy to put Peter the Great's daughter Elizabeth on the throne. [15]

In any event, even the Russian tsars were strange. For example, the state earnings in France at the beginning of the 18th century amounted to 145 million French *livre*. The estate of one member of the royal family, the Duke of Orléans, was valued at 114 million *livre*, and his debts at 74 million *livre*. The legendary diamond studs that the king presented to his wife were worth 800 thousand *livre*.

Let's compare: the budget of the Russian Empire in 1899 amounted to 1.5 billion rubles, but the value of the estates of the royal family were worth maximum 125 million. The Russian tsars were much less well off than the state they presided over. It is well known that during the first census in 1897, Nicholas II wrote under "Occupation": "land owner". This land owner and his immense family took at most 8% — and according to some sources 2–3% — of the annual Russian state budget.

Officialdom — a striking trend

Russian officials throughout history have had a terrible reputation that was well earned. It is thought that Russian officials' lust for bribes goes back to the tradition of *kormlenie*, literally 'feeding', when the royal administration would live on money earned from the local population for the length of their term of service. Representations of the local royal administration received their *kormlenie* usually three times a year, at Christmas, Easter, and on the Feast of Saints Peter and Paul. When such an official (these were called *kormlenshchiki*) entered office, the population paid him a *kormlenie* right off. The *kormlenie* was rendered in kind: bread, meat, cheese, etc.; the horses of these officials were supplied with oats and hay. Besides these material items, those officials extracted various taxes for their own use: judicial, trade-related, and other kinds. With these levies they supported themselves and their servants.

Initially *kormlenie* was only an occasional thing, but the 15th century gave rise to arbitrary demands and abuse of power on the part of local authorities. For this reason already in the 15th century the great princes of Moscow set down regulations for the revenues of the officials that received *kormlenie*. In the mid 16th century under Ivan the Terrible, the liberal elites achieved a great land reform, which replaced the feudal system of *kormlenie* with a fairly European system of local governance and court juries.

Around this time, Rus' began to create an institution of civil service. Becoming a civil servant began with swearing an oath, and even in the 17th century there was already an anti-corruption clause. In swearing the oath and kissing a cross, the clerk pledged "to carry out all business and make all decisions honestly, to take care of all state funds and not embezzle from the state, to not take gifts (i.e. bribes) from anyone and for anything, and to not disclose confidential state affairs to anyone".

However, though it had been officially repealed, there remained a practice of giving incentives to officials for things which they carried out in their official duties, and this survived almost at the level of legal recognition. "The people's expenses on voivodes and podyachyes," wrote the historian S. M. Solovyev "were an everyday thing, which did not cause any complaints or murmurings of discontent." The exceptions were isolated cases when "a particular voivode demanded an excessive amount of food." In such circumstances, the line between a legal demand and an abuse of power was a fine one. As a result, in 1648 Moscow saw a revolt against corruption that ended in fires and the deaths of ordinary townspeople. In order to calm the population, Aleksei Mikhailovich, the tsar at that time, executed two senior officials for corruption.

Starting in 1715, accepting a bribe in any form was considered a crime, and officials began to be paid fixed official salaries. The state administration of the 18th century was fundamentally different than the medieval of the 17th, but it nonetheless retained the depraved practice of receiving gifts from petitioners. Due to constant wars, however, their salary was often delayed or not paid out at all, and many officials, especially those from the lower classes, lived in poverty, so often extracting bribes was their sole means of surviving.

Peter the Great took desperate measures against bribery. During his reign, a whole set of laws were adopted to combat bribery, including the Military Code of 1715, which was the first attempt in the history of Russia to systematize the country's criminal law. At the same time, it was under the rule of Peter the Great that the reform of all areas of Russian administration brought embezzlement and bribery to unprecedented levels, affecting every part of government. Abuses of power on the part of civil servants, who often had no other means of getting by, were negligible compared to those done by the closest associations of this reform-minded tsar. "Governors care only about their own pockets: the governor of Kiev brings money to his house in Moscow not in bags but by the cartload," an unknown Russian informer wrote to Peter the Great from Holland. "Foreign merchants send silver and gold out of Russia, which is forbidden in other countries. Noblemen put their money in foreign banks: Menshikov, Kurakin, the prince of Lvov." Indeed, after his exile to Siberia, it was discovered that the tsar's favorite Prince Menshikov had 9 million rubles deposited at banks in London and Amsterdam, 4 million rubles in cash, valuables worth over a million rubles and 105 pounds of gold bullion and vessels. For that era these are completely fantastical sums. The entire annual budget of the Russian Empire in those years did not exceed 15 million rubles. A state official or military officer was paid between two and 14 rubles a month — or rather, they should have been paid such, but the state treasury almost never paid out salaries on time. A wooden farmhouse cost 3–10 rubles, and a two-story stone house in the city cost 100 rubles. As some excuse for Menshikov they sometimes say that he kept and renovated some buildings in Saint Petersburg for his own money; that unlike Peter's palace, his own palace was constantly used for diplomatic receptions and meetings. Even assemblies and balls were paid out of his own pocket. It appears that by the end of his life, he had simply ceased to understand where his own pocketbook stopped and the state treasury began.

CHAPTER 2

People in Russia stole terribly until Anna Ivanovna came to the throne (1730–40). At her court, her favorite Ernst Johann von Biron had especially immoderate tastes. During this time Biron, as S. M. Solovyev writes, "was not a depraved monster who would commit evil just for the sake of being evil; but it was enough that he was alien to Russia, a man who did not restrain his mercantile aspirations in favor of other, higher ones. He wanted to make a profit from his position and from his times, the fact of being favored by the empress in order to have a good life off of Russia's money. He needed money but he did not care how it was collected."

While the fight against corruption continued, attempts to eradicate it failed. Catherine the Great issued a special decree that forbid any kind of "*accidentia*", a Latin term for supplementary income from petitioners (i.e. bribes). The names of any official taking bribes were to be published for all to see.

An indicative tale of corruption dates from the region of Nicholas I and resembles Nikolai Gogol's play *The Government Inspector*. It ended in a great scandal and the trial of a certain Khmelnitsky, then governor of Smolensk. For several years, officials had been carrying out costly repairs of bridges and roads, but many of these expenses existed only on paper. When Nicholas I saw that for every mile allegedly 35 thousand rubles had been spent, over ten times the actual costs, he exclaimed, "It would be cheaper to pave this road with silver coins than stones!"

The idea of building a church in Moscow in honor of the country's victory in the War of 1812 was declared as early as December 25, 1812. In his manifesto, the emperor Alexander I declared: "To eternally commemorate the unparalleled courage, loyalty and patriotism that the Russian people have shown in these difficult times, and to express our gratitude to Divine Providence for saving Russia from impending doom, we have decided to build in our first capital city of Moscow a church in the name of Christ the Saviour... Let this church endure for centuries." A competition was held in which 20 proposals were examined and the project was awarded to Alexander Witberg.

Witberg proposed building the church between the Smolensk and Kaluga roads on the Sparrow Hills, which Alexander I poetically called "Moscow's crown". The reasons for building the church on this location included:

1. The emperor's wish to build a church outside the city, as Moscow "does not have sufficient space for an elegant building";

2. reference to St. Peter's in Rome and St. Paul's in London, which were initially situated outside the city (though both are now within the centers of their respective cities);

3. a good geographical location (the Devichye Pole field stretching at the foot of the Sparrow Hills allowed the entire cathedral to be seen from far away;

4. and the final argument – a historical one – was that the Sparrow Hills are located between the routes that the enemy took: they entered Moscow on the Smolensk road and retreated on the Kaluga road.

The church was to have been the highest in the world at 237 meters from the foot of the hill to the cross on top. The height of the church itself itself would be 170 meters and its main dome would be 50 meters across (by comparison, the height of St. Peter's in Rome is 141.5 m and the Ivan the Great Bell Tower is 80 m).

The construction of two enormous triumphal columns was envisioned, which would each be the height of a 30-story house. One of the columns would be built from guns captured by the enemy on Russian territory and the other with guns captured abroad.

In 1817 a ceremony was held to mark the start of construction on the church on the Sparrow Hills, but two curious details quickly became apparent. The first was that the ground on the Sparrow Hills was soft and watery, and the slopes were full of ravines and hillocks. The right place for such a huge structure should have been carefully sought out and examined, as it required immense foundations. Surprisingly, instead of halting construction, the contractors continued to quietly and successfully appropriate the funds invested for building the cathedral and so the construction soon began to "drift". Only under the reign of Nicholas I was a special committee appointed to determine whether it was even possible to build such a structure on the slopes of the Sparrow Hills. The committee included all of the leading architects of the Russian Empire. Their results found that building on the slopes was impossible, but there was a superb site on top. This is where today the high building of the Lomonosov Moscow State University is situated. This was only half of the problem, however. The main obstacle was the embezzlement that had occurred on a colossal scale. The treasury had suffered damage amounting to 300,000 rubles, an enormous sum for that time for a single construction project.

Witberg was a man of impeccable honestly, a fine architect, but clearly useless as an administrator and financial controller. In 1829 a new competition was held, after which Nicholas I approved a new, more modest proposal by the architect K. A. Ton. This project led to the building of the Cathedral of Christ the Saviour on Moscow's Volkhonka Street.

What seems unbelievable in this story is simply the scale of corruption. Squandering and plundering practically all the allotted funds without building anything, just turning the earth over, must be some kind of record. It is no less surprising just what kind of building project they were plundering. This was a church and, what's more, built in memory of the heroism and victims of 1812. The affair of the unbuilt church is mentioned in Nikolai Gogol's play *The Government Inspector*, where a police inspector talks about a church that they had long been building, but it ultimately burned down in a fire.

Alexander II complained to Count Mikhail Tarielovich Loris-Melikov about the "reckless disloyalty of the officials who serve not their sovereign but their own purse". In his fight against corruption, Alexander II also ordered officials to disclose their income and assets, not only their own but also that of their wives. At the beginning of the 20th century corruption could be discovered just as before, and corrupt officials, even high-ranking ones, could expect punishment. The height of bribe-taking in Russia under the last tsar Nicholas II was linked to an increase in the number of state officials, military spending, various real-estate transactions, and exploitation of mineral deposits. Corruption drastically increased during the Russo-Japanese War. This forced the tsarist regime to take further measures to strengthen the consequences for taking bribes in wartime. If officials were caught extorting bribes during this time, they were not granted any amnesty. They were sentence to prison, where they would do hard labor from sunrise to sunset.

The battle against corruption continued into the Soviet era. True, the word "corruption" was not used yet, but Soviet officials referred to "bribery", "permissiveness", and "abuse of authority".

The watchful eye of the OBKhSS (Department Against Misappropriation of Socialist Property), with varying success, kept an eye on the relations between officials and representatives of the "private sector". The Soviet Union eventually collapsed, and the violent ushering in of a market economy saw a completely different scale of corruption at all levels of administration. Alas, such is the sad pattern of Russian history: according to contemporary accounts, Russian political reforms have inevitably been accompanied by an increase in corruption.

CHAPTER 3
Myth 2: On widespread dirtiness

Russia lacks a European way of life, resulting in a peasant country where unsanitary conditions, sloppiness, and perennial grime reign, and Russia has not been able to rid itself of this to this day.

The roots of the myth

Today it is hard to say how the idea arose of the infinite dirtiness and unsanitary nature of Russian towns. Does the reason for it lie in the autumn streets of the past flooded by the rain, broken asphalt, rubbish in the street, and dirty elevators in the cities? It's fair to say that the country is changing, it is becoming nicer on the eyes, and there are fewer and fewer traces of the devastation that perestroika wrought. Or perhaps the term "unwashed Russia" became entrenched due to an emotional comparison with Europe during the time of Peter the Great's reforms. Maybe this is all part of the Russian intelligentsia's tendency to self-flagellation, as a major characteristic of members of the Russian intelligentsia is searching for and revealing in one's own vice, a trend that especially developed in the 19th century. "Unwashed Russia" may mean nothing more than the spring thaw common to the Russian climate. The matter lies rather in the difference of the Russian way of life. There is no basis to speak of an innate filth and lack of hygiene from ancient Rus' to the present day.

Characteristics of Russian plumbing

> On Saturdays Russian peasants go to the steam bath as regularly as English workers go to pubs.
>
> —*James Alexander, British officer in the 1830s*

Bathing customs

Usually visitors to Russia in the 16th and 17th centuries set down opposing accounts of the Russians' customs and way of life. However, they all wrote independently of each other on the Russian tradition of the steam bath.

Baths themselves and the regular habit of washing in them are older than any modern peoples. The inhabitants of the ancient East had baths, and often washing became linked with the religious idea of ritual purity. If you are clean on the outside, that means that you are clean on the inside, in your soul. To bathe was to prepare oneself for communicating with higher powers. According to legend, when one washes, one's thoughts, emotional experiences, bad moods and cares flow away with the water. You switch off, are refreshed, experience the pleasant feeling of a healthy body, and are imbued with an influx of energy.

The peoples of the ancient East also considered it necessary, before communicating with the gods, to set one's body and clothing in order. It would have been considered terrible ignorance to appear dirty before a deity or a worshipped ruler. Thus one finds an emphasis on water, cleanliness, and bathing in India, China, Japan, and ancient Greece and Rome. The Bible,

CHAPTER 3

Mahabharata and Homeric epics all speak of the ancient custom of washing the feet of an honored guest. As a rule, the more important and honored a guest was, the more stately the person who was to wash his feet in the basin. The task of washing an especially honored guest fell to the master of the house.

The cleanliness of one's body has never been considered anywhere simply a matter of hygiene, nor has the bath ever been considered just a place to wash. In all places and at all times cleanliness was a means of harmonizing one's existence, of becoming more pleasing to the gods, closer to perfection.

What is today called a sauna, steam bath, or Russian bath in fact appeared earlier in history than the Russian people. Writing in the 5th century BCE, Herodotus spoke of the inhabitants of the Black Sea steppe who "pour water onto stones and sweat in huts." [16] The ancient historian was writing about the Scythian plowmen, self-sufficient farmers who lived in a traditional way.

Long before this time, the common ancestors of the Slavs and Germanic peoples were already familiar with the steam bath. Archaeologists have found these structures which used heated stones in settlements dated to 2–3 millennia BCE. It is likely that these steam baths with their hot stones were not just a place to wash up but a kind of primitive temple. The birch twigs that Russians today use to thrash themselves and fellow bathers are directly descended from the birches that shepherds in forest regions would feed to their livestock during times of scarcity. Ancient Russians beat themselves with birch twigs in the bathhouse, made themselves clean, prepared for communicating with the gods, with the same birch twigs that were then fed to their cows — the most valuable animal they owned.

So the bath wasn't only about cleanliness. It was a path to harmony. It was a way of staying healthy and warding off disease. The steam bath was therapy, massage, and keeping warm. A good example is Prince Vladimir's order that steam baths be built as a "repose for the infirm", that is, for the sick.

According to legend, it was a bath that cured Master Peter, the builder of Novgorod's St. Sophia Cathedral. The old man fell ill during the construction and was afraid that he would not have time to finish the church. In the steam bath he was restored and finished his great task.

According to another legend, in the first century St. Andrew the Apostle was welcomed with a steam bath when he came to Rus'. If that is just a legend, it is an illustrative one.

The Russian tradition of the steam bath was remarked upon by almost all travelers. The German diplomat Adam Olearius described a country where there was a bath at every turn and the people, who loved the hot water and birch twigs, regularly bathed. The Russian steam bath made a great impression on him. Like many other visiting foreigners, he viewed the steam bath not as the Russians' way of getting clean but rather as some kind of national masochism: to willingly enter such heat, let people flog you with some kind of whip, and then jump in the snow, or even into a hole cut in the ice! Clearly with such cruel practices, the Russians were trying to drive the devil out of each other.

> What Russian doesn't love the steam bath? It's a pastime and a social club. Most importantly, the steam bath is the key to staying healthy, as it is a unique synthesis of the four elements: water, fire, earth and air. It is for this reason that, since ancient times, the steam bath has been considered a holy place, where one could literally wash away one's fatigue and stress, where one could set right one's weary soil and a body worn down by everyday cares.
>
> A clear mention of the Russian steam bath was recorded in the 11th century. In the Primary Chronicle there is a story about the Slavic way of bathing, put into the mouth of St. Andrew. An even earlier description of the prototype of the Russian steam bath can be found in Herodotus. According to the ancient Greek historian, the baths of the Scythian tribes resembled yurts or teepees. They stood poles in the ground, bound them together at the top, and wrapped felt around them. In the middle of this tent they set a cauldron filled with an herbal

infusion and into it they threw stones that had been heated on a fire outside. This produced a powerful steam full of herbal essential oils that had an antibacterial effect on the space inside the steam bath. It is know that among the Scythians there was the custom of using tree bark softened with stones to clean one's skin. Such hygienic practices allowed them to stay healthy during long migrations. The convenient design of these mobile baths allowed the Scythians to transport them on carts and quickly set them up whenever necessary.

The 5th–6th centuries mark the appearance of the Russian steam bath as we know it today in one form or another. This is a small log cabin with a a single small window at the ceiling. The basic features of a Russian steam bath are a stone or cast-iron stove, wide wooden shelves with a place to rest one's head, benches placed at the walls, buckets, sponges and loofahs, and of course oak or birch twigs. In front of every steam bath was a waiting room where one could change clothes and freshen up afterwards.

Practically every family in Rus' had its own steam bath, which was fired up once a week (mostly on Saturday, the traditional day for bathing). Towards the 15th century, public baths appeared where men and women could bathe at the same time. Only after a decree of Catherine the Great was mixed-sex bathing banned. It should be noted that before that, public baths offered female attendants for so-called "massage" services. It's not hard to guess that we're talking here about the prostitutes of the time (what time and place has not had them?). In Europe city baths were not always used for their intended purpose. As Giovanni Boccaccio wrote of 14th-century Naples in his *Decameron*, "When the ninth hour had come, Catella took her waiting-woman and without anywise changing counsel, headed to the bath that Ricciardo had named to her. The chamber was very dark, wherewith each of them was well pleased."

The Russian steam bath has a powerful effect on a person's health and well-being. When foreigners saw that Russian bathers strike one another with birch twigs and compared this to ritual torture, they did not realize that by doing this Russians were getting cleaner and afterwards felt great. From that time the renown of the Russian steam bath, where people rid themselves of every ill, has spread throughout the whole world.

The Russian steam bath has not been purely a place for personal hygiene but for recreation as well. No holiday or important event in the life of a family, went by without a trip to the steam bath. After giving birth to a child it was held obligatory to "wash" the child in the steam bath. Before a girl was offered in marriage, her female friends would take her to the steam bath in order to "drive foolish thoughts" out of her before the wedding. On the second day of a wedding feast the whole crowd gathered in the steam bath. They considered such a ritual essential for the happiness of the new family and the health of their offspring. The steam bath also played the role of a tourist attraction for foreigners. Crowds of visitors came to Russia to see with their own eyes how steaming Russian men came out of the steam bath to roll around in the snow and jump into freezing pools of water. It was thanks to the repute of these "strong men" that Russians were feared but respected.

Originally anyone who had sufficient land could build a Russian steam bath. Sometimes in the middle of the 17th century a law was proclaimed that a Russian steam bath could be only be built at a considerable distance from houses in order to prevent fires. Russian steam baths soon spread widely throughout Europe thanks to Peter the Great. The state ordered that baths be built for Russian soldiers in Amsterdam and Paris, and from these the local people learned the Russian art of bathing. By the 19th century, in Moscow alone there were already around one and a half thousand private steam baths and hundreds of state-run baths.

As the English poet and diplomat Giles Fletcher wrote about baths in Rus' at the end of the 16th century, "You shall see them sometimes (to season their bodies) come out of their bath- stoves all on a froth, and fuming as hot almost as a pig at a spit, and presently to leap into the river stark naked, or to pour cold water all over their bodies, and that in the coldest of all the winter time." [17]

Théopile Gaultier observed, "Under his clothes the Russian peasant has a clean body, until like the models of Ribera or Murillo." [18]

And in the 17th century, we hear from Charles Howard Earl of Carlisle that "There is no city in their country, where there would be no public and private steam baths, as this is almost a universal treatment against all diseases." [19]

Other descriptions of Russian bathing customs have come down to us by Samuel Collins, Stanislaw Niemojewski and the early 18th century Danish ambassador to Russia Just Juel. In the 19th century under Alexander II, the English military attaché Frederick Arthur Wellesley was still very surprised at Russians' weekly bathing ritual. [20] It seems that under Queen Victoria, in Britain's "golden age", such bathing was still something new and unusual for Englishmen. For that reason in the 19th century the British officer James Alexander recommended the Russian bath to his compatriots, not just as a tourist attraction but as a cure for many diseases. [21] He went on to describe in detail the steam bath procedure and expresses his amazement.

Germans too also had to persuade their fellow countrymen to bathe in the 19th century. A soldier in the Prussian army was issued underwear and two pouches with tobacco and powder for brushing one's teeth. The army had to teach men to wear underwear, bathe, and brush their teeth.

One last historical witness is interesting, this time not from Russia's neighbors to the west but from Arab travelers from the Middle East: "The country of the Slavs is flat and covered with forests. They have no vineyards or arable fields. They have a kind of barrels made of wood in which there are beehives and honey. They keep their clothes clean, their men wear golden bracelets. They have a lot of towns and they live freely." [22]

The Slavic god Bannik

The Russians' relationship to the steam bath was typical for many peoples of the world, but for the Russians it took on a truly spiritual significance. It is curious that nowhere, in no other religion in the world, was there a god of cleanliness. Not even among the Romans, who were very fond of thermal bath and made them a sort of hangout. In the baths the Romans met with friends, feasted, and celebrated festivals. The baths were a place to talk, where reputations were made or destroyed. People would make deals and exchange opinions. It's very probable that the ancient Russians gathered in steam baths or directly after in just the same way and for the same reason. If that's true, then the tradition of sitting together at table after going to the steam bath, the gathering of a "steam-bath club", is of very ancient provenance.

But I repeat that the Romans had no special god, no "Thermicus" or such, but the Slavs did. In traditional Slavic belief, we find a description of a slight, scrawny, and naked old man covered in birch leaves. This old man's name was Bannik. It seems that the steam bath was so important an element of the ancient Slavs' culture that it led to the recognition of a dedicated pagan deity. Bannik, the spirit of the bath, remained part of the popular consciousness until the 20th century. People would set out a little bowl for Bannik with milk, they would ask him to "let them into the steam bath and not be angry", people tried to maintain a good relationship with him just like with the other spirits in their home.

There was once an old wedding custom connected with the steam bath and Bannik. The mother of the bride would bake special bread called "Bannik bread" and sprinkle it with salt. With this bread she would bless the young couple before the wedding. They would wrap the bread along with roast poultry and two pieces of cutlery in a cloth and sew it up. The next day the matchmaker would open it back up again and present it to the young couple when they came out of the steam bath. The young couple was obliged to eat some of the Bannik bread.

They would make supplication to Bannik in the evenings at Christmastime, when young girls told their fortunes. At midnight they came to the steam bath to find out who was fated for them. For Russians starting a family, having children is a symbol of purity. For that reason this ritual was linked to the steam bath and the deity Bannik.

The holiday of Ivan Kupala

Russians even today celebrate a festival from pagan times: Ivan Kupala, also known as St. John's Day. This is one of the most lively and revered holidays on the Slavic calendar, which falls on the same day as the feast of the John the Baptist. Its pagan nature has survived through the centuries. In pagan times, the festival was held in honor of the Sun God, whose spouse was the light-bringing Dawn, a beautiful maiden.

After the Russians adopted the Gregorian calendar, the feast came to fall on July 7, that is, the eve of July 7. Some European countries celebrate the Feast of St. John the Baptist in a way similar to Ivan Kupala according to the old date: the summer solstice from June 20–26, on the boundary between the two halves of the solar year, which formed the basis of the old agrarian calendar. This was the time of the year when the sun was at its height, and it was followed by a change in the sun's course across the sky that brought it towards winter. As a result of this change in the sun's course, over the next months the days would be shorter and the nights longer.

It was at this time of the year that nature was most flourishing, trees were blooming and starting to bear fruit. The longest days of the year and the shortest nights were registered. Farmers believed that at this time of the year, the magical power of fire, water, earth and growing things was so great that they were ascribed protective, purificatory, fertility-inducing, and healing qualities. A person who took advantage of this power would have success for the coming year.

In folk believe, the days around Ivan Kupala were considered the most dangerous (on the same level as Christmastide), as at this time otherwordly powers were active. The eve of Ivan Kupala was especially frightening for peasants, it was the height of the feast and at this time that they would perform the major rituals.

Ivan Kupala was connected with the natural elements, namely with fire in its two forms, the earthly and heavenly (the sun), and with water. The observances of Ivan Kupala, celebrated on the night before the holiday, involve a rich ritual complex. There is gathering of plants and flowers, weaving twigs together, painting buildings green, lighting bonfires, destroying effigies, jumping over fires or over bouquets, fortune-telling, hunting down witches, and wild nights.

A traditional thing to do on Ivan Kupala Eve is to look for the fern's flower. Ferns were considered one of the most mysterious, magical plants. According to folk belief, a flowering fern not only makes one's most secret desires come true, but it also helps to find buried treasure.

Water has a special place in the rituals. There was mass bathing of crowds in springs of water, washing with water or dew, having a steam bath, or pouring water over oneself. The water rituals could be done at night, at dawn, or in between the morning and midday church services. Everyone believed in the healing power of bathing on Ivan Kupala. Anyone refusing to bathe was suspected of sorcery.

The old meaning of the name of the deity Kupala (from Russian *kipet'* 'to boil') was gradually forgotten and the name came to be associated with the word *kupat'sya* 'to bathe', so the central theme of the holiday was mass bathing.

Ivan Kupala is commonly considered a holiday for the youth and young lovers. On this day the young men of the pagan Slavs sought wives and "stole them away out of the water". Simply put, they pretended to abduct them.

After Rus' adopted Christianity, this holiday was kept and became the Feast of St. John the Baptist. In the Christian worldview, the image of the departing sun came to be seen as a symbol of St. John, whose birthday fell on the summer solstice.

CHAPTER 3

In traditions of both East and West the saint was granted such epithets as the light preceding the rising of the sun (correlated with the image of Jesus Christ

As is well known, Christianity was opposed to pagan holidays and pagan deities. However, it proved impossible to eradicate the custom of the Slavs to bathe on this day. It was not possible to do away with these rituals. The only change was that women were no longer "abducted".

City life

> It is impossible to imagine anywhere in Russia so filthy as one can easily see in the suburbs of this City of Lights. In our country people at least cover it up, but the French are utterly indifferent to the stench.
>
> —*Vladislav Khodasevich, Letters to Nina Berberova*

From antiquity to the present day

The cities of antiquity were built in healthy locations. When the Romans chose a site to found a new city, they checked whether people there lived long lives, what illnesses they suffered from, and what they died from. The cities were built to be spacious so that wind would blow through and ventilate them, so that they could supply it with enough water, and so that the city had room to expand.

Originally Rome too was founded in such a place: far from the sea, at the mouth of the Tiber, on hills. [23] It was a good location both strategically and in terms of the environment. However, as the centuries went by, the population of Rome grew enormously (over one million people at the time of the Caesars, although houses taller than two stories were rare — just imagine the population density). This caused catastrophes affecting essentially the whole society.

As we all know, history repeats itself. Contemporary Moscow, having taken on all governmental functions, along with the headquarters of major corporations and cultural institutions, has grown to unbelievable proportions, and no one can tell just how many people really live there, [24]. It already has come to face a mass transit crisis and now it is gradually approaching the same societal collapse that Ancient Rome faced. Two thousand years ago the Romans managed to ward off such a catastrophe (at least by the standards of that time, of course): they build aqueducts, a rudimentary sewage system, and places to dump waste, and most importantly, they attempted planned development of the center of Rome — all this made a city of a million people a relatively habitable place. Let's hope that Moscow too can somehow overcome its capitalistic growth hormone. Otherwise it will destroy both Moscow and the Muscovites.

The crisis of the Roman Empire put an end to "eco-friendly" cities without walls. Already by Late Antiquity walls and towers were popping up around the city, for barbarians were bursting into the empire. In the sixth and seventh centuries, when everyone was fighting everyone, the city retreated into its own walls. The population within these walls was increasingly pressed together and the knowledge of building good cities was lost.

It's hard to imagine the unsanitary conditions that the European population lived in during the Middle Ages. Within the walls of cities there was not enough space to start with. Thousands of people were packed into a space of between two or five, maximum ten, hectares. Some of them might have had their own houses with gardens, but the majority lived cooped up, with several people to a room. The water supply? If they had any, it was mainly what remained from Roman times. Every housewife had to go to the municipal fountain herself to get water — a great way of spreading disease. In the north of Europe, where the Romans never built cities, they took their water straight from rivers or wells. This was already more hygienic, but still wells could be contaminated with human waste.

CHAPTER 3

There was no sewage system whatsoever. The chamber pot, a European invention, came about because cities had no sewage systems and houses had no toilets. People used these chamber pots and then poured them out straight into the street. The street is also where dishwater and food scraps ended up. They did not dig gutters like the Romans did. The contents of chamber pots, together with water from washing, flowed in malodorous streams along the road, entered the ground, and filtered through to the same water they used for drinking.

Practically every household in European towns of the Middle Ages had stilts or wooden boots. The filth in the streets was so awful that sometimes, especially after it had rained, these tall wooden boots, which could be easily washed, were not enough to cross the streets without getting one's ordinary shoes dirty. The wooden boots were rarely worn alone as they are rough on one's feet. They acted as galoshes. Rich city dwellers would put them over their shoes and then leave them outside in front of their homes for their servants to wash.

The man of every household was responsible only for his own property, but no one cared about keeping public spaces like yards, streets or town squares clean. [25]

The municipal authorities of wealthy times sometimes organized cleaning brigades, but the townspeople themselves were opposed, as they didn't want to pay for it. Travelers in the Middle Ages many times mentioned that when they approached a large town, they first smelled its unbearable stink and only then caught sight of its walls. Knights' castles were not any better. Small and unbelievably cramped, they served of course for defense against attack, but they had no sewage system or water supply.

The word "alcove" is certainly familiar to the reader, but not everybody knows where it came from. Only in the 16th century did the rooms of a noble lady come to be called alcoves. Initially the word meant a niche in a wall of a knight's castle. Into this niche a bed was put over which a canopy was placed. The canopy was not a protection from mosquitoes but it was supposed to protect the feather bed from drops of condensation falling from the ceiling. The alcove had no windows and it was never ventilated. The feather bed was never dried or washed. The alcove was so full of bedbugs, lice, and other insects, that the Arabs who came to visit the court of Charles the Great said that the feather bed was moving.

Isabella I of Castille, queen of Spain at the end of the 15th century and beginning of the 16th, claimed that she had only bathed twice in her life, when she was born and on her wedding day. This terrible lack of bodily hygiene was characteristic not only of secular society but also the clergy. Several popes suffered from diseases caused by lack of hygiene. For example, according to historians, Clement V died from simple dysentery. But he was luckier than pope Clement VII who died of the itch.

The glory of France, Versailles, architectural marvels, the Enlightenment and an army that dominated Europe, all this is linked with the name of the king Louis XIV. He was an energetic, intelligent and, so some have considered him, enlightened despot. We can add one more title characteristic for that time, the Unwashed. Russian envoys residing at the court of Louis XIV, from "savage Muscovy", wrote that "his majesty stinks like a wild animal." Louis seldom bathed, and only under doctor's orders, because he suffered from hydrophobia.

Monks, servants of the Church, served as an exceptional example of dirtiness and lice-infection. Lice were called "divine pearls" and for some reason they were considered not a sign of a person's lack of hygiene, but the result of some inexplicable saintliness and holiness.

Here is what the doctor Friedrich Eduard Bilz wrote in his popular medical textbook *Das Neue Naturheilverfahren* (The New Natural Healing): "There are people who do not dare to bathe in rivers or baths, because from childhood they never set foot in water. There are no grounds for this fear, after and five or six baths people become used to it."

The first general cleaning of Paris was organized only in the 17th century. In the eyes of Parisians this was such a solemn event that a medal was stamped to commemorate it.

Cities in Rus'

In Russian cities there were no medals in honor of street cleaning, but for very different reasons than in Versailles: in Russia cities were cleaned regularly. One of the reasons for general cleanliness in cities was communal solidarity. In Western Europe the master of a house was responsible, as mentioned above, only for his own property, while sewage ran through city streets.

In old Russia people lived in houses that shared common yards. This meant that the streets were shared property, and no one could dump a bucket with dirty water right in the street like in Paris, showing that they cared only for their homes and not about other people in their neighborhood.

Russians had a different approach to cleanliness. In every homestead there was a steam bath and a privy. These privies were regularly cleaned by people hired by the community. For example, it is well known that in Novgorod in the 14th century, cleaning of these holes was organized on a regular basis, namely twice a year in April and October. In the 17th century an amusing term appeared for these cleaners of toilets: golddiggers. The content of these outhouses was "night gold". The golddiggers would work at night and in that way make their living.

The Russian words for privy and the "golddiggers" are very old and original to the language. In many European languages, however, the words for cleaning and waste disposal are quite recent.

Russian towns of the Middle Ages were less constrained by fortified walls. For one, there was not a permanent state of warfare going on between everyone, but also walls were usually built from wood, and these could be easily and cheaply replaced.

Houses not only in the villages but also in the towns of

old Russia were not pushed up tightly against one another but widely spread out. Houses had spacious yards with fresh air. Few descriptions have come down to us, but here is one from an archaeologist working in Moscow: "In the direction of Nikolsky Gate there was the courtyard of the Simonov Monastery with the Church of the Presentation of Mary, which was built back in 1458, with chambers. Behind it there was an alley some 4 meters wide, going from Zhitnitskaya street to Nikolskaya street. The Simonov courtyard occupied from its side the entire alley opposite to the church. The location of the Church of the Entry into Jerusalem stretched along the road for over 50 meters. The courtyard was 25 meters long and around 8.5 meters wide. Just next to the altar part of the Church there was a fence of the Church of the Annunciation's priest's courtyard, which was a little over 30 meters long (along the street), 20 meters wide and was 27 meters away from the Rozhdestvensky courtyard." [26]

The plans of Russian towns in the 18th and 19th centuries are well known, how much land was within a homestead and how those homesteads were organized. The great Russian historian Vasily Klyuchevsky [27] wrote that in Moscow, "next to each home there was a wide yard (with a steam bath) and a garden," and that its inhabitants had plenty of water, for in their yards they had a well.

Foreigners who visited Russia from the 16th to the 18th centuries emphasized the cleanliness and orderliness of Russian towns. When the Englishman Wallers wrote about Russian towns in the 19th century, he observed that the streets were wide and straight, with houses either wooden or made of stone, but mainly single-storied and are separated from one another by large courtyards. [28]

It was also obligatory to clean one's house on every holiday. One old Slavic holiday has been maintained in Russia from pagan times to the present day, namely Christmastide. [29] During Svyatki it was a tradition to dress up and act like different characters from folk myth, including animals. One ritual that these costumed revellers performed was a house cleaning, where they swept the corners of homes and splashed the people present with water. They made sure that their hosts observed the standards of ritual behavior, such as sweeping the house on certain days, putting their household tools back where they belonged, and preparing special dishes for the holiday.

While travelling in what is now Ukraine, the British officer James Alexander made special mention of how clean the peasants' homes that he stayed in were, with polished pine tables and chairs that shone like mirrors, and white and red embroidered cushions. I must point out that he is not talking about the homes of the aristocracy, but the simple homes of the peasantry.

Alexander noted that the local men were good-natured and smoked pipes, while the women were very neat. He wrote that his Swedish servant could not live up to the cleanliness and hospitality of these Ukrainians, as he was constantly drunk and unhelpful.

The only town in Russia that was truly dirty and stinking, not in its lovely squares of course but in its gateways and residential areas, was Saint Petersburg. Dostoyevsky gave a realistic description of this in *Crime and Punishment*, and this was already the 19th century. And so it happened that the city became the image of European Russia.

Epidemics

One can hardly dispute that hygiene and cleanliness have an enormous importance for one's health. Russians had an unusually high resistance to disease, thanks to among other things their habit of having a steam bath once a week or more often.

History underlines this: both in the Middle Ages and the modern era outbreaks of disease occurred much more rarely than in Western Europe, though they often came from that direction. Until the 11th century serious disease was unknown in Russia, but since the 6th century Western Europe had suffered a terrible epidemic every hundred years.

European historians used to say that the Normans feared the dead of their enemies more than the living: [30] a heap of bodies could lead to an outbreak of plague. In 842 the Normans broke off their siege of Paris and retreated in a panic: a plague that had erupted frightened them more than the Franks' cavalry.

At that time mass epidemics did not reach Rus' at all. Only in the 11th century, five years after the outbreak of ergotism (gangrenous poisoning known as "Saint Anthony's fire") in Western Europe, was the first serious epidemic registered in Russia. This was such an extraordinary event, it so struck the people of Rus', that it was reflected without exception in every chronicle. Nonetheless, the epidemic occurred only in Russia's western provinces and therefore was doubtlessly brought from Europe.

In the 14th century the universal outbreak of bubonic plague, known as the Black Death, began with the Tatar hordes sweeping into Crimea and besieging the citadel of Kafa (now Feodosia), which belonged to the Genoese. In three years of siege they could not manage to take the city. In the third year the plague came to their encampment. The inventive Tatars used catapults to throw the bodies of their dead over the walls.

The Genoese hurriedly boarded their ships and fled back to their homeland, but some of them were already infected. Thus in the mid 14th century the Black Plague arose first in Italy, spread to France and Spain, and then reached England and Ireland. It went on to hit Germany, Scandinavia, Iceland and even Greenland. In total, two thirds of all Europeans fell ill, half of whom died, that's 25 million people. Because of the Black Plague, England and France even broke off their Hundred Years' War.

Europe at the time had no real way to fight the plague. As a bitter memorial to the epidemics, in many European cities dating back to that era columns were erected with bas-reliefs, so-called plague pillars.

CHAPTER 3

This terrible plague hit Russia in the 14th century as well. However, it came not from the south but from the west. In Russia the Black Death appeared first in Pskov, which had the most intense trade relations with Western Europe. A chronicle from Novgorod offers important evidence for this: "And throughout the towns and the land there was a great and terrible dying. The living could not bury the dead faster than they perished, the dead lay everywhere in the towns and villages, in houses and churches." [31]

The historian Alexander Goryanin notes that, according to Western European sources, the plague "swept through all Western and Central Europe, reaching the most remote areas there, but stopped somewhere in Poland." [32] To be more precise, it stopped on the borders of the Grand Duchy of Lithuania (whose population was 90% Russian, for which reason it has been called Lithuania-Rus'), i.e. on the borders of where steam baths were found, the line separating good hygiene from the lack thereof.

According to scholars, several Russian cities visited by foreigners suffered (Novgorod first of all), but the scale of the tragedy was not comparable to what happened in countries to the west. Much later even the most severe outbreaks of plague in Russian history — especially in 1603, 1655 and 1770 — did not present a demographic crisis for the country.

The Swedish diplomat Per Erlesund noted in his writings on Muscovy that "the frost ulcer more often appears along its borders than in its inner regions" [33]

According to the testimony of the English doctor Samuel Collins, who lived for nine years in Russia, when this same ulcer appeared in Smolensk in 1655, everybody was amazed, especially because nobody remembered anything like it. [34]

Even venereal diseases were unknown in Russia until the 15th century and then came from Western Europeans, namely Italians who appeared in large numbers in Russia at that time. There were many of them, for example, among Aristotele Fioravanti's builders who were raising the Uspensky Cathedral in Moscow. It is believed that these amorous Italian builders first introduced the women of Moscow to syphilis, or as it was then called, the Latin disease. This shameful legacy of the Italian Renaissance was left to naïve Russia along with architectural wonders.

Dramatic population growth

An objective measure for the health of a people might be the rate of population growth. Because there were no effective contraceptive measures then, birth rates were usually high almost everywhere. As a result, the indicator of population growth and the ratio of births over deaths clearly demonstrates the quality of life of different peoples in Russia and what the situation with disease was. It is easy to see that from this perspective, Russia before 1913 had a quality of life no worse — or even one better — than Western Europe. If today rapid population growth is characteristic for the third world, in times past it was the complete opposite.

Judge for yourselves: from the time of the Roman emperor Augustus, when 26 million people lived in Western Europe, to the end of the 15th century (i.e. a span of 1500 years), the population of the region had hardly doubled. In the three centuries from 1500–1800 — just in the time when foreign travellers showed especial interest in Russia and many documented the Russians' way of life — the population of England doubled and in Germany, which did not have overseas colonies, it grew by 170%. In Russia, it grew threefold from 15 million to 45 million people! [35] And that's not all.

Systematic records on the Russian population began in 1897. That was the year of the first full census. In the year 126,411,736 "men, women and children" lived in Russia. [36]

Thus we see that during the 19th century, from 1800 to 1897, the population of France grew by 1.8, in Britain by 1.6, and in Russia by 2.6 from 45 to 126 million people. Only the USA,

CHAPTER 3

which drew a large amount of immigrants, saw faster population growth than Russia. In 1500 the Russian population was lower than in all large countries of Europe. Between 1700 and 1800 it became more or less even with the other large countries. In the course of the 19th century Russia became the most heavily populated country of Europe.

From 1897 to 1913 the Russian population grew at the rate of 2–3 million people every year. In 1913 the Russian Empire was already home to 135 million people. [37] According to some authorities, it had over 150 million people. This means that from the time that Russia stopped extensively grabbing up new territories — and it had even lost Alaska and a strip of California — within 25–30 years of the reigns of Alexander III and Nicholas II (until 1913) the population grew by one third due to an exceptional rise in life expectancy. Let's remember that in 1913 the GDP of the Russian Empire was the fifth highest in the world. At the same time England and France remained the strongest colonial powers. Germany had much greater territory than it does today. Russians inherited good genes from their ancestors that ensured that they stayed healthy. Documents of the 14th to 17th centuries attest to the fact that Russians were very fit and could live to the age of one hundred:

> Many Russians live to the age of 80, 100 or 120, and only in old age do they experience illness.
>
> —*Jacob Margeret, a French mercenary in Russia in the early 17th century*

> Many Russians live to a very old age, never suffering from any kind of illness. You can find men in their 70s who retain all of their vigor, with such strength in their muscular arms that they can take on work that our youth today could not.
>
> —*Augustin Freiherr von Meyerberg,*
> ***A Journey to Russia***

Sadly, in the 21st century Russia is looking at rather different indicators. It is appalling that in spite of such good genes that should ensure longevity, Russian life expectancy has dropped in recent decades and is lower than in many developed countries. According to the Russian Federal State Statistics Service, at the beginning of the 21st century men in Russia lived on average 60 years and women 72 years. At the same time, men in the USA lived on average 73 years and women 79 years. Alas, in Russia today this is not a problem of sanitation but completely different factors.

CHAPTER 4
Myth 3: A tradition of serfdom and lack of democracy

Russia has never had a democratic tradition and for that reason it cannot survive without a "strong hand". Its entire history — from prince Sviatoslav I of Kiev to Suvorov and Zhukov, from Sviatoslav's shield that (according to legend) he nailed to the gates of Constantinople to the Cossacks in Paris, Soviet tanks in Vienna, and missiles in Cuba — is one of the perpetual expansion through force of arms by a bureaucratic, militaristic state. But if we take a careful look, it turns out that Russia has a venerable democratic tradition.

The roots of the myth

The image of Russia as a place fundamentally hostile to democracy is based on two main historical arguments: the Russian princes for over a century were politically and economically (through payment of tribute) dependent on the Mongol-Tatar khans, and Russia long practiced feudalism.

The first postulate was profoundly formulated by Karl Marx: "The cradle of Muscovy was a bloody bog of Mongolian slavery, not the rough renown of the Varangian era. Modern Russia is nothing but a metamorphosized Muscovy." It is hard to deny the impact that the Mongol invasion had on Russian history. Some scholars are convinced that the Mongol invasion was disruptive for the growth of Rus', which was at a higher level socially and economically than the invaders, and it preserved for a long time the natural character of farming. "Rus' was set several centuries back and in those times when Western guilds were entering an era of primitive accumulation, Russian craftsmanship had to repeat a part of the historical path which it already gone through before the Mongol yoke," as the Soviet historian Boris Rybakov put it.

Georgiy Vernadsky, while not denying the cruelty of Mongol rule, highly respected the Mongols' religious tolerance and compared it to Catholic aggression in the West. The great Russian historian Nikolai Karamzin claimed that the Tatar-Mongol yoke played a crucial role in the evolution of the Russian state. Another Russian historian, professor Vasily Klyuchevsky, followed these lines and suggested that the horde prevented further civil wars in Rus', which had been wrecked with infighting. "The Mongol yoke was disastrous in its effects on the Russian nation, but at the same time it was a school where Russian statehood and autocracy was forged, where the Russian nation recognized its own identity and took on the character which later eased its struggle for survival"

Feudalism in Rus' is another aspect of history, from which, like a rabbit from a magician's sleeve, the image of a Russian national tendency to slavery is drawn. Let's not forget that serfdom — which arose in the early Middle Ages in Central and Eastern Europe and saw peasants bound to the land they lived on — was implemented in the 15th-16th century in Russia and long remained a crucial element in the socioeconomics of agriculture. Serfdom (like slavery in America) prevailed in practically all countries in Europe and around the world, but Russian serfdom is nevertheless singled out and demonized. In spite of all its flaws, however, one cannot call Russia's system slavery. It was a kind of service under conditions of a constant fight to survive, an opposition with East and West. Often the relations between a landlord and peasants were patriarchal, when the aristocrat took care of the peasants. He would not let them go bankrupt, lose themselves to drinking, he supported them in times of hardships, etc. As a result, the peasantry for a long time remained as a whole and did not become divided into paupers and rich kulaks. In addition, in Russia not all peasants lived under feudalism. There were entire social classes — Cossacks, Siberian settlers, Pomors, and other farming people who did not experience this form of dependence.

Those quick to accuse Russia of allowing slavery don't see that in the West the situation was no better and often it was even worse. It was in Russia that feudalism existed in its tamest form, it never lead to ridding the peasants of what they had and it did not reduce them to "property" like in Europe. It was in Russia that peasants always had the larger share of the land, while in Europe up to one hundred percent of arable land and pastures were in the hands of landlords. In Austria and Germany feudalism ended not long before it did in Russia, in 1848. In the USA, slavery (and real slavery, with masters and "two-legged property") lasted until 1865. During the American Civil War, England and France supported the southern, slave-owning side. Slavery in Brazil and in the Ottoman Empire, with which the West tightly cooperated, lasted even longer than in the USA. Until the beginning of the 20th century, there was slavery in the Transvaal. In the European colonialist holdings, even if slavery had been banned, for the white overlords the local aborigines were second-, third- and fourth- class citizens. If Russian feudalism allowed corporal punishment, in England it was allowed until the 1880s, and in the English navy until the beginning of the 20th century. In the British colonies, including India, corporal punishment still existed as late as the 1930s. Corporal punishment in state-run and some private schools in England was outlawed only in 1987; in other private schools in

Britain it was outlawed only in 1999 (England and Wales), 2000 (Scotland), and 2003 (Northern Ireland).

In the majority of European countries democratic institutions did not arise earlier than the mid 19th century, i.e. Alexander II with his reforms (military, legal, devolving power to regional levels, etc.) was a ruler of his time. In that fortress of democracy England, in the 18th century no more than 2% of the population had the vote. Women received the right to vote in the USA only in the 1920s, in Great Britain in 1928, in France in 1944, and in Switzerland in 1971. In the USA people of color (African-Americans and Native Americans) received the same rights as whites only in the 1960s.

Nonetheless, it is Russia that gets accused of a lack of a democratic tradition. Richard Pipes, for example, considered it was not democracy that was characteristic of Russia but rather "a bureaucratic police state, which in practice is in power today". Pipes clearly explains that this was the reason for which he sought the roots of totalitarianism not in Western ideology, as the majority of historians did, but in Russian institutions. In this he differs little from Karl Marx, already mentioned above, who consistently held that Western civilization, its historical path, was a model that all other countries and peoples should follow. Marx saw the qualities peculiar to these civilizations mere deviations from the "norm", a backwardness and "atavism" that prevented normal development. Considering the Russians to be a people "without a history", Marx seriously claimed that "hatred of the Russians was, and still is, the first revolutionary passion", and called for a decisive campaign of terror against the Slavic peoples. During the revolutions of 1848 he urged the German and Austrian militarists to "trample the delicate flower of Slavic independence."

Meanwhile, Russia had no less real democracy than in Europe, and in many periods of its history it actually had more. This can easily be proven. A wide devolution of local government bodies made Russia a country with a free spirit. It was a country that in 1917 had 6–7 or even 20 times fewer officials per capita than Britain or France.

It was not in European monarchies but in Russia that a tsar could shake hands with representatives of the people in the square at the royal palace. It was not in the US, the land of an "American Dream" long unavailable to everyone as slavery was abolished only in the 1860s, but in Russia in the time of serfdom that even commoners would make a brilliant career. The son of a village priest became an all-powerful minister and reformer, and the son of a farmer became a patriarch and officially the second ruler of Russia, while the architect of Moscow's Kazan Cathedral was a former serf. Let's consider this in greater detail.

Was ancient Rus' a democracy?

> Why is liberty such a rarity? Because it is one of the greatest goods.
>
> —*Voltaire*

The beginning of the Eastern Slavs' statehood

According to the Primary Chronicle from the 12th century, in 862 Rurik the Varangian [38] with his brothers was invited to rule in Novgorod. [39] This event is traditionally considered the beginning of Eastern Slavic statehood. Rurik arrived in Novgorod, which until then had been ruled by an assembly of the people called the *veche*. Such a popular assembly in ancient and medieval Rus', where the people present considered affairs and decided common issues, was a historical form of direct democracy in the Slavic states. Such governance in the form of a "boyar republic", limiting the power of the prince, existed then throughout the Russian lands, both in towns and villages. Rurik the Varangian did not or could not change this system and the Novgorod popular assembly lasted for over six centuries, longer then the assemblies of other Russian lands, finally ending only in 1478.

Towns in those days were not detached, isolated settlements. On the contrary, they were centers of large administrative regions. If it was a large town like Novgorod, each of its districts had its own popular assembly. They were called *konchanskie vecha*. These meetings of an area's inhabitants decided many issues. The common town *veche* presided not just over the town but over the whole region.

Thus the Novgorod *veche* was not just a big city council, it was the lawmaking body for that entire part of Russia. There were however two exceptions to this. The first was that it was not simply elected deputies who took part in the *veche* but everyone who was willing and able. The second was that in that time, the territory of Novgorod was larger than present-day France.

This kind of management was very distinct from European city law and was closer to Greek politics in the time of Aristotle. In Greece the *polis*, or city-state, consisted of a city itself and the countryside around it. Part of the population of a city-state lived in this surrounding countryside. The city-states were small and to get to the national assembly one had to walk a maximum of 20 or 30 kilometers, but it was often much less. The decisions taken by the national assembly considered the surrounding countryside as well.

The national *veche* is described as if the entire male population of Novgorod, ten thousand people, met in the square and decided all issues in a democratic way, but it wasn't quite like that. The entire population of Novgorod totalled 20–30 thousand people, women and children excepted. Able-bodied men made up 15–20% of the total population, so only 4–5 thousand.

For comparison, at different points in history the number of citizens of Athens varied from 10 to 40 thousand people. In most city-states of Ancient Greece the population was smaller, from 5–8 thousand adult males. Athenian citizens chose their officials in the assembly. Just like the people of Novgorod chose their *posadnik* (mayor) and *tysyatsky* ('thousandman', a military leader who commanded the volunteer army of a thousand men). It was classic direct democracy, when everyone knew not only the people they were voted for but each other as well.

The Novgorod *veche* was the highest state body in Novgorod, which was respectfully called "Master Novgorod the Great". The *veche* invited princes, kept watch over them, and sometimes expelled them. It decided issues of peacetime and during war. It commissioned the building of churches and leased the land for this on a temporary or permanent basis. It chose the archbishop. It tried Novgorod citizens for serious crimes, and upon finding them guilty it could sentence them to punishment, confiscate their property, or exile them.

The *veche* had its own chancellery with a *veche dyak*, a clerk who would write down the decisions and place on them the seals of Novgorod the Great. And, of course, the city had its own home guard, which was larger than the prince's armed forces. Novgorod was one of those medieval societies which could set an infantry of its citizens against a feudal cavalry, and the prince had an important role of an organizer and inspirer of their victories.

> The victories of Alexander Nevsky in the battles with the Swedes in 1240 and the German knights of Livonia in 1242 are often treated as due to the prince's first-rate armed forces. This is, of course, far from the whole truth.
>
> Alexander Nevsky's armed force (2–3 thousand cavalry) was only a small part of Novgorod's army (15–17 thousand men). Novgorod had its own cavalry, consisting of two to three thousand men. The main striking force of the Novgorod army was the home guard, consisting of infantry troops wearing armour (this was precisely the time when infantry came into the historical arena) and armed with long spears and battle axes.
>
> A heavy battle axe in those times was a formidable weapon, almost like a sword. Besides, swordsmanship is an art, and a sword in the hands of someone untrained would not be an effective weapon. An axe is different, what counts here is the power of the blow. A battle axe could easily crush an enemy's shield or hack armor apart.

The use of armed militias, unprofessional soldiers, says nothing in this case about the poverty or illiteracy of the Novgorodians. The undefeated Czech who led armies during the Hussite Wars, Jan Žižka deliberately armed his soldiers with such "unconventional weapons."

Žižka was himself a knight, but as fate would have it, he led an army consisting mainly of peasants. His success came from arming his men with these weapons, for he believed that teaching a farmer to use a sword is a futile endeavour. In Europe it was said at the time that a knight is born on horseback with a sword at his belt.

For that reason, the clever Czech commander felt that it was unnecessary to specially train peasants in fighting if they had tools they had been used to since childhood. Žižka was a rural landowner and knew how peasants lived. His entire forces were militias armed, for example, with peasant whips.

It was also Žižka who developed the famous tactic of using carts as mobile fortifications. Carts were arranged into squares or circles, joined wheel to wheel by chains and positioned aslant, and connected at their corners so that horses could be harnessed to them quickly, if necessary.

Instead of a spear head, Žižka attached sickles to the wooden shafts of a spear. With these sickles the Taborites who were hiding behind the wagons could deftly strike at the legs of the knights' horses that were unprotected by armour. Just imagine a knight in his suit of armour charging a peasants' wagon, while his horse's legs are hacked by a sickle and from above a blow lands on his helmet, which splits apart. Thus two peasants could defeat one knight.

In a Russian battle of 1242, which has entered history as the Battle on the Ice, infantry regiments played the decisive role. The traditional account of the event is that the army of the Teutonic Order crossed the ice at its narrowest point, at the strait between the Lake Pihkva and Lake Peipsi. Alexander Nevsky had foreseen which way the enemy would go and thus he set up the Novgorod forces as follows: in the front, on the ice, he put archers, behind them were heavy infantry, and at the flanks were elite troops. He made his personal guard stand in reserve.

The Teutonic Knights crossed the lake, created a wedge formation (called a "boar's snout"), and attacked the central Russian forces which they managed to shatter. However, Alexander Nevsky's flanking troops stroke the "boar's snout" from the side and his reserves struck from the rear. The Russians' central forces were smashed, but this was Alexander Nevsky's plan: to surround the Teutonic army and not let it leave the lake.

And who were those soldiers who struck from the sides? Where they Alexander Nevsky's elite troops? No, they were the choice squads of Novgorod and Ladoga! It was the town militia, the heavy infantry that stopped the offensive of the Teutonic cavalry and did not let it escape from the treacherous spring ice. The same heavy infantry attacked the enemies from the sides and held off the threatening "boar's snout".

Alexander Nevsky held his personal forces in reserve until the last moment. The enemy was retreating, it was done for, and then Alexander Nevsky's personal force struck from the back to finish the enemy off. He inflicted a crushing, devastating blow by drowning them in the lake. Since the infantry could not catch up with the cavalry, Alexander's professional force was especially effective.

The *veche* was not regularly convened but was called when necessary. It was announced by a special bell, which theoretically any townsman could ring. Between the times it was convened, the *veche* was managed by a Council of Lords, which served as the government of Novgorod the Great. It was composed of a *tysyatsky*, a *posadnik*, along with the former *posadnik* and *tysatsky* (in this way continuity of government was ensured!) and other administrative officials.

The decisions of the administration were carried out by specially designated officials. Still, the vast tradition of self-governance permeating literally all aspects of life made a large bureaucratic apparatus unnecessary. Indeed, what are officials for? Managing? The local *veche* independently appointed people who would be responsible for all public matters, it formed brigades of yeomen (*obshchinniki*) and delegated tasks. It saw greater success than a whole army of bureaucrats.

Self-governed communities prevented crimes from being committed on their territory, built roads, organized wayfarers and merchants, set up places for trading, hired guards to protect shipments, built ports on the river, and prevented people from poaching. In short, they did themselves everything that officials would do if there were no local self-governance. And bureaucrats would do the same thing but worse and for much more money. One can only be amazed how small an administration was necessary for such an enormous country. Rus' under Yaroslav the Wise (ca. 978–1054) had a population of over a million, but the entire central authority, including all the officials under the prince's authority, were no more than a thousand people! Officials remained in large cities, on portages, where trade was carried out, on the borders — but there were not many of those either, a couple of hundred people at most.

To compare, under Philip IV France had a population of around 7 million people. Royal officials alone numbered 20 thousand. The amount of officials in the counties, towns, customs authority, and trade authority was four times more. So we have 100,000 officials for 7 million people and less than one thousand for one million. That means that in France, for the same number of citizens there were 14 times more officials! This was the price that the state had to pay for denying local government.

The rule of law

The Pskov Judicial Charter was a legal act that regulated mainly the civil relations of feudal Russia in the 15th century. It was compiled from the beginning of the 14th century. The last changes to its text were made between 1462 and 1471. The sources of the Pskov Judicial Charter were legislation found throughout Rus' as well as local traditions that had developed according to the sociopolitical realities of northwest Rus'. The Charter consists of 120 articles, and half of them are dedicated to civil law. The Charter reflects subtle legal distinctions. Real estate (*otchina*) is clearly distinguished from movable property (*zhivot*)

CHAPTER 4

and the legitimate ways of coming into both types of property are specified. A distinction is made between a legacy left by a will and an inheritance acquired by the decision of a court.

The Pskov laws regulated in a very detailed way those aspects of law which modern lawyers call obligations: the relationships between people in building and selling, exchanging things, the right of lien, gifts, lending and borrowing, employment, use of property — basically any situation where people are legally bound to do something for each other. According to the Pskov laws, a woman could hold property and inherit from her father and husband.

It is hard to call the Pskov criminal law severe, especially by the standards of the Middle Ages. One could avoid penalties in most cases by paying a fine. The death penalty was reserved only for serious crimes, namely treason, theft from Pskov's kremlin, arson, and theft after one has already been caught doing so twice before.

In English law of the 15th century over 80 articles called for the death penalty. Compared to this, the Pskov Judicial Charter was more than humane. Acceptable forms of evidence were written documents, the accounts of witness, one's own testimony, and the judicial duel. As in other countries of medieval Europe, a judicial duel, or trial by combat, was used only in cases where it was impossible to determine the truth by questioning witnesses, but neither party would admit guilt. In such a case, a dispute was settled by a fight between the parties: the winner would be announced the one who won the dispute. Essentially, the judicial duel was a duel carried out with the sanction of the state.

It is of course hard to consider the judicial duel a perfect form of evidence. For that reason there were ever fewer judicial duels with time; people to some degree relied less on divine providence, and relied more on themselves and on evidence.

There was no trial by fire or water in Pskov. Judging a person's guilt or innocence was a practical embodiment of "God's judgement" and was referred to as the ordeal (from

Anglo-Saxon *ordol*, Latin *ordalium* 'examination, trial'). The ordeal is considered a very ancient legal tool, first attested in the Code of Hammurabi. The trial by fire consisted in forcing the subject to keep his or her hands in a flame, walk through a bonfire, or keep a tight grip on a red-hot iron. Those who could withstand the test were found innocent, while those who could not were found guilty. In the trial by water, the subject was forced to pluck a ring out of boiling water, jump into a river with a rapid current, or was tied up and placed in freezing water. The ordeal spread through many nations in the Middle Ages, but the people of Pskov did not accept such methods.

The popular assembly had the power to try those accused of a crime. The judges were appointed by the popular assembly, the princes' representatives, the representative of the Novgorod representative and the *bratchina* — the village or town's guild of artisans. The people of medieval Pskov were able to try the accused without the help of state administration by having the community simply come together. By the standards of that time, the Pskov Judicial Charter is well thought-out, subtle, and humane.

When did the popular assembly come to an end?

At the beginning of the 13th century Rus' consisted of around fifteen principalities, among which centers of association gradually formed. However, the natural course of centralization was interrupted by the Mongol invasions (1237–1240). In 1243 after the Mongol nomads had carried out numerous devastating raids on Russian soil, the Russian principalities accepted becoming subjects of first the Mongol khans until the 1260s and then the Golden Horde in order to keep the peace. Later they were forced to pay tribute as well. The relationship of the Russian principalities with the Golden Horde [40] during peacetime was restricted by the princes' taking of charters (written grants of authority or rights) for ruling the principality and by paying tribute.

CHAPTER 4

In 1262 the popular assemblies of the whole of Rus' rose up against the Mongolian collectors of tribute, or more precisely, the Muslim Besermen merchants who carried out this lucrative business for the Golden Horde and demanded double or sometimes triple payment. The people rose up in Suzdal, Yaroslav, and Vladimir. [41] As the writer of a chronicle attests, "in all Russian cities *veches* were called and everywhere people fought against the Tatars and did not accept their aggression."

Naturally news of the uprising troubled the Golden Horde and the Mongol-Tatar troops were ready to put down the rebels. Then Alexander Nevsky, considered by the Horde to be the senior prince of all Rus', sought to prevent a punitive expedition and went to the Horde to negotiate, and he also ordered that the *veche* bells in these cities be removed and that they not call an assembly.

In Novgorod and Pskov the *veche* bells remained. In the Russian lands that passed under the Grand Duchy of Lithuania, the *veche* survived into the 14th and 15th centuries. It existed in Kiev, Lviv, Minsk, Turov, and other cities. Even after the 15th century the *veche* did not disappear. Russian cities simply gradually received permission to govern by Magdeburg (German) law. As the result of a mutual adoption of two traditions of democracy, a different system of city self-governance arose, one not as strict and formalized as in the Roman and Germanic West.

Democracy in Russia under Muscovy

> Democracy is a device that ensures we shall be governed no better than we deserve.
>
> —*George Bernard Shaw*

Muscovy in the 16th and 17th centuries was the forebear of the Russian Empire. This state held northeast Rus' with its harsh climate, poor soil, and enormous distances. It was the personification of the Russian peoples' perennial fate, the development of places adverse to life. A small population was scattered over a large territory. Under these circumstances Moscow, the capital, began to naturally play the key role. A rising country needs a single center. The realities that Muscovy faced made its political tradition necessarily autocratic and stern. It brought to the fore the decisions of the tsar, behind whom a group of senior officials and aristocrats stood.

But at the level of local government in this large, extended state, democracy was flourishing.

Local democracy

The wide expanses of Muscovy, agriculture as the main way of life, and the need to work unproductive plots of land gave farming a communal character. Land belonged to the community, and the fate of the individual was also in its hands. Through elected officials, elders, the community decided where and what family would plow and sow, it set taxes and duties, determined who would maintain roads, and who would cart elected officials around. The community was part of every event in a person's life, from birth to death. The government did not interfere in the affairs of local communities and treated them as collective owners and managers.

The communal principle of self-rule was applied to administrative units of the country, which were equivalent to modern regions. After the reforms of 1550–1555 they became formally enshrined rights to self-rule. These reforms were carried out by none other than Ivan IV, or Ivan the Terrible. At that time Ivan was quite a young, healthy, and "progressive" ruler. His advisers, called the Selected Council, backed by the tsar's will and power, initiated many remarkable transformations in Russia, until in 1560 the tsar's beloved wife died an untimely death. Around this date Ivan started to move away from reforms and gradually turned to full-on autocracy, the abolishment of his Council, his secret police called the *oprichnina*, and a reign of terror. Many historians made the serious claim that Ivan simply went mad from the loss of a loved one and illness. Thus in 1555 Ivan IV had taken Kazan, for which he won the epithet "the Terrible", but he had not yet deployed the secret police. The tsar was halfway on his road to strengthening the power of the central government — and, as it turns out, local democracy too. His district constitutional charter was a kind of a Russia-wide circular (a kind of decree), which set out: "In order that there be no damage or penalties to the peasantry and so that we [the tsar] are not burdened with petitions, and so that settlements (*posad*) and rural districts (*volost*) do not become deserted, we have ordered that in all cities and rural districts elders (*starosta*) be appointed, who will rule over the peasants and who will be chosen by the peasants from among themselves."

Regional self-rule proved a successful project for a whole century. This system lost its significance only towards the middle of the 17th century, when governors began to be appointed to every major town. These governors gradually accumulated all power in their hands, they had their own bureaucracy and military troops for maintaining order. "The Moscow state [in the 16th century] can be called autocratic-regional." wrote Mikhail Bogoslovsky. [42] "but from the mid 17th century it became autocratic-bureaucratic," However, even then self-rule did not disappear, it was only transformed. The town bureaucracy had to cooperate with local democracy. For example, the representatives of the tsar were responsible for collecting state taxes, but the primary duty of elected peasant authorities was to ensure that these taxes were collected in a timely manner. As a result the most hardworking and respected peasants became direct assistants to the tsar's administration.

This is already not the life of a self-sufficient society existing in itself and for itself. This is a collaboration with the state. The regional principle of governance was universal in Russia. It easily adapted to changing political realities. Sometimes a *zemstvo*, a form of local government, played a less noticeable role, but at other times it was enormous, and it existed throughout history until it was abolished by the Bolsheviks.

Free peasants and serfdom

One more persistent myth about the deep-rooted "servitude" of the Russian people is connected to serfdom. Meanwhile, there was a wave of extreme forms of serfdom throughout Europe. The arrival of serfdom corresponds to a particular stage in the development of sociopolitical relations. But since the development of the various parts of Europe happened at different rates due to each region's climate, population, proximity to trade routes, and external threats, in some European countries serfdom was a feature only of medieval history, while in others it lasted until practically modern times.

In many large European countries serfdom appeared in the 9th and 10th centuries (England, France, the west of Germany), while in others it appeared much later, in the 16th and 17th centuries (northeastern Germany, Denmark, eastern parts of Austria) Serfdom began to disappear either fully or to a significant degree already in the Middle Ages (the west of Germany, England, and France), or it persisted more or less until the 19th century (Germany, Poland, Austro-Hungary, Russia). In the Russian state at the turn of the 15th and 16th centuries, a manor system began to form. The Russian peasantry at that time formed up to 90% of the population. A portion of the population continued to work lands that were communally held, but belonged directly to the prince. Such peasants were called *chernososhnye krest'yane*, from Russian *cherny* 'black', as state-owned land was called, and later, in the 18th century these peasants were called state peasants.

The prince gave part of his lands to feudal lords, who in turn were obliged to serve in his military. The peasants living in these lands were called *pomestnye* (from *pomestye* 'landed property, manor') or *vladelcheskie* (from the verb *vladet'* 'to own'). But these and other peasants paid a tax, and the taxes for peasants under manor lords was significantly lower than for the "black" ones, but in total they nevertheless paid more.

The serfs of Muscovy

Originally a farmer was a free man and worked a piece of land under an agreement with the owner of the estate. He had right of departure or refusal, that is, he had the right to leave the landowner. The landowner could not send the farmer away from the land before the harvest, and the farmer could not abandon his piece of land without having settled his debt towards the owner after the harvest was finished. According to the law there was a uniform time for leaving serfdom, when both sides could settle with each other. This was the week leading up to St. George's Day (November 26) and the week starting from that day.

A freeman became a farmer from the moment that he "set his plow" on the portion of the land that belonged to the landowner (i.e. he began to fulfill his duty of land cultivation) and he ceased to be a farmer when he left agriculture behind and took up another occupation.

Only under the tsar Alexei Mikhailovich did the Sobornoye Ulozheniye (Code of Law) of 1649 [43] establish a perpetual attachment of peasants to their land — the inability of farmers to leave the estate — and manorial rule, i.e. the power of landowners over the farmers on their land.

However, even according to the Sobornoye Ulozheniye, the lord did not have the right to infringe on the lives of his serfs and deprive them of their plot of land. Peasants were allowed to transfer from one lord to another, and even in that case there was a duty to establish the peasant on a piece of land and give him necessary property to do his work. Thus, the Sobornoye Ulozheniye was the first printed law to take into account officials abusing their power. Of course, its application in practice was not complete enough to call it a true codification of rights, and yet there was nothing like it in the European context of the time.

"Even after the Sobornoye Ulozheniye of 1649 the Russian state did not cease to see serfs as its subjects: they paid state taxes, they were not deprived of individual rights, lords were prohibited from 'foraging' in their lands, and the government did not give up its right to hold lords accountable for abuse of their power."

Yes, in practice lords constantly violated the rights of their serfs, sold them without their land, turned them into slaves, and broke up families. Historians rightly point out that such cases became ever more common towards the end of the 17th century. But when feudal lords separated spouses in order to get their hands on young women they liked, they knew quite well that they were criminals and their actions could have serious consequences.

> Darya Nikolaevna Saltykova, nicknamed Saltychikha – was a Russian feudal lady, who has gone down in history as a sophisticated and sadistic serial killer, who murdered dozens of serfs under her.
>
> After she was widowed at the age of 26, Saltykova gained full control of the seven hundred or so serfs on her estates in the Moscow, Vologda, and Kostroma regions. While her husband was still alive, Saltykova had not shown any marked tendency towards abuse. She was still a blossoming and very devout woman, but over time she began to show signs of mental illness that caused her to commit terrible crimes.
>
> Around six months after the death of her husband, she began to beat her servants regularly. The main grounds for which she punished them was negligence in washing the floors or laundering. The abuse started with beating the delinquent peasant woman with any object that fell into her hands (most often with a stick). Next the victim was whipped by stablemen and footmen, who sometimes beat the unfortunate victim to death. Gradually the severity of the beatings she gave increased and they became more elaborate. Saltykova would pour boiling water over her victims or singe the hair off their heads.

CHAPTER 4

In one case, even an aristocrat faced the wrath of Saltykova. The land surveyor Nikolai Tyutchev (grandfather of the great Russian poet Fyodor Tyutchev) maintained a long love affair with Saltykova, but eventually he decided to marry a girl named Panyutina instead. Saltykova decided to burn Panyutina's home down and gave the people under her some sulfur, gunpowder, and hemp. In the end, the people were too scared to carry out the act. When Tyutchev and Panyutina were married and went to their estate, Saltykova ordered her serfs to kill them. However, these serfs instead told Tyutchev of the threat to the couple's lives.

Complaints grew against Saltykova under Elizabeth I and under Peter III, but the cruel landowner belonged to a famous aristocratic family, so all the cases against her were dismissed. Furthermore, she did not hold back from giving great gifts to those in power.

But when Catherine II ascended to the throne and complaints reached her, they were treated more seriously. The investigation lasted six years. Saltykova's accounts were searched, which allowed investigators to establish a circle of officials who had been bribed. Investigators also looked at records of the movement of serfs, where they could determine which farmers had been been sold off, which ones were sent to work elsewhere, and which ones had died. Saltykova's trial lasted another three years. In the end, she was found "guilty without mercy". By the decision of the senate and Empress Catherine II, Saltykova was stripped of her titles and sentenced to imprisonment in a monastery, where she eventually died.

For such crimes against peasants, the state punished, exiled, or stripped owners of their land. Without that land, lords lost their livelihoods and social status. To some extent the law protected serfs.

In general, however, it was not necessary to rush to anyone's defence. Our idea of what serfdom was is very far from the reality of it. Some researchers now suggest that the feudal economy was a cooperation between serfs and lords, that these serfs and lords, who came together in the same church, could not seriously be antagonistic to one another. Everyone had their own role, their own responsibilities, and their own duty to the country. Basically, the evolution of serfdom was a matter of historical necessity. Serfs were transferred to lords on a temporary basis and were not subject to ownership but control. This lessened the burden on the state treasury in maintaining an army. The forces of the landed gentry were constantly used in wars against Lithuania, the Commonwealth of Poland, and Sweden, and to defend the southeastern borders tens of thousands of noblemen were conscripted every year for military service.

Even land was given to the nobility on a temporary basis, to be held as long as they provided services to the state. If a nobleman's sons continued this service, they would inherit the estate.

If a noble family had no sons, after his death his widow and daughters would take a tenth of his estate for their sustenance, and the rest of the estate along with its serfs would go into the state treasury. For centuries it was like this: the larger an aristocrat's estate, the more men he would have to contribute to the war effort. The more money he took in, the more he had to pay.

This was especially strict under Peter the Great: if there was a report that a lord was avoiding national service, hiding his son, or did not want to send his children to receive an education in the capital, punishment was inevitable. The guilty man was put in chains and his estate divided equally between the state treasury and the accuser.

Thus when on February 17, 1762 Peter III's manifesto freeing nobles from obligatory service was proclaimed, peasants could not understand what was happening. They found it strange that lords would now become institutionalized layabouts, not obliged to provide any services to the state. "Many peasants believed that from this moment on serfdom was illegal and they awaited the next proclamation, which would free them," the scholar Alexander Goryanin observes, [44] "but they had to wait for another 99 years and one day." Of course, not everyone inherited such patience from generation to generation. Within little more than a decade a large part of Russia, including Orenburg, the Urals, Western Siberia, and the Middle and Lower Volga were swept by the uprising led by Pugachev. The peasants did not forgive this breaking of the social contract.

Free peasants in Muscovy

Unlike peasants attached to manors, state peasants were always personally free, they did not come under serfdom. In the center of the country there was a mix of "black" peasants and bonded serfs, but over a large portion of Russian territory there was no serfdom at all, in the Cossack Hetmanate, [45] the Russian North, most of the Urals and Siberia, and in the southern Cossack regions.

On state "black lands" there were peasant householders. They belonged to a community of peasants, paid state taxes, and could not leave their households and farmlands without finding someone else to work it. As the historian Vasily Klyuchevsky wrote in his course of Russian history, "Such an attachment to the land had of course nothing to do with serfdom." Each peasant household was a sort of cooperative with a large and varied membership. Besides the master of the house, they were home to large families, often three or four generations under one roof, and also distant relatives or hired laborers. The master of the household was responsible to the community, but everyone else living in the household could freely leave.

Some of the "black" peasants were quite rich, some were middle-class ones, and others were utterly poor. They were engaged not only in farming but also in trade and various crafts. Mikhail Lomonosov [46] came from precisely such "black" peasants and as a young man travelled with his father on their own ships to hunt sea animals hundreds of miles away. They owned hunting grounds there.

Besides peasants in "black" communities there also lived so-called *bobyli*, who were craftsmen or hired laborers, i.e. a free rural population. One also found *pashennye bobyli*, craftsmen who owned plots of land. Their existence proves that land could be bought and sold. Otherwise, how could these *pashennye bobyli* have come into them? As the Russian historian Mikhail Bogoslovsky (1867–1929) aptly wrote long ago, "Owners of black land could dispose of their lands as they pleased: they could sell them, put them in pledge, give them as gifts, present them as a dowry, and bequeath them, whether in whole or in part."

This "peasant capitalism" went so far as to create a society on equal footing through unions of shareholders or co-owners. In parts of the peasant world too, everyone had shares and could do what they liked with them: sell them, lease them out, buy the shares of other members, or demand that their share be isolated from the common property.

The great Russian writer, dissident, exile, and Nobel laureate Alexander Solzhenitsyn admired Swiss democracy, calling it a "direct product of the traditions of the community" and considering it the most perfect and most "popular" system. Perhaps democracy everywhere in Europe grew out of such community-level forms of government. In the beginning there were territorial-level groups of people who were able to decide things for themselves and choose "good and preferred" leaders from among themselves, and then at the country level a House of Commons (called that for a reason!) would spring up.

But in Muscovy in the 17th century such "grassroots" democracy became ever stronger; communities increasingly took on lower levels of power. Moreover, this process was not limited to highbrow intellectuals and wealthy people in the cities, but it involved the masses, the peasants. And there were a lot of peasants — in the 19th century "black" state peasants made up around 45% of all Russian peasants. They knew how to defend their rights, even by force of arms.

CHAPTER 4

Moscow bureaucrats and the "staff elevator"

Muscovy had a very rich tradition of local government, election of officials, and cooperation between democratically elected authorities and civil servants. Centralized bureaucratic institutions in Russia appeared very late, in the 16th century under Vasili III. These ministries were called *prikazy* and they arose from the chancellery which aristocrats ran to carry out what the tsar commanded. In the 1660s in the entire country there were around 100 clerks, as the managers of a ministry were called, and around 1000 petty officials. Towards the end of the 17th century the number of officials in the ministries in Moscow alone grew to three thousand people. But this "bloated apparatus" was an insignificant amount of people when one considers how big the country was.

In France with its its population of 20 million at the end of the 16th century, the royal administration alone involved more than 30 thousand officials. There were around the same number of lawyers, who offered their services in a free market system but were an important part of how the state functioned. Thus in Muscovy there were ten or fifteen times fewer officials per capita than in France. This small number of officials may come as a surprise, as the population of Russia amounted to 10–12 million people. Russians of old, accustomed to getting things done on their own, did not rate officials highly. In Europe, however, officials enjoyed high social status, even in Britain with its proud democratic tradition, let alone countries of the East. Even in Japan, the most demographic country of Asia, officials were held in great respect. In China, where everything was done in a bureaucratic fashion, becoming an official was bliss. There is evidence that in order to get them into the elite circles of the imperial administration, Chinese parents often had their children castrated — eunuchs had a better chance than most at an honorable and, most importantly, a lucrative government position. In India and the Muslim world too, officials were respected.

But not in Muscovy; the general opinion of bureaucrats in Muscovy was low. They were considered dishonest, thieving, not behaving according to the rules, and bad people in general. They were accused of a multitude of sins: buying their offices, delivering biased verdicts and biased interpretations of the law, and sharing their illegal income with their superiors who in turn covered up for them. People were extremely disturbed by the corruption and self-serving behavior of officials. In folklore clerks are depicted in the worst possible light. And what can one say about minor functionaries?

The army was much more respected in Muscovy. There were not many serving in the military: about 300,000 men for the whole country. Feudal lords made up around 30 thousand, and the same number were those with the same rights but who were not landowners. In France there were around one million aristocrats, 5% of the entire population. In Muscovy they were only 60 thousand, or 0.5%.

The highest ranks of the aristocracy were boyars who owned not manors were granted for a specific period of time, in exchange for service, but rather held inherited estates called *votchina*. There were 30–40 boyar families, but this number grew. People were constantly nominated to the position of a boyar for good service. Among these were 16 eminent families. The average number of adult males in all those families did not exceed three hundred in the mid 17th century.

In France of that time we find up to a thousand titled families. Among them there was an active male population of 12 thousand. It turns out that in France there were 20–25 times more aristocrats per capita than in Russia. Andrei Burovsky [47] writes that in France at that time, almost no one rose to the aristocracy — one had to be born an aristocrat. In Britain a squire was anyone whose income was more than forty pounds a year, but there too people were born lords and hardly ever became lords.

The Russian aristocracy had seats on a council under the tsar: the Boyar Duma. [48] The Boyar Duma was relatively democratic considering its composition. Under Alexei Mikhailovich, of the 60 members of the Duma, five were boyars who did not come from distinguished clans, five were Duma nobles and four were Duma clerks (the lowest rank in the Duma). In total, out of 60 people, 14 were not of aristocratic birth but were from the common folk. In 1688, already 35 out of the 57 members of the Duma were appointed ones, self-made men of a sort.

Assemblies of the lands — the Russian parliament of the 16th century

From the middle of the 16th to the end of the 17th century, an important role was played by a Russian state legislative body called the Zemsky Sobor ('assembly of the land'). In this assembly representatives of most social classes came together to discuss political, economic, and administrative issues. Foreigners who visited Moscow in the 16th and 17th centuries immediately understood what the Zemsky Sobor was. A Pole, Filon Kmita, compared the Zemsky Sobor of 1580 to the Sejm of the Republic of Poland; an Englishman, Jerome Horsey, called the Zemsky Sobor of 1584 a parliament; and the Livonian aristocrat Georg Bruno identified the Sobor with the Swedish Riksdag. The German Johann Gotthilf Vockerodt concluded that it was a "kind of senate". A Russian ambassador to England, in 1646, Gerasim Dokhturov, described the English parliament with similar symmetry: "They sit in two chambers. In one of them there are boyars, and in the other there are representatives of the common people." The boyar chamber is like the House of Lords. The Zemsky Sobor existed under the conditions of a class-representative monarchy and its powers were not less than those of the British parliament, the Estates-General in France, or the Cortes Generales in Spain. Only at the beginning of the 17th century, five years after it appeared, did the British parliament became a de facto fundamental institution in the government of that country; only then did a legislature defy the power of the king and wield executive power directly.

In Muscovy already the assembly of the land, which Ivan the Terrible founded in 1549, determined the course of reforms in law and finance and discussed taxes; it was involved in the governance of the state. Elections of representatives to Zemsky Sobor (the number of members was not strictly set and ranged between 200–500 people or even more) were held in provincial capitals. After the meetings finished, a record of the assembly was written down and certified by all the participants of the elections. They sent this record to Moscow and then the elected people themselves set off for Moscow, taking with them necessary supplies or money. Sessions of the assemblies could go on for a long time and one had to stock up on everything one needed. Imagine the warehouses on the Okhotny Ryad in Moscow, where food is stored for today's deputies in the State Duma! The usual order of the day at the assembly included discussions over issues posed by the tsar, and every rank and group discussed all the issues among themselves, separately from the others.

After a matter was discussed, every group submitted its *skaska* (from the word *skazyvat'* 'to tell a story'). Historians love working with these "stories", because from them one can easily determine the wishes of various social groups of *posadsky*, civil servants or "black" peasants. Of course, let's be objective here: the serfs did not choose their representatives. But in Britain too neither servants nor pirates had anyone to represent them in Parliament. However, all the other segments of the population chose their representatives to the Zemsky Sobor. We find that in Muscovy, about 15% of the population elected representatives to the Zemsky Sobor. That is a substantially larger amount than in Britain.

In the 17th century only 2% of the English population had suffrage, the right to elect their representatives in Parliament. Realistically, only a significantly lower number of people, all in all 1% of the population, had the ability to vote. Alexander Goryanin has estimated that in France, until 1849 only 2% of the population had the right to vote, and in Spain in 1854 the number hardly exceeded 0.2%, while in Japan, where the first elections were held in 1891, the right to vote was accorded on the basis of paying a tax of 15 yen, which only 1% of the population could come up with.

Both Russian and Western historians speak of a "weakening of the Zemsky Sobor" under the tsar Aleksei Mikhailovich. For them it is important to find the same features of societal development as in the countries of Europe. If there were absolute despots in Europe, their thinking goes, there must have been some in Russia as well. If there were, it would somehow reflect poorly on Russia.

Alas, they don't want to notice that the differences are in Russia's favor. If we are searching through history for the development of democratic institutions, then in that epoch Russia was ahead of Britain.

The theory that the assemblies withered away is based on the fact that the Zemsky Sobors met regularly only until 1653. After that time, they were convened in a more irregular, episodic fashion. Over 135 years (1549–1684) there were a total of 57 of them. The last took place in 1684, which decreed an everlasting peace with Poland.

Only Peter the Great's coup in 1689 dealt a final blow to the Zemsky Sobors, however. He himself together with his brother Ivan V in 1682 was elected by an assembly consisting of clergy and delegates. At that time the assemblies took such a truncated shape.

Electing of tsars

The British parliament never established a new dynasty. It was never officially acknowledged that Parliament enthrones or invites a new king. It did once determine who sat on the throne: it invited the Duke of Hanover, who gained the right to the British throne through his mother, the princess Sofia of Hanover, the granddaughter of James I, and through the Act of Succession passed by the British parliament in 1701. According to that Act, the throne of England and Scotland could not fall to a Catholic. Princess Sofia happened to be the closest Protestant relation of the House of Stuart. But this was not a case of Parliament exercising statuary powers, but rather backroom dealing over which voters had no input.

Likewise the French Estates General never chose a ruler or put a new dynasty on the throne. They never even put forth a candidate chosen by the aristocracy.

The Zemsky Sobor, however, chose a new tsar. Some assemblies bore precisely this constituent character! In 1584 and 1598 the assemblies of the land convened specifically to chose new tsars: Fyodor Ivanovich and Boris Godunov respectively. In 1606 the assembly elected Vasily IV tsar and in 1610 deposed him from the throne.

In the formidable year of 1612 it was the assembly of the land, not the Duma, that constituted the country government. During the Time of Troubles (the period of Russian history from 1598 to 1613), the role of the assemblies became even greater: the dynasty of Rurik in a direct male line became extinct. In a situation where the rules of monarchial succession did not hold, the assembly decreed its will. The nation did not want to establish a republic, rather it decided to bring a new dynasty to the throne, just as some Greek city-states had elected their kings. Aristotle approved of this way of governing, where the monarchy became an expression of the will of the people.

There were a large number of pretenders to the Russian throne, a total of about 30 candidates. A true pre-election battle arose between them. One who wanted to be tsar was Dmitry Mikhaylovich Pozharsky, of whom it was said, "He ran for the throne and it cost him twenty thousand." He even had a budget allocated for his election campaign. Such famous aristocrats as

CHAPTER 4

Dmitri Cherkassky, Petr Pronsky, and Ivan Golitsyn also sought to come to the throne

Prince Dmitry Troubetskoy, an acknowledged Cossack leader, ran a very active election active campaign. According to one of his contemporaries, "He lay rich tables and organized numerous feasts for Cossacks and for one and a half months he received all of them, all the forty thousand, invited them to his courtyard on all days, treated them, gave them plenty to eat and drink, and pleaded with them that they vote for him to be the tsar, saying that they would later praise him for his rule."

However, such English-style bribery of voters did not bear fruit on our Russian soil. "The Cossacks though, after they accepted his invitations, ate and drank and praised him, later they left for their regiments where they cursed him and laughed at his folly."

When the Cossacks in February 1613 broke into the Zemsky Sobor and demanded Michael Romanov instead, poor Troubetskoy was so embarrassed that he became seriously ill: "His face blackened from sorrow and he fell ill, and he lay in bed for three months, and did not leave his home."

To this day people ask why the choice of tsar fell precisely on Michael Romanov. There are as many different viewpoints as their are historians. What is beyond doubt, however, is that Michael Romanov received the votes of over six hundred representatives, among whom were the representatives of "black" peasants too. One cannot forget that Michael Romanov was the closest relative of the last Muscovite tsar of the House of Rurik. Alas, when he came to the throne, Michael Romanov did not sign any agreement with his subjects, and unfortunately no constitution came about.

It is true that some sources speak of a certain document. They allege that when Michael Fedorovich came to the throne, he wrote a "note" with certain promises, [49] but the text of this note, or even a detailed description of what the tsar promised to do (or not do) has not come down to us. Maybe he made a commitment to rule by calling assemblies of the lands? We can only guess at whether he wrote that note for himself alone or for his descendants as well. But what use is there in guessing at that? In the history of Russia there is another such secret, namely the secret document that was supposedly drawn up when the Romanovs came to the throne.

Democracy in the Russian Empire

> A state's regime fits the nation, like a dress fits a person's figure
>
> —*Anatole France*

In the Russian Empire, self-government among the people persisted in one form or another. The authorities repeatedly sought to establish broader representation of the masses at the top level of government. As Sergei Polsky writes: [50]

Aristocratic constitutionalism became an important intellectual movement, which had significant effect on Russia's political life in the 18th century. Its origins were connected to limiting of despotism by aristocratic elites in 1730. Its ideological roots grow from the republican tradition of the Western political thought of the 17th and 18th centuries. This radical attempt was not understood by the "enlightened" aristocracy of the second half of the 18th century, who tried to realize Montesquieu's idea of "true monarchy". In response to a series of aristocratic projects of "indispensable laws" during the reign of Catherine the Great, government constitutionalism was born, which tried to go around the issue of the special role of the aristocracy in a monarchy.

The political structure of the Russian state was never distinguished by absolute monarchy. It was a complex combination of democracy, bureaucracy, monarchy, and the aristocracy. The significance of each of these elements varied at different times. Let us consider a few attempts at democratic transformation in Russian history.

CHAPTER 4

An attempt at an aristocratic constitution

After the sudden death of Peter II, the nephew of Peter the Great and the son of the executed tsarevich Aleksei, the Supreme Privy Council [51] was gathered and decided to invite Anna Ivanovna, Peter the Great's niece and daughter of his half-brother Ivan, to the throne. At first glance Anna Ivanovna had far less of a right to the throne than Peter the Great's daughters. However, Elizabeth and Anna, Peter the Great's daughters with Catherine, were born out of wedlock: Anna was born in 1708, Elizabeth in 1709, before Catherine had officially married Peter the Great. [52] How could someone born out of wedlock ascend to the throne? Of course, this was just an excuse, but everyone accepted it.

The members of the Supreme Privy Council were prepared to bring to the throne someone with fewer rights, suggesting that such a person would be easier to control and his or her power would be weaker. They decided to appoint Anna Ivanovna on certain conditions. Prince Golitsyn, one of the members of the Supreme Privy Council, set down terms which demanded that the Supreme Privy Council of eight people should exist in perpetuity and that she could not take certain actions without the consent of the Council, namely:

1. to start no wars;
2. to make no peace treaties;
3. to not impose any new taxes on the loyal citizenry;
4. to not appoint people to high ranks, civil or military, on land or sea, above the rank of a colonel, and below this rank not delegate any matters of national importance, and the Imperial Guard and other regiments be under the jurisdiction of the Supreme Privy Council;
5. to not deprive the Polish gentry of their life, property, or their honor without trial;
6. to not grant patrimonial estates and villages.
7. to not appoint, without the advice of the Supreme Privy Council, Russians or foreigners to court positions;

8. to not spend revenue generated by the state;
9. to be merciful to all loyal citizens. [53]

This was essentially an attempt to establish a constitutional monarchy, just one without a parliament — it was replaced by a narrow circle of aristocrats.

The curious thing about the Conditions is that the document remained unpublished by the members of the Supreme Privy Council. Most of the aristocracy could only guess at what it contained until the conditions were read out at the meeting of functionaries on February 2, 1730. Only from that moment did a schism appear in the Russian aristocracy, which caused, among other things, the emergence of a court opposition. [54]

The Conditions, for the people of that time, were only a preliminary document. The members of the Supreme Privy Council did not propose their own project for a future state, but they did suggest to the aristocrats of the time that they do something themselves.

Several major initiatives appeared, and none involved maintaining an absolute monarchy. [55] Some suggested limiting the power of the monarchy as in the English and Swedish systems, others called for an elected emperor as in Poland, while still others advocated for establishing a republic led by the aristocracy. The most popular initiative, supported by 364 people, set forth a "Supreme Government" of 21 people and introducing elections of members to this government, of senators, governors, and chairmen (in this proposal the Supreme Privy Council would be abolished, so most members of the Council opposed it). Besides this, many young junior officers thought that Golitsyn and the Supreme Privy Council wanted to usurp power. Such an interpretation led to the agitation of the Russian Orthodox archbishop Theophan Prokopovich.

Protests broke out. When Anna Ivanovna arrived in Moscow, a delegation of aristocrats came to meet her and demanded that the Conditions be abolished and that absolute monarchy be restored.

CHAPTER 4

According to official sources, on February 25, 1730 the empress Anna Ivanovna, the Supreme Privy Council, and the delegation of aristocrats (around 800 people) gathered in the Lefortovo Palace. A petition was read aloud in which it was said that the Conditions "contained such provisions that made the people fear that in the future troublesome events may arise, which enemies of the nation could take advantage of." Right after this yet another delegation arrived. It first brought Anna Ivanovna a request to "give permission to all generals, officers, and Polish gentry to gather and send one or two representatives of each family, to examine and investigate all the Conditions, and according to the opinion of the majority, to create a scheme for ruling the state." She accepted this.

However, the Imperial Guard threatened the opposition with execution, and after this a second position was penned and read aloud by Antiochus Kantemir: "We humbly present you with and submissively ask you to accept absolute monarchy as your great and outstanding ancestors ruled by and to destroy the Conditions offered to your Imperial Majesty by the Supreme Council and signed by Your Majesty's hand." After these words the officials cried out, "We do not want the empress to be limited by laws; she should be an absolute ruler like all the ones we've had before."

At four o'clock in the afternoon the state councillor Maslov brought Anna Ivanovna the Conditions and she tore them up before the crowd. The next day Anna Ivanovna tasked him with writing an oath of absolute monarchy, which was approved. On March 1, 1730 in all the cathedrals and churches of Russia the people swore an oath to Anna Ivanova as their absolute ruler.

Thus a constitutional/aristocratic monarchy lasted in Russia for only ten days. The next day Anna Ivanovna re-established a Senate of 21 people, but she appointed all senators herself and no elections were held. The Supreme Privy Council was dissolved and it never returned in any form. Nobody ever came back to the notes of the aristocracy and limiting the power of the monarchy was not discussed any further.

After Anna Ivanovna was firmly established on the throne, almost all opposition was repressed. Only Golitsyn was pardoned, probably because he was responsible for the initiative of bringing Anna to power (however, in 1736 he was thrown into Schlusselburg prison for interceding for his condemned son-in-law and he later died there).

The 1734 project of emancipating the serfs

In 1711 under Peter the Great, a Senate was established to replace the Boyar Duma, which became the supreme governing body of Russia. It was in this Senate that the first project of emancipating the serfs was born. Anisim Maslov headed a department responsible for collecting taxes from the peasantry. Shortly before he had written several reports to Anna Ivanovna and her favorite — and the *de facto* head of her government — the German adventurer Ernest Johann Biron, in which Maslov denounced the idleness and bribe-taking of senior officials. Maslov gave such a convincing description of the plight of the peasantry that he was tasked with leading the discussion of the new law in the Senate.

Maslov's project of 1734 empowered the Senate to legislatively oversee the obligations of the peasantry. Placed on a draft decree that he prepared was a note by the secretary of the empress, stating "withhold". The Senate delayed action as long as possible until finally Maslov died. They buried the proposal with him.

The aristocracy knew that if they were given rights, the peasantry would demand them as well. [56] Thirty years later a project for a new Constitution arose, prepared by count Nikita Panin.

Panin (1718–1783) was a Russian diplomat and statesman, one of the most influential people in the Russian Empire. Catherine, the wife of the heir to the throne Peter III and the future empress Catherine the Great, approached Panin [57] and

CHAPTER 4

he decided to join in a palace coup. The conspirators plotted to overthrow Peter III in the hope that a limited monarchy would result, along with the introduction of a constitutional government.

At Christmas 1762, Elizabeth I, the young daughter of Peter the Great and Catherine I died. Peter III was supposed to be her successor. He was the grandson of Peter the Great, and the son of Peter the Great's daughter Anna Petrovna and Karl Friedrich, Duke of Holstein-Gottorp. Those around the court understood that the simple-minded Peter could not rule a country. Many sought ways to get rid of him. This was possible by transferring his authority to his son, the underaged Pavel Petrovich, and his mother Catherine II (Catherine the Great) would become regent.

Peter III came to the throne on December 25, 1761. His reign not only did not get the approval of the people, but it also caused general discontent. No wise guidance from his cautious advisers could help Peter compensate for his lack of tact, correct his mistakes, hide his overtly hostile attitude towards his wife and his preference for his favorite, Elizaveta Vorontsova. Catherine was popular among high society and her grief was one of the reasons for the negative attitude towards Peter. According to contemporary witnesses, murmurings of discontent were universal: all but a dozen members of the court wanted him overthrown and spoke about this openly. However, Peter III treated this matter lightly and was in no hurry to be crowned.

This helped the development of the conspiracy, which arose, as was the custom in the 18th century, among the court and the Imperial Guard. They favoured Catherine. The plot was known to the most senior people in Peter III's administration, attorney general Alexander Glebov, chief of police Korf, diplomat Nikita Panin among others, but they did betray the conspirators, though they did not play a direct role themselves.

The younger members of the plot centered around the family of Grigory Orlov. Of several brothers, two are most well known: Alexei Orlov (the youngest), famous for his physical strength, was a treasurer of the Imperial Guard artillery and played a great game under the pretext of which he gathered around himself the Imperial Guard youth. The other brother was Grigory himself. He passed Catherine's instructions to the plotters. In the summer of 1762 Peter acted as if Catherine would soon be killed and because of that the plotters were ready to take action although they did not dare to begin anything. Peter's name day was coming and on this day Peter, who at that time lived in Oranienbaum, wanted to celebrate with Catherine in Peterhof. Everybody expected that on June 29 he would decide about the fate of his wife. However, on June 27 an indiscreet soldier who had heard that Catherine was in danger, blurted out the secret of the conspiracy to an officer from outside the plot. Out of fear that the plot would be discovered the plotters decided to take action right away and on June 28 they launched a successful coup.

Catherine had recently been living alone in Peterhof and these days had been restless for her as she had been waiting for the payoff. She regularly received news about the state of affairs in her allies' camp and in the enemies' camp. Under the pretext of vacating all the rooms in the palace for the emperor who was going to come with his retinue, the empress moved to a separate corner of the Peterhof gardens, to a pavilion called Monplaisir. By doing this she avoided the eyes of the sentries. In this pavilion, on June 28, Catherine was woken up early in the morning by Alexei Orlov. She dressed and together with her female servants she entered Orlov's carriage. Orlov whipped the horses to as fast a speed as possible. At seven o'clock in the morning Catherine reached the barracks of the Izmaylovsky Regiment. Some of the soldiers lined up quickly. The soldiers swore to die for Catherine and they fell down to kiss her hands and her dress. Meanwhile the officers brought the rest of the Izmailovsky soldiers, a priest with a cross appeared, and the entire regiment made an oath to Catherine II. She got into the carriage and proceeded to the barracks of the Semenovsky Regiment, the Coast Guard, and the Horse Guard. Everywhere she was greeted with cries of "Hurrah!" and everywhere the soldiers joined her. The artillery too followed the example of the Imperial Guard and went over to Catherine's side.

In the meantime to the site of the action came general Rozumovsky, Nikita Ivanovich Panin, prince Volkonsky, Ivan Ivanovich Shuvalov, and

CHAPTER 4

many other noblemen who joined Catherine's retinue. Surrounded by this army she set off for the Kazan Cathedral in Saint Petersburg. There she met with the Bishop of Novgorod and other church dignitaries. They celebrated a thanksgiving service and announced Catherine as grand empress of all Russia and the Grand Duke Pavel Petrovich was announced the heir to the throne.

At that time Peter III was in Oranienbaum, intending to begin the celebration of his nameday in Peterhof and Catherine was supposed to be waiting there for him. As soon as he arrived at Peterhof, the emperor investigated the pavilion in which Catherine had been living and found that she was gone. Everything indicated that she had not just gone away for a while but that she had fled. Some old noblemen, under the pretext of finding Catherine and talking sense into her, went to Saint Petersburg and there they joined her side. Having found himself in this hopeless situation Peter decided to go to Kronstadt. When he arrived there he was not accepted. The harbor was closed and people shouted from there that there was no emperor and that there was only Catherine the empress. Peter was stunned and instead of fleeing to Revel he waited for Catherine in Oranienbaum. In the morning of the 29th she arrived at Peterhof accompanied by the army and she sent her advance guard into Oranienbaum. The troops immediately surrounded the palace and Peter was taken into captivity. Everything was over.>>>

The coup was not supposed to bring Catherine to the throne but Pavel, who was the legitimate heir to the throne. Catherine would fulfill the role of regent until Pavel was of age, and when Pavel I came to the throne, his power would be limited by the Governing Senate. This name was given to the body by Peter the Great, but its composition was different. It was intended that a portion of the Senate's members would be appointed by the tsar for life, but the majority were drawn from the aristocracy, although that is also a position held for life. Catherine pretended to agree with this, but she signed no document.

After the coup Catherine did everything she could to be confirmed on the throne herself, and not simply stand on the sidelines as regent. The Decembrist Mikhail Fonvizin has written an account of this time. [58] Based on the testimony of his father, he writes, "In 1773 or 1774, when the tsarevich Pavel came of age and was married, Count Nikita Ivanovich Panin, his brother, the field marshall Petr Ivanonich Panin, Princess Yekaterina Romanovna Dashkova, Prince Nikolai Vasilyevich Repnin, one of the church hierarchs … many of the noblemen of that time entered into a conspiracy to depose Catherine, who had no right to the throne, and elevate her grown son instead. Pavel Petrovich was aware of this, and he agreed to adopt the constitution that Panin had proposed, sign it, and swear that as tsar he would not violate the basic laws limiting the absolute power of the monarchy."

A detailed constitution was worked out. According to Mikhail Fonvizin, "Underneath the Senate, in a hierarchical structure, there would be assemblies of the nobility at regional levels. The Senate would be invested with full legislative power, while the emperor would remain an executive authority who would approve and make public the laws adopted by the Senate."

The constitution mentioned the need for a gradual emancipation of the serfs. This act was prefaced with the statement, "Power is entrusted to the sovereign for the good of his subjects. Tyrants know of this truth, but good rulers heed it." [59]

Somehow word of this drafting of a constitution and a new coup reached Catherine the Great. The young Pavel recanted, showed remorse for his actions, and Catherine, to her credit, did not massacre her opponents but only quietly separated the conspirators from Pavel. The thing is that making a fuss, a show trial of the "traitors" and "oath breakers", was not very convenient for Catherine II herself, as she in fact was ruling illegally and any trial would have revealed this to all Russia and Europe as well.

Catherine the Great understood that Russia needed a new code of laws, as the Code of 1649 and the Decrees of Peter the Great were by now incredibly out of date. She sincerely wanted to put things to rights and satisfy the widest possible swath of society. On December 14, 1766 she proclaimed a Manifesto on gathering deputies to form a Commission for creating a new project for a constitution. The committee consisted of representatives of the governing bodies (the Senate, the Synod, [60] collegiums, and chancelleries) and of deputies from various segments of the population.

The system of electing members to the Commission was dizzyingly complex. One deputy was elected for each town by those owning property, one deputy was elected for each region by landowners, and from every province there was one deputy from among the *odnodvortzy* — 'owners of one homestead' descendants of the pre-Peter the Great nobility serving the state, now impoverished to the extent that they had no serfs — as well as from among soldiers owning arable land, state "black" peasants, and domiciled foreigners, and a representative came from each people whether christianized or not.

A total of 564 deputies were elected. The Commission did not have any representatives from the serfs. For the most part there were deputies of towns, although Moscow with its enormous population and the regional capital Buy with only a few hundred inhabitants each sent one deputy. Towndwellers formed less than 5% of the total population of the Russian Empire, but the 39% of the Commission nonetheless consisted of deputies from towns. The breakdown was: state governing bodies (5%), the aristocracy (30%), towns (39%), inhabitants of rural districts (14%), and Cossacks, foreigners, and other classes (12%). [61]

Catherine took the work of the commission very seriously. The deputies were made state employees with a government salary. They received greater privileges than anyone had in Russia at that time. All of the deputies were under the empress's own protection for life. No matter what crime a deputy might be accused of, they were immune from the death penalty and corporal punishment. Their property could only be confiscated in the event of debt. Crimes against a deputy received double the punishment, so their personal safety was ensured. In addition, deputies were allowed to wear special badges. After completing their service, deputies from the nobility were allowed to incorporate those badges into their coats of arms " to remind their descendants of the great cause they had served".

The 564 deputies brought over fifteen hundred mandates. These mandates are valuable for historians, because one can seem how people in various parts of Russia lived and what their concerns were. Both the mandates and the minutes of the Commission's meetings show that such different demands were presented that there could be no talk about drawing up a common law for the entire Empire. It became evident that the Commission could not accomplish anything. When Catherine the Great saw that her project was not producing any coherent body of laws, only great expense to the state budget, she gave up her idea of creating a code of laws for the whole nation.

One step from a constitution

Another attempt at a constitution came from Mikhail Speransky (1772–1839), an illustrious statesman of the early 19th century. It is an example of how outstanding abilities received an adequate reward.

Speransky was born in 1772 in the Vladimir Governorate in the family of a village priest. His blind grandfather taught him how to read: during church services the boy would read from hymnals, and his blind grandfather (himself once a priest) would correct him if he made a mistake. Speransky gained notice early on for his abilities and, thanks to his acquaintance with the influential nobleman who owned the land of his native village, he made it into the seminary at the St. Alexander Nevsky Monastery in Saint Petersburg. After his studies he was designated a teacher of mathematics, physics, oratory, and philosophy. At the same time Speransky became the private secretary to Prince Kurakin and lodged in his house.

Under the tsar Alexander I, Speransky entered the service

CHAPTER 4

of the ministry of the interior. Alexander became personally acquainted with him in 1806, when Speransky's superior, Prince Kochubey, fell ill and began to send Speransky to report in his place. The tsar valued the young officer's outstanding ability. In 1808, Speransky was in the tsar's retinue during his meeting at Erfurt with Napoleon. Knowing French, Speransky could easily communicate with the French generals and politicians.

If we believe in some of the testimony from this time, Alexander I asked Speransky what he thought about France and the French people. "The French have better laws," Speransky answered, "but we have better people."

"This is exactly what we should talk about, so that our laws could become better too," said the tsar.

In the autumn of the same year the tsar tasked him with an overhaul of state institutions. Alexander I often spent whole evenings with him in conversation and reading works on this subject. They were preparing for broad democratic reforms.

Speransky's complete proposal is not known; not everything has survived and many documents are attested in different versions. As far as we know, the main themes of the overhaul were to have been the following:

1. a legislative assembly (the State Duma);

2. legal reforms; members of the judicial class would be freely elected by the people, but supervision of observance of the laws and guarding public safety would lie with the state;

3. executive power should belong to the state, but in order to ensure that it does not distort the law, the state must be made accountable to the legislature.

These general principles were developed by Speransky and justified in the *Introduction to the National Constitution* that he compiled in the autumn of 1809. According to this initiative, political rights would based on ownership of property and would be granted to the aristocracy and the middle classes. The lower classes of society, such as serfs, artisans, their employees, and domestic servants, would have civil rights but no political rights.

People could rise from the lower classes to the middle class by buying property.

If this proposal had been realized, Russia would have become the most democratic country in the world, as 90% of free peasants and many townspeople owned property. The British parliament of the time was elected by only 2% of the population. The State Duma of Russia would be determined by an absolute majority of the country's inhabitants.

However, the majority of the aristocracy was against popular representation, because they realized this would immediately undermine their power. Many accused Speransky almost directly of treason: he widely used the Napoleonic Code and drew on many French laws of the time. Furthermore, despite the state of war with France, Speransky continued to correspond with French legal experts. In 1812 Alexander I had to offer a response to accusations that his chief reformer was in contact with the enemy. During a two-hour audience he explains to Speransky that in view of the enemy approaching the borders of the Russian Empire, he was not able to confirm all the allegations against him and on March 17, 1812 Speransky was exiled to Nizhny Novgorod.

Though exiled, Speransky's fate was not a tragic one. He became governor of Penza, and from 1819 he was appointed governor-general of Siberia. In a handwritten letter, Alexander I said that with this appointment, he wanted to show how unfairly maligned Speransky had been. From 1821 Speransky was again a member of the State Council.

It bears reminding that the son of a village priest lived the life of a key official and member of the court, became a prominent dignitary of the Russian Empire and received the title of count. If the population of Russia grew six times larger between 1700 and 1900, the aristocracy and other classes that had the rights of appointed aristocrats grew by forty times. Members of the new aristocracy had commoner ancestors and had often only recently been elevated to that class.

CHAPTER 4

Local democracy

Alexander II unleashed so many reforms on society that distortions of social development were inevitable. It was, among other things, due to the judicial reform, introducing trial by jury, and a reform of the army replacing the traditional recruiting policy, and urban reforms. But the most significant and important of these was the so-called *zemstvo* reform. In accordance with his new law, starting from January 1, 1864 elected bodies of self-government in the districts and governorates called *zemstvo* would be introduced. District and provincial governments functioned initially in 34 governorates, and by 1914 in 43 (out of 60). These local bodies, a sort of mini-parliament, consisted of representatives of all social classes, but the right to vote was still granted only to men who owned property.

New executive bodies were created as well, provincial and district boards. These boards had their own funds. From the raising of local taxes, insurance was provided for fire, floods, and other disasters, as well as credit for small entrepreneurs.

The *zemstvo* assemblies were introduced gradually and not in all areas of the Russian Empire. The ministry of the interior and governors had the right to revoke decisions made by the *zemstvo*. The authority of the *zemstvo* assemblies was constantly limited by the state. In spite of all this, they played a key role in Russia's economic development at the beginning of the 20th century, as well as in the cultural development of the Russian people. The *zemstvo* assemblies were responsible for education, public health, partly for public safety, they organized fire brigades, etc. In 1865 the *zemstvo* assemblies were even permitted to establish their own local postal service (alongside the national one) with separate rules and tariffs. At the same time the *zemstvo* assemblies received the right to have their own postal stamps, but only on the condition that the design of these stamps would not have features in common with those of the national post.

The status of *zemstvo* doctors and teachers was so high that memories of this have survived in Russia down to our time. At the very end of the 19th century, under the tsar Nicholas II, a Zemstvo Movement arose. Supporters of this movement came together in illegal underground organizations and demanded that the *zemstvo* assemblies be given political powers, along with autonomous government at the small rural district level, a constitution, and democratic reforms. [62] Only the interim government acting from June to August of 1917, finally brought the *zemstvo* assemblies to all parts of Russia.

The Manifesto of October 17th

On October 17, 1905, during the revolution that shook Russia that year, a "Manifesto on the Improvement of the State Order" was proclaimed. It granted freedom of conscience, freedom of speech, freedom of assembly and association, universal suffrage, and it required that the State Duma approve any new laws.

The country saw a wave of new political parties springing up, with legal recognition, each of which offered different demands and ways of changing the political system.

It seemed that Russia was moving towards a parliamentary monarchy like Britain, Holland, or Sweden. In fact, the activity of these parties often had contradictory consequences. Alexander Solzhenitsyn even believed that a parliamentary multi-party system was not right for Russia. He thought that Russia would do better with a non-party democracy that was based not on party platforms, but on the personality of the candidate running for office.

In any case, the Manifesto allowed Russian society to widely participate in political life, and Russian society proved quite capable of doing so.

The State Duma

The establishment of the State Duma was a direct result of the Revolution of 1905. Under pressure from the liberal wing of the government, especially prime minister Sergei Witte, tsar Nicholas II decided not to further aggravate the situation in the country and proclaimed the manifesto convening the Duma:

CHAPTER 4

A time has come to call elected people according to their good deeds, from the entire Russian land, to permanently and actively participate in the creation of laws, and to include for this purpose into higher state institutions a special legislative body which will be appointed to discuss and decide on national revenue and public expenditures.

Already on October 11, 1905 a decree was issued "On a change to the election statutes of the State Duma", by which the right to vote was granted to practically all male citizens older than 25, except for soldiers, students, day laborers, and some itinerant peoples.

Among the deputies were people of very modest means. The bureaucratic institutions, aristocracy, monarchy, and local direct democracy were augmented by parliamentary democracy, and the nation was fully prepared to take part in it.

The provisional government of 1917

During the period of the provisional government between the February and October Revolutions of 1917, Russia became the most democratic state in the world. Unfortunately, it did not do any lasting good. From March 22 to April 12, 1917 the Provisional Government adopted a number of resolutions, annulled discrimination based on religion or ethnicity, made all people equal before the law and allowed the masses to freely use their political and civil rights.

On September 1, 1917 the Provisional Government proclaimed Russia a republic. Regulations were set for elections to the Constituent Assembly. For the first time, not only in Russian but in world history, the right to vote was granted to both men and women once they turned 20, and active-duty soldiers could vote as well. Elections to the Constituent Assembly, and to councils at all levels, were held without any limits or special qualifications, which was utterly remarkable considering the level of Russian society at the time.

What kind of informed and responsible choices for the

future of Russia could voters make in a country where over 70% of voters were illiterate? They even paid their taxes not individually, but collectively, as entire communities and social classes. The principle of quotas and qualification requirements (depending on education, property owned, etc.) that existed in tsarist times constituted a kind of a sieve that limited power to certain kinds of people. As a result, the new democracy could not guarantee a government accountable to everyone and instantly turned into mob rule. This was one of the reasons that the October Revolution succeeded.

Democracy in the USSR

Around the world the USSR is often depicted as an "Evil Empire" and linked to appalling tyranny, where there was neither democracy nor human rights.

Russians, especially older generations, disagree with this opinion, simply because they remember the Soviet Union. The USSR indeed lacked democracy in the Western sense of the word: the right to vote and to be elected to state authorities, the right to openly express one's opinions and publish them, the right to disagree with the decisions of the government and to not participate in its policies. All of the rights ascribed to the people by the constitutions, from the one of 1924 to the one of 1977, existed only on paper. In the reality it was not even the Councils at various levels that ruled the country but the Communist Party, the CPSU.

> Soviet rule in its pure form lasted less than a week in Russia. By seizing the Winter Palace and arresting the Provisional Government, Lenin and Trotsky did not act in the name of the Bolsheviks. The October coup set up a half-legitimate Congress of Soviets, which then met in Petrograd, as Saint Petersburg was called at that time. These workers' councils had no control over the army, state organizations or finance, but they had their own paramilitary, the Red Guards, and had influence in a number of military units.

CHAPTER 4

The most important thing was that the Soviets were assertive, full of energy, and they did not hesitate to move from words to actions, which was a quality lacking in the liberal politicians of the time. After Lenin overthrew the Provisional Government in the name of the "second power", i.e. workers' councils, he appeared at the Congress on the same night (between November 7 and 8 according to the Gregorian calendar), where he gave his famous decree and called on all workers' councils across the country to take power into their own hands in the same way, putting an end to the monolithic state that had prevailed in Russia.

What happened next is the most interesting part of the story. The Bolsheviks at this convention were a minority, but they had tight control over the Red Guard paramilitary, bridges, telegraphs, railways, and government offices. It is clear that the Congress of Soviets was an unorganized and uneducated group (consisting of 649 delegates) who did not move in the top layers of society.

But as the mob could get nothing done, the question was raised of forming a new, permanently acting body of the Congress – the All-Russian Central Executive Committee, in short VTsIK (exactly from that moment the word *ispolkom* 'executive committee' began to deeply entrench itself in the Russian political lexicon, because, in principle, it is not always important who makes decisions and how; the most important thing is who is going to carry them out). At this stage, a portion of the delegates, the SRs (the Socialist Revolutionary Party), known as the Mensheviks, left the convention in protest, leaving Lenin and the leftist revolutionaries to become the majority. The VTsIK still included representatives of multiple political parties (among its members, let's say, there were 29 Left SRs), and for that reason on November 9 one further, real authority was established: the Council of People's Commissars. The CPC became over the following years the true decision-making and executive authority. The difference between it and the VTsIK (the half-government) and even more between it and the Congress (half-parliament) is that the CPC from the start consisted of only one political party, namely the Bolsheviks, Lenin's associates.

Thus Soviet power in the original sense of the word — workers' councils — lasted only a few days, though it officially went on until the signing of the Brest peace treaty and the departure of the last Left SRs from the CPC. After that, the Bolshevik's single-party dictatorship took hold, or rather its "leading role" in the state. The Party did not deny this: at each of its congresses, this leading role grew bigger and bigger.

But there was another side to Soviet rule: equal social opportunities. When it all comes down to it, democracy is simply the protection of every ordinary individual which allows them to change their position in life. In this, the Soviet system was at least no worse than Western democracies, and perhaps even better.

The essence of the Soviet system

The classical position of supporters of democracy is the following: democracy begins when a body comes together to work out the basic principles of the new political structure. It was just like this in the USA: "We the people of these United States do ordain and establish this Constitution."

In Soviet Russia this body was the workers' councils, whose roots go back to the *zemstvo* system. In 1917 councils of workers and representatives of soldiers and farmers were formed at different regional levels.

The first workers' councils oversaw paramilitary operations, the economy, the life of society, even marriages and divorces. At first glance these workers' councils were a very primitive form of government, a sort of cross between a parliament, executive branch, and even elements of a judicial authority. The indivisibility of the functions of a workers' council was hard for Europeans to understand, as well as for Russian urbanites who looked towards Europe. Nonetheless, for most Russians at that time it was difficult to envision the need for a separation of powers.

In the first year of establishing the Soviet (from the Russian word *soviet* 'council'), people were elected for those councils from different parties. In June 1918 the Fifth All-Russian Congress of Soviets adopted a constitution for Soviet Russia. This made the new political order official.

CHAPTER 4

There was no longer any struggle between parties in the councils: the Bolsheviks had destroyed and banned all parties except their own. For that reason already by the 1920 the authority of the councils mean little compared to the authority of the one Communist party. In spite of its shortcomings, however, the Soviet system did provide for large groups of people — the urban class, the federal subjects, minorities, and workers' unions — a certain possibility to express their feelings.

A Soviet individual could participate in the councils at various levels, elect deputies to it, and give them a mandate. This created at least the illusion that he or she was subject to the law and had real political rights. In the same way people in the West participated in the work of their country's parliament and other democratic institutions, electing their representatives, who were mainly from societal elites. Professional working men had been members of the British parliament only five times over its history, but in the Soviet Union they were continually present.

To a degree, this was a fiction. At all levels the councils had little power compared to the party leadership. On the other hand, members of these councils could make real decisions, even if they were limited to a small scope.

The ability of an individual to help in directing state affairs was predetermined: for this he or she would have to build a political career within the Communist Party, entering a small circle of people known to and trusted by the Party. But no one stood in the way of an ordinary individual entering the Party and building a career.

In such a vast country as Russia, central leadership was, as a rule, always undemocratic. Before 1917 the aristocracy acted as a barrier between the people and the direction of the state. Now this role was held by the party leadership and professional functionaries. As Nikolai Berdyaev wrote, "The dictatorship of the proletariat, by expanding state power, has developed an enormous bureaucracy, which grows like a web over the whole country and subordinating itself to it. This new Soviet bureaucracy is stronger than the tsarist one, there is a new privileged class, which can easily exploit the masses. This is already happening." However, this was supplemented by enormous social guarantees and rights for individuals in the local and professional spheres.

Social welfare

For those who emigrated from the USSR, one of the biggest downsides was always the loss of a sense of security. In the Soviet Union people used to joke, "Unions protect workers even when they don't work." It really was true. People came to work and it was nearly impossible for them to be dismissed from their jobs. Not for everybody this side of social security was so necessary, but at least it was there.

I needn't mention the guaranteed paid sick leave, maternity leave, disability benefits, retirement pensions, and scholarships for students. A resident of the USSR could work without overexerting himself — everyone had a sufficient minimum except for perhaps vagrants and lower-classes mothers with many children.

Wherever a citizen of the USSR worked, he could expect free housing or the right to buy his own apartment. At large factories the workers were offered a labor contract for several years and enticed by being shown a set of apartment keys. Poorer people worked for ten or fifteen years to buy an apartment, but after fifteen years they were eligible for a free apartment provided by the state. Once you got it, it was yours and no one would take it away from you. Many people got apartments much faster, especially in new cities or people who took jobs in high demand. The quality of Soviet housing, until the 1970s, was no worse in the West. As the Soviet novelist Vasily Aksyonov observed, "Soviet living spaces are cramped, but they are warm and comfortable," and they did not demand frequent repair. When repairs were necessary, they were provided free by the state.

CHAPTER 4

When Marina Vladi set up an exhibition in Paris of women's lingerie brought from the USSR, it was presented as something horrible. Indeed, Soviet clothing lost out against things from the West. Women stood in line to get their hands on tights from East Germany or shoes from Hungary. But shoes and clothes were always available at an affordable price. A Soviet person in the 1960s and 1970s had plenty of things provided for him without particular effort and even to a similar degree as people from an average Western country, though it was easier to get food than housing, and housing was easier to get than good clothes.

One could add public transportation and leisure. Today a plane ticket from Moscow to Vladivostok costs twice the average monthly salary in Russia. In the USSR it cost less than one month's wages. Even people of modest means could use the trains. Residents of Moscow and Leningrad, even students, could take the train on Friday evening to Tallinn or Riga, walk around the next day, and take the next evening train home again.

Many families, even from Kazakhstan or Siberia, regularly took their vacations on the Black Sea. Vacation packages were provided by unions for free or at half price. Public transport was very cheap.

One can add to this an equality in income that seems absurd to us today. A driver in the Russian North, a member of the Academy of Sciences, and a specialized industrial worker would all make at most 800–100 rubles a month. The minimum wage was 90 rubles a month, and the USSR average salary was 140 or 150 rubles a month.

Thus the income gap between rich and poor in the USSR was less than tenfold. No one could have imagined people living with the same city with not a ten, but a hundred or ten thousand times difference in incomes like Russia today. Long ago, in the 1960s, some commentators outside Russia claimed that it was precisely the experience of the USSR that was pushing to West towards socialism. If there was a country that so guaranteed social welfare than other countries should catch up to it. In the postwar era, the West saw a wave of socialist reforms, providing more and more state welfare, which was uncharacteristic of capitalist societies.

Social mobility

The USSR had considerably less social stratification than the countries of the West, thanks to people having the right — and real possibility — of working in any profession. The Soviet Union considered talented young people sacred. It seemed utterly immoral to hold them back in learning and taking on the work they wanted to do. The availability of free vocational training, for a time (in the 1960s and 1970s) the best in the world, really gave equal opportunities for professional development.

The principle of equal opportunity also applied to vertical stratification, and simply put — to one's social career. Soviet citizens were bombarded with loud propaganda slogans saying that all paths were open to them, that they walked through the country as its masters and could easily go from an unskilled worker to a state minister. In the United States the same classical stereotype was born: someone could go from a shoeshine boy to a millionaire. But how many such people were there?

But in the USSR not just the representatives of the elites, but also people who ruled the country began as working people, rural laborers and truck drivers. Khrushchev came from a mining background, Brezhnev was a land surveyor. The road to becoming a minister or party official was essentially open to everyone. People, even from the most humble walks of life, really felt that the laws were looking out for them, that the people ran the state. Of course the laws were not looking out for them, and the state was run by the party elites, not the people, but a feeling of empowerment was widespread.

The "promoted workers" of the 1930s–1950s constituted a vast elite specialized intelligentsia in the USSR, and they even managed the factories, industrial districts, and ministries.

CHAPTER 4

The state of affairs finally changed when the positions at the top of the Party became semi-hereditary in the 1970s and 1980s. This period is sometimes seen as a "defense of Soviet rule against outsiders". This was not a bitterly ironic statement but a real description of what was going on in the country. In reality, the party finally changed from a career ladder, albeit in poor state and wobbly, into a monolithic wall without doors or windows.

Of course, it makes no sense to compare parliamentary democracies with the Soviet system, they are apples and oranges. But it is an undeniable fact that Soviet rule was not primitive totalitarianism and lacked any element of democracy.

The population of the USSR lived in its own Soviet socialist democracy, though a somewhat peculiar, perverse kind of democracy. In many ways it fell short of parliamentary democracies, but in other ways it even surpassed them.

CHAPTER 5

Myth 4: Russia as a prison for peoples

The myth of Russia as a prison for peoples arose in the 19th century. According to this myth, the chauvinism of ethnic Russians always led to the widespread oppression of the "colonized" minority peoples. Thus all other ethnicities in this multicultural country were conquered by force of arms and became half-slaves, doomed to disappeared from the face of the earth.

People who know something of the history of medieval Russia claim that the Slavs, leaving their homeland northeast of the Dnieper River, first colonized the autochthonous Finno-Ugrian lands (Moscow, Vladimir and Novgorod), and then the state of Muscovy burst out and crushed the Ugrians, Permian peoples, Tatars, Bashkirs, Sakha, Kalmyks, the peoples of Siberia and the Russian North, and then the Poles, Finns, Krimchaks, peoples of the Caucasus, and the inhabitants of Central Asia.

Such people say that the "colonialist policy of the tsars" differed from, for example, the British Empire only in that the British conquered territories overseas through their navy, while the Russians did it by moving over dry land. Through their advantageous geographical position, the Slavs were able to take over territories stretching from Berlin to the Kamchatka Peninsula. They even managed to cross the Bering Strait to Alaska and set up fortified colonies all the way down to California. If it hadn't been for the Pacific Ocean and the difficulties in staying in touch with the Russian homeland, Russia might still have its "American" colonies today.

The phrase "prison for peoples", first used to describe the Tsarist era, came to be applied to the national policies of the USSR. A modern interpretation of this myth of "prison for peoples" or "evil empire" now circulates in former Soviet republics to justify their declarations of sovereignty during the collapse of the USSR.

The roots of the myth

Russia was first called a "prison" by a French writer and traveler, the marquis Astolphe de Custine (1790–1857). His book, *La Russie en 1839* was published in Paris in 1843. It was not translated into Russian until the 20th century, but nearly all of the tsarist aristocracy knew French (sometimes better than their native Russian) like many educated people of that time. Custine, like no one else, in a talented journalistic manner managed to create a vivid picture of the gigantic empire, a country where individuals were defenseless against the mighty state. As he concluded, "However immense this empire is, it is nothing but a prison, the key of which is held by the emperor."

At the same time, Custine said nothing about international relations. Notions of the nation-state and national sovereignty, which arose during the Enlightenment and the French Revolution of 1789–1793, had only begun to spread across Europe.

By calling Russia a prison, Custine wasn't referring to how the country's minorities were treated, but what he saw as the humiliating status of all peoples and social classes, all of the Russia Empire's subjects in general. He wrote of the lack of a civil society in the country, independent public opinion capable of resisting the tsar.

The slogan of Russia as a prison for peoples was taken up by the Bolsheviks, who gave it a wider interpretation. The revolutionary rhetoric of the Bolsheviks was meant to provoke the feelings of smaller peoples, to encourage them to free the "inmates of this prison", who consisted of a great many different ethnicities, to free all peoples, even the ones fewest in number. These seeds led to a bountiful harvest in 1917.

In the Soviet era, the tsarist-era statement that Russia was a "prison for peoples" was frequently quoted in histories of the country. George F. Keenan, an American ambassador to Russia, wrote, "Even if we admit that *La Russie en 1839* was not a very good book about Russia in 1839, we are confronted with the disturbing fact that it was an excellent book about the Russia of Joseph Stalin, and not a bad book about the Russia of Brezhnev and Kosygin." [63]

Keenan was one of many who believed that it would be a good thing to free these "captive peoples" from their prison. Winston Churchill also believed that helping the peoples of the USSR to break free was the best tool in the fight against Soviet power. Not without reason a joke was popular that the USSR was not a prison for peoples but a communal apartment of all peoples from which some people just needed to be moved to other apartments. Zbigniew Brzezinski and Richard Pipes also referred to the "prison for peoples" in their speeches. [64] Western analysts were convinced that the USSR was not a new state but simply an expansion of the Russian republic, [65] and that in dealing with the USSR, the world was facing a new type of colonialism. [66]

The American historian Terry Martin has described the USSR as an "affirmative action empire". The party elites *de facto* created a centralized power, while at the same time the national republics *de jure* made it a federation. Thus there was a kind of compromise between the center and the periphery, and the USSR had to generously offer opportunities to the elites of the different minorities in order to avoid separatist tendencies.

CHAPTER 5

In the end, this recognition of minorities produced separatism nonetheless. During perestroika, complaints that the USSR was a "prison for peoples" arose in every republic, among nationalists and democratic forces of all stripes. The notion of Russian colonialism allowed them to substantiate their claims to independence. [67]

The enormous potential of the movements for various people's liberation was deftly used by the Bolsheviks. Even during the Civil War of 1918–1920 they managed to brilliantly play the national card, artificially stimulating local forces that convinced the elites to secede from the Russian Empire and thus seize power for themselves. According to some scholars, the Red Army's victory in the Civil War is due to, among other factors, Lenin's nationalities policy. They even say that Lenin's genius lay in detecting this desire for liberation among Russia's minorities. Along with a small army of Russian laborers he sent into revolutionary battles an innumerable multitude of different nations who longed for liberation. [68]

Lenin was improvising, according to professor Gregori Derlugyan. "In the autumn of 1918 Denikin's volunteer army smashed the Red forces in Kuban and on the river Terek. [69] The remains of the Reds sought refuge in the mountains of the Caucasus, where Kirov and Ordzhonikidze entered into a longstanding dispute with the Muslim authorities of Chechnia and Ingushetia. As a result of comparing the teachings of Marx and Muhammed, a wonderful fatwa was proclaimed that recognized the Bolsheviks' struggle as a jihad for justice. When Denikin was only a hundred miles from Moscow, he was hit from behind by the 'red-green' partisans from the Caucasus, as well as the Ukrainian insurgents of Nestor Makhno. Similarly, the offensive of the ataman Dutov was halted by Bashkir troops which had joined the Bolsheviks, Admiral Kolchak was held back by Latvian gunners, the Baku Commune was defended from the Turks, and the Azeri Musavat by the Armenian Revolutionary Federation armed with Mauser guns and Georgian Mensheviks were defeated with the help of Abkhaz peasant militias, the Kyaraz." [70]

The anti-Bolshevik forces, known as the White Army, wanted to restore the Russian Empire [71] and inevitably came into conflict with the new nation-states. Even if the new governments of the countries that were part of the Russian Empire offered them help, the Whites often refused to work jointly. For example, the Finnish general Mannerheim [72] was prepared to lead the forces of the Finnish army against Petrograd, which was controlled by the Reds. If it were successful, an independent Finland could count on Russia as a huge ally. A small country like Finland very much needed a strong neighbor as an ally. In other words, if the the White forces recognized Finland's independence, as Lenin already had, Mannerheim was ready to cooperate with the White Army.

The White Army leader Admiral Kolchak [73] gave Mannerheim non-commital answers, however. Sazonov, the former foreign minister in the Provisional Government, was then in Paris and refused to allow Yudenich to conduct negotiations with Mannerheim. On the other hand, General Denikin, who had always been polite and tolerant, this time made a serious statement that he would of course first of all hang Lenin and his associates, but the next in line would be the members of independent Finland's government. After all this, naturally the Finns did not strike Petrograd.

Estonia too refused to fight against the Bolsheviks after the White Army refused to recognize its independence. In the North Caucasus, Denikin was forced to assign special forces to hold off the constant onslaught of the mountain peoples, but the Bolsheviks were able to rely on these mountain peoples in their fight.

Of all the subject peoples of the Russian Empire, only the Poles fought against both the White Army and the Red Army. Denikin felt that the Poles had prevented him from taking Moscow: they launched an attack at the most decisive moment of "Operation Moscow", in October 1919, and thus crippled the White advance. [74]

And then Poland started to fight the Bolsheviks...

Later in the 20th century the Eurasian movement presented Russia not as an empire, but as a different kind of state. One can read in detail about the ideology of these people, but for us at the moment the most important thing is that the scholars who belonged to the Eurasian school of the 1920s, primarily the

CHAPTER 5

historians Petr Savitsky, Nikolai Troubetskoy, George Vernadsky, Nikolai Alekseev, and others, wrote, "Russia is a world of its own. Peoples and individuals living in this special place are capable of achieving a degree of mutual understanding and peaceful coexistence that they cannot achieve with the peoples of Europe and Asia." [75] Thus the Eurasianists saw Russia as a true "family of peoples" that brought together people of different backgrounds and religions through a common culture, from everyday life to political traditions, and through a common historical fate.

To Russians today, Eurasianism is interesting as an attempt to see Russia as a diverse country, not an empire. Even if it were an empire, it would be a vastly different one than the empires of Europe.

The road to an empire

> The empires of the future are the empires of the mind.
>
> —*Winston Churchill*

The ruler of the world

The roots of European colonialism can be traced to the Age of Discovery in the 16th and 17th centuries. Even the name of that era is extremely Eurocentric. Who discovered the world? Europeans. Who did they discover it for? For themselves, of course. Other people might have a very different idea of who discovered whom and whether it was necessary to do so. In 1971 the chief of the Sioux tribe, Standing Bull, took a flight to Genoa, walked down the gangway in his full war dress and proudly proclaimed that he had discovered Italy. Why should that sound funny to us? Columbus "discovered" America, which was already home to 22 million people.

Even before they had managed to "discover" the whole world, Europeans in the 16th and 17th centuries began to treat their new territories as their granary. Slavery is simply one example of how the Europeans managed to turn the world upside down.

Let's not dwell on this saddest page from history. Let's remember only that the world trade in African slaves was finally outlawed only with the conventions of Vienna (1815) and Verona (1822–1832). It was in fact the Russians at the Vienna conference, where the fate of Europe was decided after Napoleon had been defeated, who brought up the matter of the slave trade. Russia also proposed establishing an international police force for the seas. This proposal was ultimately rejected in the congress in Aachen in 1818.

While the slave trade finally came to an end, that happened much later than the emancipation of the serfs in Russia. Trading in slaves, transporting them over the ocean, stopped after the signing of a treaty between Britain and the USA on April 7, 1862. Already then people said that English merchants were ruined, because they had invested in slaves in the USA beforehand. Trafficking in slaves really ended only in 1890, when the Brussels Conference Act of 1890 was signed by over twenty countries in Europe, Asia, and Africa. By that time the slaves had been freed in the USA, Brazil and Peru, at least officially. As unpleasant as serfdom was, Russia had no racist theories as Europeans did. Ibrahim Hannibal (1696–1781), an Ethiopian slave ransomed from the Ottoman Empire by Russia, and the ancestor of the great Russian poet Alexander Pushkin, was a sensation in the court of Peter the Great, but that did not hinder him from becoming a nobleman, and answering every sneer directed at him with his sword. *En garde*! While he actually did do this sometimes, this mostly happened when he travelled abroad to Europe.

The Sepoy Mutiny and the Fate of Shamil

The largest colonial uprising against Britain was the Sepoy Mutiny (1857–1858), when Indian troops in the British military, trained by the colonialist authorities, rebelled against their

CHAPTER 5

masters. This riot was sparked by rumors that the Sepoys' rifle cartridges were greased with the fat of cows, animals that Hindus held sacred and forbid using for their meat or fat, or pig fat, which outraged the Muslim population.

Thus a mixed crowd of Indians from both Hindu and Muslim backgrounds stood behind the barricades. Discontent had been growing, but the British administration ignored the threat. The sepoys interpreted the British intransigence as an unambiguous disregard of their religious beliefs by the arrogant whites.

Naturally, the fat on the rifle catridges only served as a pretext. For the real reason one has to look more closely at the British conquest of India. The rebellion was led by Indians who for many years had been despised for many years by their British "fellow soldiers" and treated as second-class citizens. It is true that the Sepoys treated the British cruelly, even women and children. But what should one call the behavior of the British army and its commanders, who crushed entire villages, who officially endorsed tactics of spreading terror among the population and executed the leaders of captured Sepoys, who had surrendered after they were given the word of the British Viceroy of India that they would be spared. They were tied up with their backs against the muzzles of cannon barrels and shot.

This means of execution was intentionally meant to humiliate religious Hindus. According to Hindu beliefs the soul of a deceased person continues to live in some other form. The main condition for immortality is to bury the deceased's body (or ashes) as a whole and in one place. Vasily Vereschchagin's painting *The Suppression of the Indian Revolt by the English* is widely known in Russia. It was presented in London in 1887 and attracted huge protests from the supposedly democratic population of Britain, with newspaper campaigns against it and even the possibility of a court case. What is curious is that no one denied that what was depicted in the painting had actually happened. There was no legal case against the artist, only mere threats.

Then the law-abiding, civilized Britons simply stole the painting. Vereshchagin's work disappeared completely, and to this day it has never been found. Luckily many copies were made, and it remains one of Vereshchagin's most respected paintings, an honor it deserves.

The sepoys were executed in 1858. It was not angry natives who were executed, but fellow soldiers who had fought for the British Empire in China, Burma, Afghanistan, and in the Crimea against Russia.

At almost the same time, in 1859, the Russian army captured Gunib, where the leader of Chechen and Dagestani tribes Imam Shamil made his last stand, and Shamil surrendered. The Chechens were not subjects of the Russian Empire but a conquered people, and furthermore they had not fought for the Russians. And yet neither the assault on Gunib nor the occupation of Chechnya entailed such atrocities as the British in India. If we are talking about a promise given to an adherent of a different faith and a foreigner, in the novel *Hadji Murat* by Leo Tolstoy it turns out that the protagonist. Hadji Murat dies particularly due to the inability of the Russians to keep their promises. And this character looks much more amiable than those who have "set him up". Combat officer Count Leo Tolstoy had fought the Chechens and thus he had respect for them, he acknowledged their honor and dignity.

By capturing Chechnya, the Russian Empire put a stop to raiding, the slave trade and blood feuds, but it limited its intervention in the everyday life of the local people. The Russians did not extract vengeance on the people they conquered. Moreover, Russia gave them ample opportunity to integrate into the life of the empire, such as by serving in its army. The Chechens enjoyed the same rights as any other subjects of the Russian Empire. They could move to Saint Petersburg, and send their children to the same schools as the Russians, Armenians, and Tatars. They could receive a Russian passport and go abroad, set up a business, make money, and build a career. Tolstoy's

CHAPTER 5

depiction is no idealized version of the Caucasus, he calmly accepted the reality for what it was.

Pushkin spoke of the "force of circumstances", and under these circumstances Chechnya had to enter the Russian Empire, but the lives of the people of the Caucasus got no better or worse.

A rebel who acts against the natural order of things ought to be treated fairly: one should remember that he is a human being first of all. After Shamil surrendered, he was exiled to Kaluga, near Moscow, where he lived until 1870. There he had an active social life, receiving many visitors. Shamil spoke Russian well and quickly become a local celebrity. The authorities ensured the Shamil did not escape, but no one thought of humiliating him or executing him for his war against Russia. They even gave him a retinue of servants.

In 1870 Shamil decided to go to Mecca on a great pilgrimage. The Russian Empire let their fiercest enemy walk free, providing him with all the bureaucratic formalities he needed just as with any other Muslim in the empire. He died of old age during this pilgrimage in March of 1871. His remains now lie forever in a place sacred to all Muslims.

There is, incidentally, a curious document, released from deep within the secret police files of the Russian Empire's ministry of internal affairs. It is an extract from the rules for dealing with Muslims from the Caucasus who were serving in the tsar's army, signed by chief of police Benkendorf: "No pork shall be given to them ... There shall be no foot drill for them ... Do not inflict corporal punishment on them. Punish them only through warrant officer Tuganov who knows better how to deal with which people. [76] Efendi shall be permitted to visit the highlanders whenever he wishes ... Do not allow anyone at the court to disturb them during their prayers ... Make sure that neither the teachers nor the noblemen say anything inappropriate about the highlanders' faith and do not urge them to change it..."

Nationality means nothing

Conquering the world was a difficult, exhausting job. It was not so easy to take up the "white man's burden", as Rudyard Kipling put it in his observation on British colonialism, and head to the uncivilized world. Life found a way, however, and in India today there still live several million Anglo-Indians, the descendants of legal and illegal marriages between Englishmen or Scotsmen and Indian women.

Until the mid 20th century, the Anglo-Indians were second-class citizens. Even such talented and celebrated man like George Orwell, author of the dystopian *1984* and *Animal Farm*, personally experienced such treatment.

There was nothing like this in Russia. The main key to success was religion. It was important to be an Orthodox Christian, but one's ethnic background was utterly unimportant. For example, christianized Tatars could reach any career heights.

Boris Godunov, the Tatar prince on the Russian throne, caused all kinds of doubts because he was seriously suspected of murdering the son of Ivan the Terrible, Prince Dmitry. But if he had been a bit luckier, if he had managed to strengthen his position on the throne and carry out his reforms, maybe today we would view him just like many people see Peter the Great. Never was anyone discriminated against for his Tatar origin. Indeed, nearly a third of the Russian aristocracy was of Tatar ancestry, including the great historian Nikolai Karamzin (Tatar *kara murza* 'black prince'). [77]

A large amount of Russian elites came also from the Grand Duchy of Lithuania, and the majority of these, if not 100% Polish, had a substantial amount of Polish blood. This did not prevent the princes Golitsyn, Glinsky and Czartoryski from ascending to the Russian throne, pushing aside the great Russian nobility.

Let's not forget that even the tsar's line was not purely Russian by blood. All later generations of Russian rulers married German princesses, and they became less Russian and

CHAPTER 5

more "germanized". Over time, it was practically full-blooded Germans that were sitting on the throne. However, this did not prevent them from becoming tsar, and the Russian people did not refuse to accept them in this position.

Whatever countries became part of the Russian Empire, their population was immediately granted the same rights as all other subjects of Russia.

I have already mentioned the Tatars and Poles. When Armenia and Georgia became part of Russia, their peasants received the same rights as Russian peasants, and their townspeople became part of the same general bourgeoisie. Their aristocracy also received the same privileges as the Russian aristocracy.

Prince Bagratyon, Suvorov's and Kutuzov's comrade-in-arms, who fell in the Battle of Borodino, came from the Georgian Bagrationi dynasty. A prominent court figure in the time of Alexander II and Alexander III, Count Mikhail Tarielovich Loris-Melikov was Armenian. The conqueror of Central Asia and subjugator of Tashkent, the first Governor-General of Turkestan, General. Konstantin von Kaufman came from a Russified Austrian family.

Indeed, Count Loris-Melikov, a native Armenian, was prime minister. In the Russian Empire — like in the Ottoman Empire — the notion of "nationality" or "ethnicity" did not come up in principle, it was considered something unimportant and not noted in one's passport. The basic distinction was religion: whether you were an Orthodox Christian, an Armenian Christian, or a Jew. Moreover, people not indigenous to the Russia Empire were often placed in privileged positions. Not only were the Finns recruited into the army, but most of the Muslim peoples too. The peasants in Georgia had a very peculiar privilege that dated back to nobody knows when, namely, they were exempt from paying taxes. Although the state religion was Orthodoxy, it did not prevent the building of Catholic or Protestant churches. It's enough to walk down Nevsky Prospect in Saint Petersburg and see the many places of worship from every religion. With the highlanders from the North Caucasus and the peoples of Central Asia things were even more interesting: their entire local elite received nobility rights. Among the highlanders already someone who owned a small herd could be considered a prince. For the Turkmen people every warrior was a nobleman — everybody who had at least once participated in a military expedition. That was one third of their male population, and all of them were granted the rights of the Russian nobility! It was a kind of discrimination against the Russians, as in Russia, to become a nobleman one had to make a great effort. Kalmyks, Bashkirs, and Tatars were signed on to the Cossack military forces. The government granted them parcels of territory and guaranteed their rights to land and pasture. There were no limits to non-Russian peoples in pursuing higher education or entering military school. In fact, the opposite occurred: affirmative action was given to peoples "newly entered" into the Russian Empire.

The Polish lands between 1815 and 1914 were divided between Austria, Prussia, and Russia. Uprisings against Prussia hardly ever ceased: the Prussian state was settling the Polish lands with Germans. The Poles rose up against the Austrians twice, in 1846 and 1848.

The Poles also rebelled against the Russians, yet Russia's policies in Poland were much more liberal than the Austrian or German ones. If a Pole knew Russian, he could become an important official in Saint Petersburg. One could draw up a long list of Polish generals, governor-generals, scientists and officials in the Russian Empire, hundred or thousands of names, such as Przewalski, Dostojewski, Wojciechowski, Czartoryski, Gorbowski, Jagużyński, Siemieniewski, Kraft, Wasilewski, Kochański, Potiomkin, Dubieński, Tuchaczewski, Glinka and others. No, it is impossible to mention all of them.

However, in many histories written in Polish, even in schoolbooks, the uprisings against the Russians, Austrians, and Prussians are all treated the same, in spite of the fact that the scale of the events was almost identical — in the uprising of 1830–1831 around 10 thousand Poles were killed and about

CHAPTER 5

12 thousand died in 1846. Nevertheless, the uprising of 1830–1831 was referred to as the Russian-Polish war in which the revolt of "good" Poles was suppressed by "bad" Russians. The uprising against the Austrian in 1846 was treated as a minor conflict.

In 1846, the Krakow uprising was not supported by the local peasantry. The majority of landlords in Galicia were Poles, but the peasants were mainly Rusyns or Ukrainians. Ordinary people did not want any independence for Poland, as it was clear to them what fate awaited them in a new nation-state. For them it was better when the authorities were far away in Vienna (especially as by that time Austria had already formally abolished serfdom) than having local Polish magnates who were likely to restore serfdom.

The Ukrainians had reason to fear that they would be worse off in a ethnocentric Polish state than in the multicultural Austrian empire, and they were proven right! In 1918–1939 Poland initiated a wave of oppression of Orthodox Christians, one more terrible than the Austrians had carried out before. Both in 1830–1831 and in 1863 the Poles rebelled not as it is presented today, demanding independence for the ancient Polish lands around Warsaw and Krakow. No! What they really demanded was that they get back the former territories of the Commonwealth of Poland, that is the native Ukrainian and Belorussian lands. They wanted to break free of the Austrian, Prussian and Russian empires, and why? So they could build their own!

The 19th century was an age of geopolitical expansion and the formation of new states. As Dominique Lieven, a specialist in Russian history and professor at the London School of Economics, explains, "At that time empires were the only way for countries to survive. The idea that if Russia in the 19th century had decided to leave its territories on the Baltic or in Poland, it would have changed into a nice little democracy, is completely wrong. If that had happened, Russia would now be ruled by someone else, because it was an age of imperialism. In the 19th century there were no alternatives to maintaining a geopolitically strong empire." [78]

However, the Russian Empire was based on completely different principles than the European colonialist empires. Russians simply had no other word to describe their historically formed multiethnic state. Peter the Great was the first to call it an empire. Scholars today sometimes try to point to the terms "state" or "community", to be able to distinguish through terminology level such essentially different state formations, but no other term has caught on. We must nevertheless keep in mind that the Russian Empire was a completely different type of empire.

Dominique Lieven explains why, unlike the rest of Europe, Russia saw no wave of nationalism in the 19th century. "A significant role was played by the integrating aspect of the empire. The Russian Empire was Russian in nature. The tsar and core elites were Russia. However, the empire was open to representatives of different peoples both within the country and outside. At the beginning of the 19th century the Russian Empire was very cosmopolitan. Only towards the end of that century did pressure grow on the tsar to make the empire more specifically Russian." [79]

The Russian Empire

> Russia can do without any of us, but no one of us can do without Russia. Woe to anyone who thinks so, and twofold to anyone who can really do without it.
>
> —*Ivan Turgenev*

How it conquered its territories

The Russian Empire extended itself, according to a logic of inevitable expansion, over the plains, where stopping meant death. The Russian Empire cannot at all be compared to the European colonialist empires. The Russian state largely grew because the Russians proved a lively, hard-working and enterprising people. The natural environment was both harsh

CHAPTER 5

and generous to them. Russia had always been surrounded by sparsely populated and barely developed lands. These lands, at first glance, were cold and infertile, remote from the centers of civilization.

This is what the central belt of Russia was like. Now it is a cultivated territory, where there are cities with millions of people. Between the 10th and 13th centuries this was a region of boundless forests, without roads or towns, without any grain production. In the territory between the Oka and Volga Rivers, grain was brought from what is now Ukraine or from the Volga Bulgarian state. The Russians then established a system to cover this land with fertilizer, and what had earlier been infertile, worthless land began to produce abundant harvests. A stream of Russian settlers flowed into this land between the two rivers after the Tatar invasion.

There were lands just as cold and barren along the Volga, in the Ural foothills, Siberia and the Russian Far East. It is hard to call the Black Sea coast cold, but it too was a barren and wild place. To work this land, one had to start practically from scratch. The population of these colonized lands did not lose out from the arrival of the Russians. For proof, simply consider that in 1914, the population of every people in the Russian Empire was higher than it had been before the conquest.

The Russian advance with its colonization of new territories settled old disputes between civilizations, some dating back to the era of the Golden Horde. The Russians had long had to pay tribute to the Tatar khans, but they then freed other peoples from this burden. This development, this growth and colonization was shaped by Russia's geographical features. Moving some distance further east, the Russian army claimed new borders, but these borders were just as permeable, just as arbitrary as the earlier ones. The coming of the Slavs and later the Russians never meant displacing the indigenous peoples. Typically it only marked a transition to a greater proximity, residing together almost like relatives. It was a transition from living near one another in different villages to living together in one community, one world.

If a Slavic expansion occurred from the 11th–13th centuries from the Dnieper River northwest to Yaroslavl, Moscow, and then Arkhangelsk, that only means that Slavs and Finno-Ugrian peoples were living side by side on the same territory. Some tribal alliances of Rus' "officially" included both Slavic and Finno-Ugrian peoples such as the Vyatichi. [80]

The people of Kiev also established alliances with the Turkic-speaking Cumans and carried out trade on the same massive scale as with the Finno-Ugrians, and they even intermarried. It is well known that the Russians fought against the "united Mongols", during the famous Battle of the Kalka River, only because they were allied with their fellow Slavs and the Cumans. The Cuman khan Koten was the father-in-law of the Russian prince Mstislav the Bold.

If a people joined Rus', their everyday lives hardly changed. Rus' is not often a target of criticism against the Russian people. Russia's policies after the 16th century, however, have led to accusations of "Russian colonialism" and "Russian enslavement of the peoples of the Urals, Siberia, Far East, and Russian North" when the homelands of other peoples became part of Russia.

The first exhibit in this accusation is the conquest of the Kazan Khanate. According to one of the most prominent Western scholars of Russian history, the Harvard professor Richard Pipes, Russia won the Kazan Khanate not only through great cruelty, suppressing the Tatar's movement for national liberation, but it forever thwarted any opportunity the Volga Tatars had to develop. Pipes particularly cites Russian sayings like "an uninvited guest is worse than a Tatar" and tries to make the Russians out as the oldest enemies of the Tatar people. However, both in the history of Russia and in the birth of Russia's national myths, the Mongol invasion, Golden Horde, Kazan Khanate, and Northern Caucasus have become tangled up in such a tight knot of issues that it will have to be discussed separately.

CHAPTER 5

The matter of the Tatars

St. Basil's Cathedral, which sits on Red Square in Moscow, is one of the most famous tourist attractions in Russia. Its onion domes, the multicolored tiles on its façade, and the tented roof over its doors are known even to people who have never been in Russia. But few people know that this cathedral which is today a UNESCO-recognized monument was built by the order of Ivan the Terrible to commemorate his conquest of Kazan' and victory over the Tatar Khanate.

In histories written before the Bolshevik Revolution, the access to the Baltic secured at the beginning of the 18th century, the conquest of Warsaw in 1795, the conquest of Berlin in the middle of the mid 18th century, or Paris in 1813 pale in comparison to the conquests of Kazan and the Crimea. This victory has been elevated to a religious triumph over the "infidels", a battle between Good and Evil.

Is it any surprise? The Kazan Khanate was an offshoot of the Golden Horde, and in its heyday (the second half of the 15th century) it stretched from the Sura basin in the west to the Belaya River in the east, and from the Upper Kama in the north to the Samara bend in the south. Its rulers were descendants of Genghis Khan and related to the khans of Central Asia and Siberia. Around 10–15% of the Khanate's subject called themselves Tatars and were considered conquerors in this land. The peoples of the Middle Volga, such as the Bashkirs, Chuvash, Nogay, and Finno-Ugrians (Mordvins and Mari) were vassals of the Tatar khans.

Internal strife pulled the Kazan Khanate in two different directions. One was for peaceful coexistence and trade with neighboring Muscovy, and the other was for supporting the policy of the Crimean Khanate, which had been inherited from the Golden Horde and considered Russia merely a source of slaves and plunder.

In historical testimony and literary accounts there is no period more terrible for Russia than its time under the Golden

Horde. The chronicles of Rus' referred to the Horde as the "foul ones" and "the plague of the steppe". In the *Tale of Igor's Campaign* it is written, "Once again, chilled to the bone, Russia has felt the impact of a Cuman raid."

In the popular mind no foreign people was as frightening as the Tatars. But they were evidently not Kazan Tatars, not even Crimean Tatars, who were "famous" for their terrible raids that involved kidnapping people into slavery. From folksongs one can clearly see that we are dealing with the Tatars as collectors of tribute, the "baskaks", the officials of the Golden Horde:

If I've no gold, he'll take my horse;
If I've no horse, the Tatar will take my children;
If I've no children, he'll take my wife;
If I have no wife, he'll take my head. [81]

This sad song is only one of many. Neither the Swedish onslaught of the 17th century, nor the century of confrontation with Lithuania and Poland, nor the the two world wars against the Germans, are so imprinted in the Russian national consciousness. There are no Poles, no Germans or Swedish people remembered in folklore who would have exacted payment as mercilessly as the Mongol tax collectors.

Meanwhile, historians continue to debate the impact of the Golden Horde on the development of Russian statehood. For example, the Russian historian Nikolai Karamzin considered the Horde to possibly be the main reason for the rise of the principality of Muscovy. Vasily Klyuchevsky agreed with him, writing, "The Mongol yoke with the extreme misery it brought on the Russian people was a school of hard knocks in which Russian statehood and the Russian aristocracy were forged, where the Russian nation became aware of itself and took on the qualities that would help it fight for survival."

Richard Pipes offers his own account, considering the Mongols to have been higher than the Russians culturally.

He argues, "While in China and Iran, which had also been conquered by the Mongols, the conquerors assimilated quickly and lost their distinguishing national traits, in Russia this did not happen." The failure of the Mongols to become slavicized, in Pipes's view, shows that they had a higher level of culture than the Russians, because as a rule, peoples with a higher level of culture do not assimilate among peoples with a lower level of culture.

In opposition to him, Boris Rybakov's work clearly shows that a sharp industrial decline in Rus' took place precisely in the Tatar-Mongol period. During this time, the amount of specialized trades decreased, that is, many fields requiring special qualifications simply disappeared. This same period shows clear signs of the desolation of the Russian lands, with Rus' shrinking towards the northeast, away from its ruined and almost completely devastated south.

We could talk about cultural interaction between Russia and the Tatars only if we turned a blind eye to a long range of eloquent testimonies that the Russian national consciousness did not arise on the basis of affinity to the Tatars but on the opposite, on the basis of distaste for the Tatar yoke and the feeling that the Tatars were a foreign body in Russia. This feeling united all Russians, whether it be the simple village woman who frightened her children with tales of the "evil Tatars", the monk writing a chronicle who called the Tatars "godless Ishmaelites", or one of the princes who inevitably ended their proclamations with the hope that God would "overthrow the Horde". For almost two centuries the Russian cities of Novgorod and Pskov were forced to offer tribute to the Horde and thus ensure their relative freedom and protection from invasion from the West. Actually, it was precisely for this purpose that the free city of Novgorod employed Alexander Nevsky, who managed to raise to this task by diplomatically going along with the Horde's wishes. But there was no talk of an alliance and certainly not about equal partnership. What's more, the fact that Alexander Nevsky managed to negotiate with the Horde did not mean that the other Russian cities could do the same. There is a multitude of chronicles bearing witnesses to horrors of the Tatar invasion: the sacking of Moscow and Kozelsk, the burning of Ryazan and Vladimir, and many other woes that came upon the heads of those who took up their swords to defend their cities and their families.

According to the historian Petr Romanov, another issue is that it was not the Horde's custom to impose its culture, its lifestyle, onto conquered peoples, to destroy and burn for sheer pleasure. The cities that surrendered managed to get by under tolerable circumstances, but they were neither free nor sovereign. Moscow managed to adapt and was able to concentrate all its financial resources against the Horde. By accumulating the necessary capital and striking at an opportune moment, Moscow managed to throw off the hated Tatar yoke. The Battle of Kulikovo and conquest of the Tatar Khanate were imprinted in the national consciousness as great deeds of national and religious importance. And now someone tries to substitute all this genuine historical reality with some touching Russian-Tatar togetherness! [82] By fighting against the Kazan Khanate, the Russians were continuing their war with the Golden Horde.

The victory over the Kazan Khanate put an end to a century-long dispute. As soon as Kazan fell, the khanate's citizens voluntarily joined the Grand Duchy of Moscow, swearing an oath to the "white tzar".

This scholarly debate certainly raises sensitive issues for both Russians and Tatars, especially because both peoples live under the same state and for some many centuries have intermixed. In conclusion I would like to say this about the issue of the assimilation of the Tatars to Russia which Richard Pipes raised: up to one third of the Russian feudal aristocracy, and the bright and well-known personalities of Russia in the 14th and 15th centuries in general, were of Tatar origin.

CHAPTER 5

The multiethnic state of Muscovy

Muscovy, the cradle of the Russian Empire, was never a monoethnic state. Rus' had a multiethnic character from the start. Russia's territorial expansion did not at all come about in the same way as the European colonial empires. It was a unification of territories that sometimes happened through military force, but involved peoples who had long been joined by a common historical fate by trade, by cultural relations and even intermarriage among royals. The territories that Moscow took did not become colonies in the Western sense. The status of new lands in the Russian state is most comparable to the provinces of the Roman Empire. In essence, Muscovy had already laid the foundation for self-rule. Moreover, for the conquered lands and peoples, self-rule was a natural, common thing.

As Muscovy spread east, as a rule the indigenous peoples willingly entered into Russia. Sometimes (as in the case of Kazan, Siberia, or Astrakhan) this voluntary joining was interrupted by the intrigues of countries hostile to Russia, such as Ottoman Turkey or the Central Asian khanates.

Often these states first became allies of Moscow or even its vassals (such as Kazan and Astrakhan). It was not the policy of the tsars of Muscovy to absorb these territories by force, deny them autonomy, and establish Russian administration. Rather, it happened because the vassals broke their oath of allegiance to Moscow.

All of Muscovy's opponents were themselves multiethnic states. After the rise of the Mongol Empire and the Golden Horde, its province in northern Eurasia, the Russians, Bashkirs, Nogay, and Tatars fell under a single state. In the capital of the khanate, which was located in Sarai Batu and later in Sarai Berke, Russian, Tatar, and Bashkir aristocrats came together, Russian and Tatar craftsmen worked side by side in the workshops of the Mongol settlements, delivering tools and ornaments to the khan's court. Russian and Bashkir soldiers also took part in the Mongols' military expeditions under the orders of the khan, as during the war against the Arabs, which ended with the sack of Baghdad.

From the other side, in Russia during the era of Muscovy there lived a great many Tatars, who faithfully served the Russian princes and often held high positions. The christianized Tatar prince Peter Ibragimovich led the defense of Moscow in one of the wars between Kazan and Moscow. Sain-Bulat married a princess of the Mstislav line and for one year, in 1557, he even ruled Moscow when Ivan the Terrible had fled to his oprichnina territory. During Ivan the Terrible's march on Polotsk he was accompanied by two former princes of Kazan, Yadigar (baptised as Simeon Kasayevich) and Utyamish (baptised as Alexander Safagireyevich).

When the Tatar and Mongol princesses adopted Christianity, they could marry Russian princes or even tsars. The Muscovite prince Yuri Danilovich, brother of the famous Ivan I Kalita and grandson of Alexander Nevsky, was married to the Tatar khan Uzbek's sister Konchaka (she was baptised as Agatha). The mother of Ivan the Terrible, Elena Glinskaya was from a line of russianized Christian Tatars who had settled in Lithuania.

Ivan the Terrible thought of himself as one of the last Orthodox Christian rulers, the tsar of Holy Rus', and encouraged the Tatars and other peoples to convert to Orthodoxy. However, he never set out to eradicate Islam in the lands that fell under Muscovy. The famous words of Novosiltsev, the Russian ambassador to Turkey of the time, to the Ottoman sultan Selim bear direct witness to this: "My country is not an enemy of the Muslim faith. Its servant, the tsar Sain-Bulat, has authority in Kasimov, as does Prince Gabdulla Aqkübek in Yuryev, Ibak in Surozhik, and the Nogay princes in Romanov, they all freely and solemnly praise Mohammed in their mosques." [83]

In other Russian territories the situation was similar. In the territory of Kazan, besides Tatars there lived Mari, Mordvins, Udmurts, Chuvash, and also some Bashkir. The Siberian Khanate was populated by, besides Tatars, Mansi, Permians, and Khanty.

In the Nogay Horde other peoples besides the Nogays lived, such Bashkirs and the ancestors of today's Karakalpaks. Only the Astrakhan Khanate was a more or less monoethnic Tatar region, but it was also the most sparsely populated, stretching over the barren steppes, and it had no real autonomy as it was dependent on Crimea.

Between these khanates there were conflicts of course, but there were also prolonged periods of peace. In the 15th and 16th centuries, the principality of Moscow and the Crimean Khanate were allies in the war against the remnants of the Horde, and then against Lithuania. There were whole eras in the history of the Kazan or Astrakhan Khanates when "pro-Russian" forces were in power.

The seizure of Kazan

Indeed, the rulers of Kazan had a real opportunity to join Muscovy voluntarily, since the Kazan Tatars had many supporters in Moscow.

Several years before the conquest of Kazan, there was a project to join it peacefully to Moscow. It was planned that it would fully preserve its freedom of religion, keep the local Muslim administration in place, and give the Tatar aristocracy the same rights as the Russian. This project came very close to being realized.

Officially it even materialized: in 1551 a kurultai [84] was held in Kazan where the majority voted for a treaty with Moscow. Kazan pledged to free all Christian slaves, a Kazan government was created, headed by a Tatar nobleman, Khudai Kul. (The Kazan Khanate had over a hundred thousand Russian slaves, for a population of less than one million people.) This government pledged an oath of allegiance to the Russian governor Mikulinsky and announced that the Kazan Tatars would peacefully join the Russian state.

However, when Mikulinsky was to solemnly enter Kazan, at the last moment a change of power occurred, this time bringing in anti-Russian elements. It was headed by a pro-Turkish prince. The conspirators tricked the people of Kazan into being opposed to the Russians, saying that archers were coming to the city and planned to commit a massacre. Actually, it was a peace delegation coming to Kazan, among whom were Russian diplomatic representatives with the head of the government Khudai Kul.

As a result, 180 Russian soldiers who were already in the city, were brutally murdered, in the best traditions of the French St. Bartholomew's Day massacre that happened in Europe around the same time. This was the reason that Muscovite archers showed such cruelty during the conquest of Kazan. Such treason made a peaceful course of events impossible. What is more, it did more harm than good to Kazan citizens themselves, as it made the Tatar aristocrats who favored Moscow openly join the Moscow army, which already had Kasimov Tatars, Chuvash, and Mari fighting for it. Some Tatars, even if they did not overtly join Ivan the Terrible's army, ignored Kazan's appeal for help in fighting the Russians. This was because they did not consider Khan Yadigar, who came to the Kazan throne, a legitimate ruler, but they thought of him simply as of a "Turkish hireling".

Who served in the army of the Muscovite tsar Ivan the Terrible that stormed Kazan? Was it the Muscovites? The Cossacks? Not at all! It was a multiethnic force, practically the same as the Red Army in 1941.

To give some dry statistics, the army consisted of Russians (up to 50 thousand), Kasimov Tatars (30 thousand), Astrakhan Tatars (20 thousand), Tatars from Moscow, Nizhny Novgorod, and Kazan (10 thousand), 3 thousand Nogay, 5 thousand Meshchers, 4 thousand Chuvash, 7–10 thousand Mordvins, 10 thousand Circassians, and 10 thousand Mari and Udmurts. All in all, 60% of Ivan the Terrible's army were non-Russians. Furthermore, there were quite a few European officers and mercenaries serving in it, Germans, Poles, Dutch, and English. The Tatar element in Ivan's army was larger than the Russian.

CHAPTER 5

On the Kazan side we find the following figures: 30–35 thousand Kazan Tatars, 3 thousand Nogay, 10 thousand Astrakhan Tatars, 10–15 thousand Mari and Udmurts, 1 thousand Turks, and 1 thousand Russians. That means that against the 40–45 thousand Tatars from different states who defended Kazan, there were over 50 thousand Tatars on the side of the Moscow army.

As a contemporary historian writes, "The Kazan Khanate in the period 1467–1560 underwent a civil war, caused by the necessity to reconsider its place in the world and its choice of orientation. Eventually, the majority of Tatars took up their arms on the side of Moscow. The Pro-Turkish sentiments among part of the elite had almost no support from the population and it was doomed to failure". [85]

He goes on to write, "the Tatars joined Russia by their own free and informed choice — a choice which was difficult and bloody given the geopolitical reality of the time. One evidence for this is the fact that during the Time of Troubles, Tatars supported the Russian state and not the Poles." [86] And what was the fate of Kazan after its defeat? It was nothing comparable to the colonialist policies of the West. After the war, a Russian administration was appointed for the Kazan territory. The lands of the pro-Turkish elites were given to Russian settlers, but these elites were spared, and with their families and retainers they were taken to Moscow, where they assimilated.

Those Tatar elites who consciously supported the Russian position had a much more favorable outcome. In fact, they were made equals with the Russian aristocracy. They retained their freedom of religion.

At first, Muslim Tatars were not allowed to live in the city, but they were allowed to live in settlements. Towards the end of the 18th century, the settlements of the Kazan Tatars become part of the city. Their residents become the core of the emerging Tatar ethnicity.

Kazan became the center of an enormous territory, the capital of the eastern part of Russia. All the vast territory from the North Caucasus to Perm and Bashkiria was put under the jurisdiction of the so-called formally independent Kazan Khanate. The Kazan archdiocese that was founded immediately became the third most senior-ranking in the Russian Orthodox Church.

The taking of Siberia

In 1555 ambassadors came to Moscow from the Siberian Khan Yadigar and bowed down before Ivan the Terrible. They voluntarily admitted their status as vassals and said to him, "Take, tsar, the whole of Siberia into your hands."

The tsar naturally agreed and send his ambassador Dmitry Kurov to Siberia to collect tribute. Thus the Siberian peoples (not just the Siberian Tatars, but also the Khanty, Mansi, and other peoples in the region) also willingly came under the Russian state.

There was some anti-Russian sentiment among the local strongmen, especially the khan Kuchum. But Kuchum did not at all reflect the feelings of the Siberian people. He was not a *sibiryak*.

Kuchum was a prince from a line of Central Asian khans and an "appointee" of the Uzbeks and the Kazakhs. In 1563 Kuchum killed the legitimate khan, the descendant of an indigenous Siberian dynasty of local rulers, Yadigar (the very same who earlier had willingly declared himself a vassal of Moscow). Kuchum then broke off relations with Moscow and began raiding Russian lands, namely the territory around Perm. It was only after this that the Russian cossacks moved against him.

The fight against Kuchum was not a battle between Moscow and the Siberian Khanate. It was a battle between the central government of an established united Russian-Tatar state and an usurper of the throne of one of its provinces. It was a battle between the central authority and a separatist.

Many in Siberia were unhappy with Kuchum's anti-Russian

policies. He persecuted the Khanty and Mansi people for their loyalty to Moscow. The Russian force who threatened Kuchum included Tatar soldiers as well. One third of the population of Kuchum's state were Russian. Most of them supported the legitimate khans and, along with them, Moscow.

Many scholars believe that when a force of 500 cossacks under Yermak fought a campaign against Kuchum in 1582–1585, this operation was pushed in Siberia itself by supporters of union with the Russian tsardom. It was an ordinary sign of the affection that the "invaders" and local people had for each other. One can also understand the honors that the indigenous people of Siberia heaped on the fallen Yermak, and the myth that the locals made out of the man, just as with the folk hero Ilya Muromets.

Russian national politics

> The Russians already, thanks to the size of their country, are free of pagan nationalism, they are cosmopolitan people or at least they are one-sixth cosmopolitan, because their country makes up almost one sixth of the entire inhabited world.
>
> —*Heinrich Heine*

Often states that joined Moscow were its allies or even vassals. The annexation of these lands, depriving them of their autonomy, and the establishment of Russian administration was not a colonial policy on the part of Russia but a consequence of the vassal rulers there breaking their allegiance. This autonomy was regularly restored.

Moscow's "conquest" of Kazan, Astrakhan, Siberia, and other territories was of the same nature as the the French king's "conquest" of Burgundy and Anjou, the English in Wales, and the Spanish kings in Málaga and Seville. But it was not at all like the English conquest of India, the French conquest of Indochina, or the Spanish conquest of the Maya and Aztec empires.

The rise of the Russian Empire

Can one imagine running away from freedom into a prison? If one takes the idea of Russia as a "prison for peoples" seriously, then that is precisely a flight that many Europeans made from the 17th to the 19th centuries.

In the middle of the 17th century, the Moscow suburb of Kukuy was home to twenty thousand Europeans, mostly Germans, but also Dutch, Scots, French, Swiss, Italians, Danes, and Irish.

The government of Muscovy sought to attract more foreigners to work for it, and these "service-class foreigners" even made up a special branch of the army. In 1651 the composition of Moscow's armed forces were the aristocratic cavalry (37,596), Muscovite archers (8122), Cossacks (21,124), Tatars and Middle Volga peoples (9113), foreigners (7707), Reiters (1457), and dragoons (8462).

Thus foreigners made up a major part of the Russian army. The government sent special emissaries to recruit them and they always brought back volunteers who wanted to serve in Moscow.

Scots streamed into this supposedly oppressive place after Cromwell's campaigns. Supporters of the English parliament had not just fought against and occupied Scotland, they also persecuted the Scottish nobility, who supported their king and were quite simply their competitors.

Dozens or hundreds of innocent people died in the gallows, hid in the mountains or fled abroad. One of them, William Bruce, arrived in Muscovy in 1647. A legend has come down to us that a friend of his father, General Dalyell, advised him to go to Muscovy: Dalyell had visited Moscow during the Time of Troubles, served there for eight years, and knew the country firsthand.

What made William Bruce go from Scotland to the "prison for peoples"? Bruce was distantly related to the Scottish national hero Robert the Bruce, who in 1314 defeated the English army on the banks of the Bannockburn and became king of

CHAPTER 5

Scotland. [87] In 1328 he forced England to draw up a peace treaty that recognized Scotland's independence. In Scotland Robert the Bruce's numerous descendants were very active, and this famous clan was known for eight centuries.

Another Scotsman who decided to go to Russia (then ruled by Alexei Mikhailovich) was one Best, ancestor of the famous chancellor under Elizabeth and Catherine the Great, Alexei Petrovich Bestuzhev. What made Best go? The English "tried" and slaughtered the Scottish nobility at the slightest provocation, and in Russia a Scotsman could establish an illustrious career.

Patrick Gordon, whom many authorities call one of the first foreign teachers in Russia, was tasked by Peter the Great with establishing a regular army, and as you now know, one made up not only of Slavs. [88]

Mikhail Lermontov was a descendant of a Scotsman named Lermon, who fought in the Smolensk war and had come to Russia during the reign of Alexei Mikhailovich. In the Lermontov family there was a legend brought by Lermon, according to which they had originated from the famous poet and bard of the 14th century, Thomas Lermon. Thomas Lermon is a widely known figure in Great Britain, commemorated in one of Rudyard Kipling's ballads, "The Last Rhyme of True Thomas". It is hard to tell today whether this legend was also the reality.

In total several thousand Scotsmen came to Russia. Strange people they were! And what did they seek in "that country", where there was neither democracy nor a market economy? Which served as a "prison for peoples"?

Around 1700, up to fifty thousand Europeans were living in Muscovy. During the Northern War, Russia captured as many as twenty thousand Swedish soldiers and officers. After 1721 they were all permitted to return home, but five thousand decided to stay in Russia. What made them change their minds?

Finns and Germans, subjects to Swedish crown, also stayed after the Northern War in the lands that Russia had captured. No one fled from the "Russian invaders" to Berlin or Stockholm.

And later, in the 18th and 19th centuries the same thing happened: there was always a flow of immigrants into Russia from Europe, first a trickle and then a flood.

After the annexation of Courland in what is now Latvia, the "trophy Germans", as many as 300,000 of them, could easily go to Germany, but they didn't. They forever remained in Russia and for the most part completely assimilated. [89]

During the reign of Catherine the Great, up to four thousand Germans, French, Swiss, and other Europeans came to Russia. One of them was the Spanish baron José de Ribas (after whom Deribasovskaya street in Odessa is named), Catherine II who was born German but had long since become Russian, once asked this Spaniard if he had become fully Russian yet.

"No doubt, your highness!" de Ribas was quick to answer.

Throughout the 19th century there was a flow of settlers into the Russian Empire's eastern territories. Poles, Ukrainians, Belorussians, Estonians, Finns, Latvians, and Lithuanians came to Semirechye (now part of Kazakhstan and Kyrgyzstan), Siberia, the Russian Far East, and Manchuria. These peoples also chose this supposed prison as their home.

It is striking that a hundred thousand captive soldiers from Napoleon's army, who were given every right to return to Europe, stayed permanently in Russia. To this day we find names like Masherov, Mashov, and Shevalyev in Russia. Consider that inhabitants of civilized, rich, enlightened, and partly republican Europe chose to stay in "unwashed Russia". They chose to go from democracy to supposed slavery. Had these hundred thousand people all gone mad? It seems there was something attractive about Russia after all.

This process continued. Between 1828 and 1915, according to statistics, generalized by Vladimir Kabuzan, [90] 4.2 million foreigners immigrated to Russia. Most were from Germany (1.5 million) and Austro-Hungary (800,000). At the beginning of World War I, Russia was the second largest country for immigration after the USA, ahead of Canada, Argentina, Brazil, and Australia.

But statistics does not reveal everything. For example, the Pontic Greeks were not taken into account. They are not the descendants of Jason and his Argonauts looking for the golden fleece. Most of them came only recently, in the 19th century, from Anatolia under the Turks and from Greece itself, avoiding any census or control.

Let's note on more thing: it is one thing for an English or French-speaking Protestant or Catholic to move from Europe to the United States or Canada; it was not an easy process, but a person would remain in the same cultural sphere with regard to language and religion. But it was a hundred, a thousand, or a million times easier, more comfortable, to do that then to head East, to an unknown foreign country with a different language and with the Orthodox religion.

But people came nonetheless, over the entire history of Russia, from the "exodus of Russian Lithuanians" into Muscovy to the outbreak of World War I — the stream of immigration to Russia never let up.

The migration period

There are many examples of how Russia was settled not just by individual refugees but by literally entire peoples.

Brethren Buryats

According to Lev Gumilev, the Buryat people arose from a part of the Mongols who wanted to become subjects of Russia.

In the 17th century the Mongols were torn apart by internal strife. Some of the Mongols were fighting against China's new Manchu rulers. This Mongolia lay within the territory of China, and was called Inner Mongolia. The princes of Inner Mongolia, who were vassals of China, entered Outer Mongolia and tried to conquer it with fire and the sword.

In 1688 the princes of Outer Mongolia came together at an assembly. They did not at all want to come under China's authority, but they understood that they could not remain independent. The princes' worst fears were confirmed: from that time on, Mongolia was completely dependent on China, its independence existed only on paper. But not the northernmost part of Mongolia!

Already at their assembly, some of the princes decided to turn to Muscovy for help. The princes of northern Mongolia wrote a letter asking the tsar to make them subjects of Russia and they pledged their allegiance to the tsar. Some of these northern princes did not want to live with the Russians and went south. A stream of other immigrants flowed from the south — Mongols were fleeing to Russian territory in order to escape the attacks of the Manchus.

From that time on, a part of the Mongol people has lived in Russia. Those Mongols who wanted to live on Russian territory came to be called Buryats. [91]

The Oirat Kalmyks

The Manchus waged a campaign also against the western Mongols, the Oirats. At the beginning of the 17th century some of the Oirat tribal leaders, unable to withstand the onslaught of the Manchus, decided to move west, to what is now Kazakhstan and to Siberia. For them this was a way to survive, but in their new land they were unwelcome foreigners. The Kazakhs and the Nogay Khanate fought against them. The Oirats then turned to the Russian government, asking for protection.

The Russian government set a territory aside for the Oirats to move to and promised to protect them from Nogay and Kazakh raids. The Oirats who came to Russia took on the name Kalmyks. [92]

The Kalmyks deserved the trust of the authorities: they bravely and loyally served the Russian state. When Peter the Great went abroad in 1697, he officially assigned the "Kalmyk Ayuka Khan" to guard the southern border of Russia. During the Great Northern War between Russia and Sweden, the Swedish royal regiment, led by king Charles XII, was surrounded by

Kalmyk cavalry and almost wiped out. The king himself barely escaped.

In the war of 1812, the Kalmyk regiments under the Cossack ataman Platov threatened Napoleon's cavalry at Borodino, took part in the "Battle of the Nations" at Leipzig, and marched into Paris in the front ranks of the Russian forces.

The Khakas — tributaries of the Kyrgyz

The Russians appeared along the Yenisei River at the beginning of the 17th century. There they found several primitive states established by the Kyrgyz. The Kyrgyz where nomadic warriors, and their tributary peoples were settled or semi-settled farmers, herders, hunters, and fishermen. The Kyrgyz considered themselves the dominant players, extracting tribute from these peoples and doing whatever they wanted to them.

The Russians levied a tribute in furs called yasak both on the subjects of the Kyrgyz and on the Kyrgyz themselves. The Kyrgyz fought fiercely against the Russian authorities. Twice they nearly took the settlement of Krasnoyarsk. What was typical of the situation, however, is that the peoples under the Kyrgyz did not want to wage war against the Russians. Many of them became Russian subjects, although they were well aware that the Kyrgyz would not forgive this. These peoples died under Kyrgyz raids, were tortured and enslaved. They were attracted to the Russian newcomers, not their Kyrgyz overlords.

In 1703 the Kyrgyz were finally dislodged from the Yenisei and decided to move on to the Dzungar (Western Mongolian) Khanate. They tried to take their subject peoples with them into Dzungaria, but most refused to go. Even those who were taken away tried hard to return. The ones who remained asked to become citizens of Russia. The former subjects of the Kyrgyz came to be called Minusinsk Tatars or Khakas. Today there are over 70,000 of them. They live in the south of Russia's Krasnoyarsk Krai and in Khakassia.

The Uyghurs: From China to Russia

The Turkic-speaking Uyghurs are known from the early Middle Ages as one of the indigenous peoples of Central Asia from Tibet to the Altai Mountains. [93] Eventually the Uyghurs' homeland was conquered by China.

The Uyghurs rebelled against the Chinese many times: they could not tolerate the suppression of their people and forced sinicization. Every time they suffered a defeat, they asked to be brought into the Russian Empire.

The flow of refugees from Eastern Turkestan stopped only for a short period: in the middle of the 19th century there was a hope that Eastern Turkestan would become part of the Russian Empire. The Uyghurs ceased to emigrate to Russia, because they hoped that their homeland would simply become part of Russia. However, England (perhaps they were concerned with the freedom of peoples and the right to self-determination?) forced Russia to withdraw its troops from the region. Once it became clear that the Uyghurs' homeland would not be taken in by Russia, Uyghur refugees again poured into Russia.

After the Communist Revolution in China, in the 1950s the Xinjiang Uyhur Autonomous Region was founded. Nonetheless, even under the Maoist government, repression of the Uyghurs continued. In the mid 20th century already some hundred thousand Uyghurs fled from China to the USSR. The exact number of refugees is unknown, as they tried to stay inconspicuous so that the Chinese would not persecute their relatives who remained behind.

The Armenians in Turkey and in Russia

The Armenians are the descendants of the ancient kingdom of Urartu. After that kingdom fell, the Armenian lands became part of the Persian and then Roman empires. The Armenians grew used to being ruled by foreigners. Part of the territory of the historical Armenia briefly became a dependent vassal state called the Kingdom of Armenia. From the 13th century on, half of the entire historical Armenian territory was divided between Turkey and Persia.

The Armenian highlands are a barren place with poor soil. For this reason, the Armenians had long been forced to move to foreign lands and settle down in cities.

Within Russian territory at various points in history, a number of Armenian communities were founded, especially in the Crimea, in Kuban, and on the Don. Most of these colonies were continually replenished by new arrivals from Armenia. One should note that although the Russian Empire was Orthodox, even Armenians, who belonged to a different branch of Christianity, could rise to high positions in society, while in Persia and Turkey Christians were officially considered infidels and treated like dogs.

The flow of refugees into Russia slackened in the 19th century, as after the Russo-Turkish war of 1811–1813 and the Russo-Persian war of 1828–1829, Armenia became part of the Russian Empire. Now the Armenians remaining within the Muslim world fled not to Russia, but to Armenia itself as a new part of the Russian Empire. Up to 90,000 Armenians are thought to have made the move. [94]

But these several tens of thousands of migrants are a drop in the ocean compared to the refugees who fled to Russia from Turkey in the 20th century. The Russo-Turkic war ended in 1878 with the defeat of Turkey and the signing of the San Stefano peace treaty. Under a special article of this treaty (article 16), administrative reforms were instituted in western Armenia. The position of Christian peoples in Muslim Turkey at the end of the 19th century was grim. Armenians were second-class citizens and forbidden to bear arms, and they often fell victim to Kurdish marauders and Ottoman tax collectors. The Armenian political circles in Constantinople and the Caucasus believed that hope for liberation of the western Armenians was to be found in Russia. Under pressure from these circles, the Orthodox

Patriarch of Constantinople sent a petition to the Russian tsar Alexander II.

The Russian government agreed to include in its negotiations with the Turks a special point concerning the Armenians, which stated:

In view of the fact that the cleansing performed by the Russian army of the territories occupied by it in Armenia, which must be returned to Turkey, might cause clashes and complications, which may adversely affect the cordial relations of both states, the Sublime Porte undertakes to carry out, without delay, improvements and reforms called for by local needs in the areas inhabited by Armenians, and to ensure their protection from the Kurds and Circassians. [95]

Such moderate demands and the lack of any direct reference to Armenian autonomy was the result of diplomatic pressure that Britain had put on Russia. Britain believed that any strengthening of Russia's position would harm its interests in Asia and on the route to India. Nonetheless, article 16 of the treaty was generally favorable to the Armenians, along with articles 25 and 27 (which set a six-month timetable for withdrawing Russian troops from Asian Turkey and and forbade the Turks from persecuting any of their subjects who had collaborated with the Russians, i.e. the Armenians). The Sublime Porte was obliged to carry out reforms in Western Armenia, and part of Western Armenia (Kars, Ardagan, Bayazet, the Alashkert valley, and other areas) was given to Russia. The Treaty of San Stefano significantly strengthened Russia's position in the Balkans, and also in Asia, thanks to the annexation of Batumi, Kars, and other areas. It was precisely this part of the deal that was unacceptable to the European states, which led to a revision of the treaty at the Berlin Congress of 1878.

The result of the policy of containment against Russia was the Armenian Genocide of the late 19th century, 1909, and most terribly in 1915–1922. After every such massacre, more Armenians fled to Russia.

Russia's Koreans
As soon as Russia established itself in the Far East, a flow of Korean immigrants came into the Russian Empire. By 1920 as many as 300 thousand Koreans lived in Russia. Last names like Tsoy, Khon, and Ju have been "Russian" for a long time now.

Russia's Chinese
In the same period, the end of the 19th and beginning of the 20th century, up to 300 thousand Chinese entered Russia, and their descendants live there to this day.

The birth of Novorossiya

The 18th century was for the Russian Empire the century of the Black Sea coast and all the territories that received the designation Novorossiya, a name which was readily taken up. People supported with great enthusiasm the idea of the south being "returned" to Russia, both because they considered the Black Sea coast their land, and because farmers simply could not stand such a huge expanse lay uncultivated because it had been made inaccessible by the Tatar invasions.

The Russians considered these lands a New Russia, a natural extension of the old Russia and supplement to it. In later times, the name Novorossiya has been used also for the part of the Caucasus along the Black Sea, which is where the city of Novorossiysk takes its name from.

Before 1917 the word "Novorossiya" came to be applied to all territories gained at the end of the 18th century. In the 19th century Odessa's university received the name Novorossiysky.

Although this name might sound similar to New England in the USA or New South Wales in Australia, it expresses a different notion. It would be even more apt to call this territory not a New Russia but a Restored Russia, though that doesn't sound as good. The unity of Novorossiya was broken by the Bolsheviks. In March of 1918 they signed the Treaty of Brest-Litovsk with Germany, which gave the Germans the right to enter Ukraine.

The nationalistic Central Rada in Kiev, the Ukrainian legislature at the time, rakishly considered the Black Sea coast theirs. According to the views of Ukrainian nationalists in Kherson, the Crimea, and the Donbass, this was Ukrainian land. The Germans soon overthrew the Rada and put the pro-German hetman Skoropadsky in power, and he signed another treaty with the Germans that allowed them to bring their troops to the Black Sea coast, the Crimea, and the Donbass. After the end of World War I the Germans left, but the Bolsheviks strangely continued to consider the western part of Novorossiya as far as the Crimea, as well as the Donbass, which had been part of Russia until the Germans won them in the Treaty of Brest-Litovsk, to be Ukrainian territory. After World War II, Krushchev formally annexed the Crimea to Ukraine. The city of Sevastopol, the glory of the Russian army, also became part of Ukraine.

For the sake of historical fairness, we must point out that in terms of both international practice and the Soviet domestic law in force at the time, Nikita Krushchev's transfer of the Crimea and Sevastopol from Soviet Russia to the Ukrainian SSR was illegitimate. The constitution of the USSR required that a referendum be held before any borders were changed. Naturally, holding a referendum was not even brought up. Furthermore, when the area was handed over to Ukraine, Sevastopol had a special status as a off-limits military area and was not legally subordinate to the Crimea region. Accordingly, it could not have automatically been transferred to Ukraine, and this would have required a separate decision. But back then, in careless haste, it was as if they forgot it existed and Sevastopol was not mentioned separately in any of the decisions connected to transferring Crimea to Ukraine. Of course, it's silly to blame Krushchev today for Russia's loss of Crimea. Even in his worst nightmares Krushchev could not have foreseen the insane Belavezha Accords of December 1991 and the collapse of the USSR. At that time of his decision, the move of a territory from one union republic to another was for the higher party officials a mere formality, a symbolic gesture, nothing more than moving a coin from one pocket of a wide pair trousers into the other.

The real blame for the loss of Crimea can be placed entirely on Boris Yeltsin and his team, who frittered this affair away in a drunken stupor when he signed the criminal Belavezha Accords. Against the backdrop of the catastrophe that then fell across the entire country, one could only say of the Crimean sideshow that sometimes such things just happen.

The diverse Caucasus

Russia's relations with the peoples and states on both sides of the Caucasus mountains have a long and complicated history. After the collapse of Georgia in the 1460s, the rulers of several separate kingdoms (Kartli, Kakheti, Imereti, Samtskhe-Dzhavakheti) turned to the Russian tsars with pleas for protection. In 1557 a military and political alliance was concluded between Russia and Kabarda, and in 1561 Mary, the daughter of the Kabardin king Temryuk Iradov, Kucheney, became the wife of Ivan the Terrible. In 1582 the inhabitants of the surroundings of Beshtau, harried by Crimean Tatar raids, came under the patronage of the Russian tsar. The king of Kakheti Alexander II, under attack by Shamkhal of Tarki, sent an embassy to the Russian tsar Fyodor in 1586 and expressed his readiness to become a vassal of Russia. The Kartli king George X also swore allegiance to Russia, though Russia was unable to provide substantial assistance to its coreligionists and limited itself to pleading for them before the Persian shah. In the Time of Troubles (the beginning of the 17th century), Russia's relations with the Caucasus came to a complete halt. The repeated requests for assistance that the rulers there made to tsars Mikhail Romanov and Alexei Mikailovich went unanswered.

Starting from the reign of Peter the Great, Russia's influence on the Caucasus became more definite and longlasting, although the provinces on the Caspian that Peter won during his Persian campaign (1722–1723) were soon lost to Persia again. The border between the two states remained the northeast part of the Terek River.

Under Anna Ivanovna the Caucasian border was established. Under a treaty concluded with the Ottoman Empire in 1739, Kabarda was recognized as independent and was to serve as a buffer between the two powers. The rapid spread of Islam among the mountain peoples completely separated the area from Russia.

With the outbreak of the first war against Turkey under Catherine the Great, Russia established continual relations with Georgia. King Heraclius II even helped the Russian army, which crossed over the Caucasus under the command of Count Gottlieb Heinrich Totleben and passed through Kartli to reach Imereti.

Under the Treaty of Georgievsk on July 24, 1783, the Georgian king Heraclius II, after he had made repeated appeals for help, was brought under the protection of Russia. It was decided that two Russian battalions with four guns would be placed in Georgia.

Frankly, Russia didn't even need to take Georgia under its protection. If Russia sought only to expand its territory, who could have prevented Elizabeth from bringing Russian forces into Georgia? Russia in fact only responded after Georgia had asked for help for the twelfth time! People in Russia knew that there was nothing to get out of poor Georgia, and if the Russians crossed the Caucasus, there would again be a war with Turkey, and that's what actually happened afterwards.

The rulers of Georgia wanted to unite their territory and receive Russia protection in order to avoid genocide on the part of the Muslims.

In 1795 the shah of Persia invaded Georgian territory. The Persians burned Tbilisi and became a systematic policy of wiping out Georgians who refused to convert to Islam, and their whole families with them. Sometimes the children were spared, and taken to be brought up by Muslims, and the young girls were sold to harems.

CHAPTER 5

The last ruler of the East Georgia kingdom, George XII (1798–1800) once again asked Russia to take Georgia under its protection and to save the Georgian people. As a result, tsar Paul I finally made a difficult decision, to bring Georgia into Russia, but he did not manage to ensure this came about. After his sudden death, supposedly from a stomach ailment, his son Alexander I again thought about how Russia was threatened by the situation in the Caucasus. Did Russia really need Georgia? For six months he wavered, ignoring the Georgians' persistent pleas for protection against Muslim genocide, and finally the young tsar made his decision. He did issue a manifesto about a protectorate on September 12, 1801, which had already been prepared by Pavel.

Let me repeat: Russia answered the twelfth official request sent by the Georgians.

Soon the Mingrelian prince swore an oath to the Russian tsar. Somewhat later the provinces of Guria and Abkhazia joined in. Of course, the result of this process of joining Georgia to Russia was a war with Persia in 1804–13 and another with Turkey in 1806–12. Both of these wars saw the participation of Armenian volunteers. Armenia too had long sought to become part of Russia.

Central Asia

Russia's advance into Central Asia was caused by approximately the same reasons as the desire to return the Crimea to Russia. Throughout the 18th century Russians living in the south had to fight off raids carried out by slave-traders from the Central Asian khanates and the intrusions of nomadic tribes. The towns and fortresses of the Orenburg Line, which Pushkin brilliantly described in his *The Captain's Daughter*, were typical fortifications along the Russian borders. The Bashkirs and Kazakhs raided Russian settlements for the same reason the Crimean Tatars did: to capture people and sell them to the Central Asian states as slaves.

The country needed to strengthen its borders, protect its citizens, and make peace with its neighbors. Russia gradually began to negotiate with the Kazakh khanates, selling bread in exchange for livestock and animal products. From 1731 to the 1740s, when the Kazakh khans became Russian vassals, Russia defended its new subjects from raids from the steppes and sought to bring security to its new borders. Since the Kazakh steppe was as easily passable in all directions as the plains of Russia and Siberia plains, the Russian Empire built fortifications in Kazakhstan. In the book *A Journey from Orenburg to Bukhara*, the Russian military officer Egor Meyendorff writes of how he reached Khiva and Bukhara, which were located in oases cut off from other places by a terrible stretch of desert, and here he saw that "between 500 and 600 Russians languished in slavery: they were sold by the Kyrgyz or Turkmens, who captured fishermen after they were shipwrecked on the eastern shore of the Caspian, or by the Khivans." [96]

Meyendorff went on to write, "The fate of slaves in Bukhara is dreadful. I saw one slave whose master had cut off his ears, pierced his hands with nails, poured boiling oil over them, and flayed the skin on his back in order to make him confess where a fellow slave had run away to... Most of the Russian captives were locked up and forced to work with shackles on their legs, and they worked ceaselessly for the several weeks that we stayed in this town. I cannot describe the immense joy of the ten Russian slaves which we bought out of slavery in Bukhara during our journey." [97]

Meyendorff urged the Russian government to take extreme steps, such as taking hostages: "to take hold of the Khivans and Bukharans living in the empire and all of their possessions", in order to "return these thousand of people torn away from Russia to their homeland, to their families and their faith."

The tsar did not act on this recommendation; he had no right to take hostages, so the Khivan and Bukharan merchants were not detained. But Russia's desire to clamp down on the slave trade only strengthened.

CHAPTER 5

During the "storming of Samarkand" — something that has to be put in quotation marks — one of the oldest cities of the Orient, the jewel of Asia, etc., the Russian army lost two people. Only two! This only goes to show how advanced the Russian military was compared to the medieval Central Asian khanates, but it also shows how the Russians met no resistance in annexing Turkestan.

After taking Samarkand and losing two men, the Russians decided to be as merciful as possible. They gave gifts to the elders of the city, and as they moved on, they left behind only a symbolic garrison of one and a half battalions, around 600 people.

This is where the Oriental trickery comes in. The emir of Samarkand raised a huge army and made a surprise attack on the Russian garrison. What happened next is amazing.

For several days, until the main forces arrived, these 600 men defended Samarkand. They held out against an attack from all sides, on foreign soil, in a hostile city, and faced by an army of 65 thousand men. 600 against 65,0000! Among the defenders of the city was a young officer named Vereshchagin, who would go on to become the renowned painter of war scenes.

In 1868 Bukhara signed a treaty with the Russian Empire. One of its stipulations was that Bukhara would return to Russia all its Russian slaves that had not converted to Islam.

How Alaska was sold

There is a myth that Alaska was never sold off, and instead it was only leased to the United States. The lease was for a period of 99 years, so now the Americans should give it back.

Alas, this is no more than a pretext for patriotic pop songs and political manoeuvring. The document signed on March 30, 1867 says nothing about any lease. On that day, the Russian diplomat Baron Edward de Stoeckl, serving as an envoy to the USA, and the American secretary of state William H. Seward signed a treaty by which the United States bought Alaska from the Russian-American Company for 7.2 million dollars (i.e. 2 cents per acre of land).

Much in this deal was typical of both sides. For Russia it was the confidence that it managed to sell the territory and that's that. Thank God, it's signed, and that does it. Russia's reach would never extend as far as Alaska anyway, so it would forever remain an undeveloped territory... That Russia's reach later extended to the Far East and the Arctic are just dull trifles. Myths ignore such trifles as facts.

In that long ago time, the tsar's brother Grand Duke Konstantin Nikolaevich wanted greatly to sell Alaska. He whispered to the tsar that if Russia did not sell the territory, the Yanks would soon annex it without paying anything. To provide an example of how money could be earned, Nikolaevich pointed to the Louisiana Purchase, when Napoleon sold its French territories in the American Midwest to the USA for 15 million dollars.

Why did Russia sell it for so "cheap"? It didn't go for 15 million dollars but only $7,200,000. Sixty-four years after the Louisiana Purchase, and after Civil War, the dollar had a different value than it had had in 1803. Where did they get such a price? Seriously speaking, the were some "scientific grounds" for such an amount.

During the Crimean War of 1853–56, the British threatened to seize Alaska, and the Russian-American Company insured its holdings in Alaska for that amount. Ten years passed, but the figure stayed the same. Thus the price agreed was $7,200,000. This was 2.5% of the Russian Empire's annual budget. In general, it was a pittance for such a vast territory. It was a rare case of mismanagement, and people who did not believe in their own strengths and abilities made a significant contribution to it.

For the Americans too this deal was very typical. In 1866, the year before, the Americans had brought out a telegraph line to Novoarkhangelsk, the capital of Russia's American holdings. As they hammered poles into the ground, they found grains of gold in the deep holes they had dug. Naturally, the Russian authorities were not notified of this discovery. By 1913, the Americans had extracted 200 million dollars from Alaska in gold alone, 100 million in other minerals, and 80 million in fish and furs.

However, not everyone in the USA understood at first that buying Alaska was a good deal. In the press it was called such disparaging names as "Icebergia" and "Walrus-sia". Congress had actively sought to persuade against the purchase of Alaska and lawmakers had to be convinced of the idea. Newspapers wrote many things about the methods used to convince them. A special commission was even founded to investigate corruption among members of that august assembly. The commission gradually ended its activities without finding anything against anyone. Only in 1912 did American historians find interesting documentation, such as a confidential memo to the American secretary of state, which contained the names of all congressmen, "Russian lobbyists", and even certain sums. It turned out that it cost Russia $165,000 to lobby American congressmen to support the purchase of America. Today these payments would be called kickbacks.

The Russian Empire sold its richest land, the value of which cannot even be estimated, and got 7.2 million dollars for it, after paying $165,000 in kickbacks. Thus, in total it took in $7,035,000.

Another myth persists that Russia never even got the money. It is alleged that the money was to be delivered to Russia on the English ship *Orkney* and it sank in the Baltic. This wasn't the case: representatives of the Russian Empire could simply withdraw the money from a British bank.

Moreover, Russia's leading expert on the history of Russian America, professor Alexander Petrov, has told me of how he was able to track down documents on how the 7 million dollars were spent. It turns out that the money was used to build the Moscow-Ryazan railway. When a Russian decides to visit the Yesenin sites in Konstantinovo by taking the train to be authentic, he or she is riding on the most expensive railway track in the world. These 200 kilometers of track are equivalent to Alaska's 7600 square kilometers of gold and oil reserves.

Those who left the Empire

It would be unfair to not mention the peoples who did not want to live in the Russian Empire and not seek to understand why they made that choice.

After the defeat of Turkey and Russia's annexation of Crimea, up to 140,000 Crimean Tatars left to Turkey. Two thirds of the Kalmyks in 1771 left for Dzungaria (of these, 60–70% were killed).

The most painful events, however, are linked with the exodus of the Northern Caucasus peoples from from Russia. One must treat these separately.

The Circassians

The Circassians lived where today only Russians do: in the Kuban River basin, on the shores of the Black Sea, and on both sides of the Tereka River. During the Caucasus War of 1817–1864 the Circassians were the last to surrender of all the peoples of the North Caucasus, giving in five years after Imam Shamil of Dagestan and Chechnya. After the war, the Circassians began a mass emigration to the Ottoman Empire, as the Muslim Circassians wanted to join their coreligionists in Turkey. [98]

At the beginning of the 1990s the Circassians started a loud call for Russia to reconsider its "imperialist policies". On June 28–29, 1991 the Regional Council of Adygea issued a declaration of the republic's sovereignty. The republic was proclaimed a formation created "on the basis of the Adyghe people exercising their unalienable right to self-determination". Many leaders of the Circassian national movement treated this event as Russia's redemption from its historical guilt towards their people. In early October of 1991, through the initiative of the leaders of the Adyghe Khase, the First Congress of the

Circassian People was convened, which stated the need for the self-determination of the Circassians "through the acquisition of political and economic sovereignty within the Russian Federation".

In 1997 the Parliament of Adygea adopted a law on repatriation in the hopes that their fellow Circassians would return en masse from Turkey and the countries of the Near East. However, these hopes for Circassian solidarity were not met. In 1998 thirty-five Circassian families from Kosovo returned to Adygea. They were allocated 150 hectares of land near Maikop. Not all were able to adapt to life in the Caucasus and some went back to Kosov in spite of the inter-ethnic strife in the former Yugoslavia.

According to various sources, the number of returnees to Adygea who received Russian citizenship stands at 350–500 people, while over a thousand more have received residence permits. A mass return of Circassians to their historical homeland has not happened.

The Chechens
After the end of the Caucasus War in the 19th century, Russia and Turkey agreed to resettle a part of the Chechen people in Turkey. In total 22,500 people who wished to move were taken, about 20% of the total population. Those leaving were allowed to allowed to take all of their possessions, their livestock and their foodstuffs, and they were even given carts for this. On their way to the Russian border, they were even given free firewood, pasture and hay.

It turned out that Turkey was completely unprepared to receive these migrants. In Turkey, close to the Russian border, this group of people formed an enormous camp. They were left out in an open field for two months and suffered great cold. Many ran out of the spare supplies that the Russian government had given them.

After a long period of waiting, the Turkish authorities decided to send these migrants to predetermined sites in their deserted provinces. The migrants however refused to follow until their elders had inspected the lands set aside for them. The elders returned and stated that these lands were poor and unsuitable for farming. The migrants subsequently refused to leave their camp, and stricken by cold and hunger, they hastened to raid the nearby Armenian settlements.

In October, two hundred migrants arrived on the Russian border asking to be let back into Russia on any terms. The number of migrants coming back the border eventually exceeded 2600 people. The Russian border authorities refused to take them back and they increased their surveillance of the border.

The Turkish authorities subsequently moved troops to the border region and fired cannons at the migrants, forcing them to leave the border region for Kars under army escort. At the same time it was decided that these migrants should be disarmed. In some cases they gave up their weapons without resistance, but in Mush they were disarmed only after a brief battle in which casualties were suffered on both sides.

As a result, many of the Chechen families decided to return to the Caucasus by whatever means possible. Large groups of migrants began to appear on the Russian border and sought to return to their homeland, but this time the Russian authorities showed a rare harshness, even in the case of people seeking asylum, and absolutely refused to readmit them.

Russia's Jews

Russia's policy on ethnicity has had its dark sides. In spite of its tolerance and democratic relationships with the peoples living within it, there has been one exception: the Jews, or more precisely, religious Jews. The Jews came into the Russian Empire in large numbers after the partitioning of Poland at the end of the 18th century. The Jews were forbidden from leaving the western provinces of the empire, they were limited to an area called the Pale of Settlement. The number of Jews allowed to study in state schools and universities was limited under a quota. Jews could not pursue official careers or become military officers. Only with the Provisional Government of 1917 were these restrictions finally removed.

However, let me again stress that all the limitations considered only those people who explicitly practiced Judaism. Formally nobody prevented Jews from converting to Orthodoxy. [99] Converts could move to wherever they wanted and take up any profession. They could serve in the army and or become civil servants. For example, one of the Russian generals serving in Turkestan, a hero in Russia's annexation of Central Asia, was a baptised Jew by the name of Kaufman. The maternal ancestors of the Russian poets Fet, Khodasevich, and Blok, and even Lenin (and one's maternal ancestry in Judaism is the most important) were all rabbis.

Of course, the restrictions still caused protests. According to various sources, between 1,800,000 and 2,500,000 Jews left the Russian Empire, most going to the USA. In Belarus to this day live close relatives of the late American science-fiction writer Isaac Asimov. Russia's pathological "friend" Richard Pipes also hails from a family of Jewish emigrants from Russian-dominated Poland. [100]

Russia's Poles

After Poland's defeat in the uprising of Tadeusz Kosciuszko in the late 18th century, up to a hundred thousand Poles left the Russian Empire for Europe. However, half of them eventually returned. After the suppression of the uprisings in 1830–1831 and 1863, another 150,000 people left Russia. Some of them had participated in the uprisings and feared reprisals. I should note that many of these Poles left not for the West but headed east to Ukraine, which was closer and which they understood better. According to family legend, my ancestors in my father's line came from these Polish migrants, one "Cossack" from the retinue of a Polish nobleman, who moved from Poland to Kiev in the 19th century.

The policy on ethnicity in the USSR

> If a madman was found today who, with one stroke of his quill, would enact political liberties in Russia, then tomorrow in Saint Petersburg a council of workers' deputies would sit, which after half a year of its existence would throw Russia into a fiery hell.
>
> —*Pyotr Stolypin (writing in 1910!)*

The Russian Empire was a unitary state consisting of governorates and oblasts. Only the Kingdom of Poland and the Grand Duchy of Poland had relative autonomy. After the October Revolution, the Bolsheviks sought to create a Soviet Russia in the same borders as it had under the empire, only without Poland and Finland.

However, seeing the rapid growth in the national consciousness of the various peoples inhabiting the country, Lenin decided on another principle of forming a state, one more popular among the masses of "foreigners", a principle of a state and at the same time a national "union of free republics", i.e. a federation of these. Consequently Soviet Russia got three more jurisdictional entities, the Baltic, Belorussian and Ukrainian republics. Their ethnic and state autonomy was recognized as part of Soviet Russia. In March of 1919, the Bashkir republic was recognized, followed by Tatar and Kazakh/Kyrgyz republics the following year. The principle of a federation, as well as the right of these peoples to freely choose whether or not to enter the Soviet federation, was legislated in the Declaration of the Rights of the Toiling and Exploited Peoples (January 1918) and later in the Constitution of the USSR.

By 1933, the country counted 5300 national *selsoviets* and 250 national districts. In Leninigrad Oblast alone there were 57 national *selsoviets* and 3 national districts (Karelian, Finnish, and Veps). Schools offered teaching in the local languages. In Leningrad at the beginning of the 1930s, newspapers were published in forty languages, even Chinese. Radio broadcasts were made in Finnish (at that time, around 130,000 Finns lived in Leningrad and the area around it.

The turning point came in the mid 1930s. Centralization of power, a transition from regional oversight to top-down government, brought many negative developments with it. The 1930s to the 1950s were a dark period in Soviet ethnic policy. In these years, historians say, deportations were carried out of Koreans, Germans, Ingrian Finns, Karachay, Kalmyks, Chechen, Ingush, Balkars, Crimean Tatars, and Meskhetian Turks. During this time, the Germans, Karachay, Kalmyks, Ingush, Chechens, Balkans, and Crimean Tatars lost their autonomous regions.

The height of forced relocation of entire peoples came with World War II. The country's internal policies sought to strengthen power and military capabilities by removing "unreliable peoples" from "dangerous" areas to more tranquil, distant parts, where it would be more difficult for them to commit acts of "treason". Between 1941 and 1944, mass deportations were carried out on the Germans, Kalmyks, Chechens, Karachay, Balkars, Crimean Tatars, Nogay, Meskhetian Turks, Pontic Greeks, Bulgarians, Crimean Roman, and Kurds. This was mainly done on the basis of accusations of collaboration with the enemy, which applied to the entire people.

These deportations caused enormous damages to the USSR, to its economy, its culture, and the traditions of different peoples. The cultural and economic ties between peoples were disrupted, the national consciousness of the masses was altered. The government's authority was undermined, and negative aspects arose in state policies on interethnic relations.

The collapse of the Soviet Union in the 1990s and the interethnic conflicts linked with it are to some degree a result of these tragedies of the Stalinist era. [101]

The process of rehabilitating these peoples began after Stalin's death. In 1956 a series of decrees from the Presidium of the Supreme Soviet of the USSR (the country's supreme governing body) removed the restrictions from the Poles, Kalmyks, Greeks,

Bulgarians, Armenians, Crimean Tatars, Chechens, Ingush, etc. In 1957–1958 the autonomy of the Kalmyks, Chechens, Ingush, Karachay, and Balkans was restored. These people were allowed to return to their historical territories. This return did not happen without complications, which even then led to interethnic conflicts. For example, clashes occurred between Chechens and the Russians who had been settled in Grozny area after the former had been driven out, as well as in an Ingush region that had been resettled by Ossetians and transferred to the North Ossetian ASSR. In 1964, twenty-three years after the deportations, the Presidium of the Supreme Soviet of the USSR issued a general pardon to the German population in the Volga region. In 1972 a decree was issued that restored their freedom of movement and allowed them to return to the places they had been driven out of.

One of the first steps towards seeing justice done to these repressed peoples was the adoption of the Declaration of the Supreme Soviet of November 14, 1989 "On recognition of illegal and criminal acts against repressive peoples subjected to forced resettlement, and ensuring their rights", which rehabilitated all repressed peoples, and declared the acts of repression carried out against them at the state level criminal and unlawful.

In 1991 a law about rehabilitation of the repressed peoples was adopted. The law admitted that the deportation of the peoples had been "a policy of slander and genocide" (article 2). Among other things, the law allowed repressed peoples to restore their territorial integrity to the jurisdictions that had existed prior to their abolishment, and it also provided for compensation for damages caused by the state.

CHAPTER 6
Myth 5: Russia as a threat

As it's supposedly well known, Russia threatens the "entire civilized world". It is an economical and political threat. Wild Tartary, Muscovy, is a threat to its peaceful neighbors. A completely militarized society, the Russian Empire, where every aristocrat was an officer and every peasant a conscript, was a threat to the peaceful and stable life of every normal independent country, which this numberless army could reach by marching overland. Bristling with nuclear weapons, delirious with ideas of an ideology of global domination, it is a threat to civilization worldwide. It is a dark side of the moon, an evil empire.

The Russia that has been revived "under Putin" is still weak, its elite divided and too desiring of luxury and comfort, too keen on having standards of living "like in Europe". Therefore it seems premature to speak of "imperial ambitions". But even the "new Russia" sometimes feels tempted to bare its oil-and-gas teeth and bite off its piece of the pie. Now that the world has become accustomed to seeing Russia as a potential aggressor, it doesn't have to be persuaded that both its gas supply and the Kalashnikov are both well-made tools. The only question is who is holding those tools at the moment.

Russia has always sought to rule the world, and only thanks to the united efforts of defenders of the true (Catholic-Protestant) faith, Western freedom, democracy, and parliamentary government has it not managed to do so.

Different countries have fallen victims to Russia's battle against freedom and open societies at different times: free Ukraine and proud Poland, hardworking Baltic countries and Finland, and the freedom-loving peoples of the Caucasus. In the 20th century the Soviet Russian plague swept halfway around the world, from Southeast Asia to the Caribbean. But in the tilted battle between Good and Evil, the Russian Darth Vader could not withstand this exertion and collapsed.

But now its successor, Russia, continues to threaten the small countries around it, and as soon as it gives the chance, it will wage war against them, annex them and annihilate them. Thanks to the help from the West, these poor little countries have been able to fend off their terrible neighbor. In the name of justice, for the sake of democracy, and simply out of self-preservation, the West must fulfill this mission.

And they really believe this. They base their decisions on this. Any provocation or unverified incident is considered to be "further proof".

The myth of Russia as a threat is very old and enduring. Without it, there's no point to any of the other myths. Let's try to understand how the myth of Russia has arisen, and who needs it and why.

The roots of the myth

The myth of Russian aggression was built up between the 16th and 19th centuries and has stayed strong down to our time. One of the bases for the belief in this myth has been proven to be a fake. This document under the name of *The Testament of Peter the Great*, was allegedly discovered in 1757 by Chevalier. d'Eon de Beaumont, a French spy and agent of influence at the court of the empress Elizabeth, and later it was sent to Louis XV of France. The document talks about how to play the European powers off against one other, how to expand

CHAPTER 6

the Russian Empire, and how to ultimately achieve world domination.

Over the following century, rumors about the secret document were brought out whenever it was necessary to convince the European public of the aggressive aims of Russian foreign policy. The essence of these rumors was that Peter the Great planned to expand Russian territory towards the north, south, and east until he had conquered most of Europe, Persia, and India.

In 1836 this very forgery arose and ended with the foreboding words, "Thus we can and must conquer Europe." Experts have long since proven that the so-called *Testament of Peter the Great* is a clumsy forgery.

The forgery nonetheless continued to be dragged out whenever Russia's foes had to intensify their aggressive intentions and actions. Thus interest in its rose in 1854–1855. The British and French press defended the aggression of these countries' allies in the Crimea by the need to prevent Peter the Great's plans from coming to pass.

The *Testament* was brought up once more in 1876 in connection with the beginning of the Balkan peoples' movement for national liberation from the Ottoman Empire, in order to claim that Russia was again working towards a global state.

In 1915 the Germans had the *Testament* published in Iranian newspapers. Their plan was simple: to sow fear and distrust among neighboring countries loyal to Russia. Watch out, the Russians are coming!

In November 1941, when it became obvious that the *Blitzkrieg* had failed, German fascist newspapers again published this purported document, titling it with the strident headline, "The Bolsheviks are realizing Peter the Great's goal of world domination".

It is well known that accusations that the Soviet Union wanted global domination, its aim to carry out what was in the *Testament of Peter the Great*, also arose during the Cold War years.

Even in the new millennium the American secretary of defense Donald Rumsfeld called Russia "a new threat" and referred to the *Testament*.

In 2006, the American press began to write of Russia's "imperialist policies". The Russian president Vladimir Putin had hung a portrait of Peter the Great in his office, which was taken a sign of his aggressive policies. Layers call such speculation "presumption of guilt". This example clearly shows how on the level of political confrontation this myth is constantly used, as it has been for over two centuries now. The government changes, wars and revolutions break out, the state of the world changes, but this myth is kept safe so that it can be taken out and used again.

No such myth in the days of Rus'

> Every uprising against foreign aggressors is permissible and the first duty of every people.
>
> —*Stendhal*

Rus': aggressor or victim?

Amazingly, no one castigated Rus' for being aggressive when it really was a formidable state between the 6th and 12th centuries.

Today the term Rus' is used to refer to all territories inhabited by the East Slavs. This is fair, but not for every point in history.

During the time of Oleg of Novgorod, until 911, only six tribal unions of the twelve known then belong to Rus'. The borders of Ancient Rus' evolved thanks to conquests of the Slavic tribes' voluntary decision to join together with the descendants of Rurik. In 860 Rurik ceased to raid the coasts of Flanders and Britain. Apparently this was the time when he was declared tsar in Ladoga. In 862 he and his band captured Novgorod. Conquest, usurping power, and thuggery — everything was in

CHAPTER 6

the spirit of the early Middle Ages. It even provoked the people of Novgorod to rise up under Vadim the Brave.

In 882, Oleg of Novgorod, a relative of Rurik, took Kiev and made it his capital. At that time only a single tribe in the south, the Polans, paid tribute to Oleg.

It is also known when the last East Slavic tribe, the Vyatichi, started to pay tribute to Kiev. This happened in 964. From that time on, all East Slavic tribes were subordinated to the ruler in Kiev and entered the state of Rus'.

Rus' constantly launched predatory raids on its rich neighbors, and it especially beleaguered Byzantium, sending expeditions in 907, 911, 941, and 944.

However, neither Byzantium itself nor Europe ever accused the East Slavs and the state of Rus' of aggression: it was obvious that their acts were no different from those of other nations. To the writers of Byzantine chroniclers, the people of Rus' seemed even less aggressive than, for example, many Germanic tribes. At least they always managed to "negotiate" with the leaders of Rus'. Thus one does not find any propaganda against Rus' during this time in any historical chronicle.

What's more, the opposite can be said, that it wasn't Rus' that conquered its neighbors. Rus' was itself a constant victim of raids. Eastern Europe was a vast plain, open to every direction, almost without any natural borders. It could be invaded from any side except the Arctic Ocean. Even from that direction, going around Scandinavia, a prince Otar waged war on Rus'. [102] In the sagas it is beautifully described how the Varangians tried to conquer the mouth of the Dvina, but they couldn't manage, because the Finno-Ugrian peoples living here didn't care for the besiegers: the uninvited guests were met with poisoned arrows. The Varangians sailed back on their way, and historians even today try to understand how the local Finnish men poisoned their arrows. The majority tend to believe that the Finns used decomposing salmon-type fish as a poison, which had a terrible effect on its victim and was an affordable choice for a population whose main industry was fishing.

The appearance in Rus' of dynasty of the Varangian king Rurik is connected with these territorial gains. Rurik's band probably came to Rus' from Scandinavia. Before that, Rurik had managed to be proclaimed ruler in Friesland and venture into England. When he brought his band to Rus', the appearance of these warriors was "most wondrous": they walked around without trousers, wearing kilts instead. But that choice of clothing is no surprise for historians, as Rurik had come with his people from noble Britain, and in that time not only in the north, in Scotland, but also in the south many men went without trousers. Trousers were a barbarian clothing, neither the Celts nor the Romans knew of them.

It wasn't just Rurik who had a Scandinavian name but all the early rulers: Oleg (from Helge), Olga (from Helga), and Igor (from Ingvar). Even Vladimir, which seems to be a pure Russian name, is said by many historians to have come from Voldemar, with the Slavs changing it to fit their pronunciation. Oleg's band consisted mainly of people with names like Farlaf, Sveneld, and Rotvold. While the possibly Slavic names Ratibor and Vsevolod are also attested, it is clear that the majority of these people were not Slavs.

Some historians have questioned whether the first rulers and notable people in Rus' were of Varangian origin. Mikhail Lomonosov suggested that the Varangians could have been Prussian Balts and arrived from what is now Kaliningrad. [103] The term for Prussian then came to be pronounced as what is now "Russian". Rurik was thus a Prussian ruler, from a tribe akin to the Slavs.

Whether Rurik was a Varangian or Prussian is beside the point. The greatness of his dynasty lies in the fact that his descendants joined all of the tribes into a single state, laying the foundation for the beginnings of Rus'.

Russia also was constantly raided by its neighbors in the steppes to the south. Even before there arose a state ruled by Rurik's descendants, the Scythians regularly raided their neighbors to the north and northwest — farmers who lived in the light steppe and in the south of the forest belt. Herodotus called them the "plowmen Scythians". He believed that the nomadic Scythians dominated the farmers, and the latter paid tribute and were considered part of the primitive state of their conquerors. Some historians believe that the "plowmen Scythians" were none other than the ancestors of the Slavs. [104]

New conquerors continued to invade Eastern Europe from the east and the south, settling its vast spaces and subduing the indigenous peoples. The reason for this is simple: the conquerors were drawn by the riches of Eastern Europe, its abundance of sparsely-populated forests and steppe, its abundance of soil and wildlife.

The Huns, Magyars, Avars, and Bulgars marched across the Eastern European steppe, without venturing into the forests, and they had a considerable influence on the history of the southern Slavs.

From the south the neighbors of the Slavs attempted to conquer their lands, and these neighbors managed to create vast, lasting states. One of them was the Khazar Khanate, which arose from the ashes of the Huns and ruled over the territory of the Slavic tribes in the 7th and 8th centuries. In 967 the Khazar Khanate fell to the attacks of Svyatoslav. This turned out to make things worse, as the Khazars had prevented the predatory hordes living in the South Russian steppe from moving through. Once the Khazars were not around to stop them, the Pechenegs rushed in.

> After Svyatoslav, the son of the great Kiev ruler Igor, defeated the Khazars in 967, the Pechenegs decided to take advantage of the route to South Russia that was now open to them and in 968 they besieged Kiev. At the time, Svyatoslav's forces were far away in Bulgaria. Kiev was defended by only a small band and a militia made up of townspeople.
>
> The people of Kiev sent a message to Svyatoslav saying, "You, prince, have gone off to a foreign land, but you have left your own land

on its own, and we are barely holding out against the Pechenegs." The letter was sent by a man who knew the Pechenegs' language: in the predawn mist, this young hero left the fortified walls and managed to walk across the Pechenegs' camping by asking if anyone had seen his horse, as he had lost it.

Svyatoslav returned and drove the besieging forces away. Three years later Svyatoslav himself died at the hands of the Pechenegs. In 971 the Byzantine emperor ordered that the Pechenegs be notified that Svyatoslav was returning from Bulgaria with a small band. In fact, he had only his personal guard with him. The Pechenegs ambushed him on the Dnieper rapids and killed him.

If one believes in the legend, the Pecheneg khan Kurya made a drinking vessel out of Svyatoslav' skull. According to pagan belief, by drinking from this vessel, Kurya himself could take on the powers of the great warrior Svyatoslav. Different accounts are given of what happened to this drinking vessel, but according to one account, it is held to this day in a museum in the south of Russia. According to another version, the skull was given to Mstislav, one of the sons of Yaroslav the Wise, and he had it cremated.

The Pechenegs raided Russia time and time again in 992, 996, and 997. In the chronicles, the most devastating raids are noted, which many cities and principalities suffered from.

In Europe the Pechenegs were known as a people of enormous build and as unbelievably strong warriors. This is how the appear in the French medieval epic *La Chanson de Roland*, as well as in other literary accounts.

In 1036 Yaroslav the Wise finally defeated the Pechenegs and their tribal union fell apart. But here it turned out that the Pechenegs (like the Khazars before them) acted as a barrier for another people of the steppe, the Cumans. In 1068 the Cumans crushed the remnants of the defeated Pechenegs and poured across the Volga. They did the same simple thing to the Pechenegs as the latter did with their predecessors: they slaughtered them down to the last man and took their land and livestock.

CHAPTER 6

The Cumans also raided Rus'. "There was great wailing in our land, and our towns were deserted as people fled from the enemy." Accounts similar to this one appear in in the chronicles for 1089, 1091, 1097, 1109, 1112.

The Cuman khans Bonyak and Tugorkan have even entered Russian folklore. In western Ukraine people tell of one Bonyak Sheludivy, and Tugarin or Tugarin Zmeyevich is known to every schoolboy.

The people of Rus' were not innocent victims of assault, saintly defenders of their homeland. On more than a few occasions they carried out retaliatory raids, which were just as cruel and involved just as much cattle-rustling, violence, and looting.

In the 12th century Vladimir II Monomakh struck a blow against the Cumans. The forces of Rus' rushed to their enemy's winter pasture land. The Cumans could not leave these pastures as grass had still not grown anywhere else. They could hardly put up a fight, as their horses were emaciated after the long winter. Over twenty khans were killed in the battle, while the Russians defending their homeland "took the cattle, sheep, horses, and camels, and the settlements with their goods and people."

Still in the 12th century, the people of Rus' took a Cuman settlement on the Don. The Yas Alans (descendants of the Sarmatians) and Bulgars, peoples that had been conquered by the Pechenegs, met the Russians with wine and fish. They had evidently suffered greatly under the Pechenegs.

A significant monument of Old Russian literature is *The Tale of Igor's Campaign* which deals with a military escapade of 1185. [105] At that time, the Cumans managed to destroy the Slavic forces, capture Prince Igor, and then responded to the raiding of their land by successfully attacking Rus'.

The Pechenegs had raided only five percent of the territory of Rus'. The Cumans however kept up various industries, farming and herding, and their state was more powerful. Now ten percent of Rus' was subject to Cuman raids. Their army freely passed over the windswept Russian plains. Force could only be met with force.

In the beginning of the 13th century Rus' was confronted with an even more terrible foe: the Mongols. Their state was incomparably bigger and stronger, they could carry out much more devastating campaigns. Now almost half of Rus' fell victim to constant raids. A consequence of these raids was that the richest, most civilized and most cultured territory, southern Rus' was desolated. After Batu took Kiev in 1240, the city was burned down and destroyed. It took time and enormous effort to rebuild it. The same fate was met by Ryazan, which was later rebuilt 12 kilometers away from the earlier site. No one remembers any more where the city that the savage hordes destroyed was.

In was in this terrible epoch that legends were born of the mythical city of Kitezh and the blessed princess Eupraxia of Kiev.

Western orders of knights took advantage of the feudal fragmentation of Rus' and its defeat under the Mongols to move east. They captured Yuryev, a town founded by Yaroslav the Wise. This town in present-day Estonia is now called Tartu by Estonians and Derpt by Germans, but it was originally named after Yaroslav's baptismal name Yuri (George). Another name founded by the same prince, Yaroslavl, is called so after his pagan name.

Only in 1242 did Alexander Nevsky put a stop to the aggression of the knights and the Swedish lords. However, gradually more and more land were gained by the Lithuanians: the Russians themselves usually went "to Lithuania" to defend themselves from the Tatars

The Polish influence on the western lands of Rus' was so strong that some territories ceased to be part of Rus' and were instead assimilated by the Poles. The Polish town Przemyśl is no other than what the Russian chronicles recorded as Peremysl, only now there were no longer any Russians there.

One has to marvel at the fact that neither the Poles, nor the popes in Rome, nor the German knights who carried out the popes' will in the 13th and 14th centuries ever accused the people of Rus' of being aggressive. They complained only of their "wayward" form of Christianity, of their "foolish and brutish habits". It is all too evident how in the 13th century Rus' was the victim of aggression at the hands of the Mongols from the east and south, and from the orders of knights from the west.

An important rule of Russian history

The sad fundamental principle of a free market economy is this: if someone has wealth, other people will inevitably try to take it away from him. Eastern Europe is fabulously rich in natural resources. That is why its neighbors have been repeatedly tempted to invade it. At the same time, any people inhabiting this vast plain open to all sides, could themselves become an object of conquest. There will always be someone who wants to take this rich land away from Russia and conquer the people living in it. The only way for Russians to defend against their dear neighbors was to be strong, to found a state capable of resisting aggression.

There is one other fact that is not insignificant: Rus' has no natural boundaries.

The sea separates Britain from the European mainland. The high mountains of the Alps form the northern border of Italy. In Europe even the biggest countries have similar borders. Both Spain and Scandinavia are bounded on three sides by the sea, while in its northeast Spain is separated from France by the Pyrenees. France is limited by the sea, the Pyrenees, the Alps and the Ardennes. Germany lies to the north of the Alps and in the north it bordered by the sea. In the place where Germany and France have a weak natural border, there one will find two perennially disputed provinces, Alsace and Lorraine.

This is not the case with Russia. All of Rus' borders were easily passable. Wherever the Russian army went, there were no quiet river valleys, no great hills or sea, no mighty mountain ranges. The Russian state would inevitably be considered an aggressor if it fought back. But unlike the armies of most other states, the Russian army was not always able to tell if it was in its own lands or in someone else's.

The vastness and "accessibility" of the Russian lands to its foreign enemies had a downside.

Thanks to its special situation vis-a-vis other territories, Russia developed and evolved as a very special civilization.

It is a special civilization as it developed with practically no constraints on its land or natural resources. Together with Orthodox Christianity, this formed a very special culture, one that is open, friendly, curious, expansionist, but devoid of ethnic arrogance, and in some ways even altruistic.

Yes, this absence of borders weakened both the people and elite. It stimulated territorial expansion, "seizing more and more new lands instead of intense economic development and focused technological innovation."

But of course these are objective laws of history, not laws of how people write this history. But a rule of writing history does also exist.

The rule of writing history

Still, why did no one call Rus' aggressive in the 10th, 12th and 15th centuries? Why is it that even today no one talks of the aggression of ancient Rus'?

Let's start with the people of that time. For people of both the 10th and the 14th centuries, aggressive states and wars between peoples and tribes were completely natural. Inversely, refusing to be aggressive attracted charges of weakness, and doubting one's own strength only provoked aggression from one's neighbors.

The descendants of Russia's neighbors continue that tradition: their ancestors didn't accuse Rus' of aggression, and they don't do so either. What's more, they realize that Rus' did not disturb the countries of Europe for a long time.

For European historians, aggression is understood only as aggression against Europe. What about aggression against the peoples of Asia? That matters only if the interests of European states and peoples are involved, such as their colonial empires.

For that reason, Muscovy's expansion towards the east between the 15th and 17th centuries is never treated as aggression. Europeans were not in the least interested in that expansion. In those centuries it never came into their minds to "defend" other peoples, to accuse someone of being political incorrect or imperialist. These same European countries had mastered seafaring and were preparing to build their own colonial empires, to trade in African slaves in order to provide a labor force for their plantations in the Americas. They themselves had committed enough sins against the peoples of the non-European world, and against the background of their "accomplishments", the expansion of Muscovy's borders to the east look somehow very innocent, or in any case of little interest.

Until the 16th century, the interests of Europe and Russia didn't clash in any way. Rather, Europe was growing larger through Rus': Poland and German forces were tearing off chunks of Russian territory. Russia did not invade Poland, Scandinavia, or Germany, it didn't vie with the European powers for colonies.

The myth of Russian aggression, cruelty, of an authoritarian and impoverished country was born only when there were conflicting interests. The myth did not emerge right away but in several stages.

The birth and death of the myth

> If we want to have peace, we must fight.
>
> —*Cicero*

"Orsha propaganda"

The first political myths of Russian aggression and nastiness arose during and immediately after the Russian–Lithuanian War of 1512–1522. During this war, Muscovy and the Grand Duchy of Lithuania sought to take hold of Smolensk and annex the land around it.

On September 8, 1514 the king and great prince Sigismund routed the Muscovite army at Orsha. The Muscovites were defeated, that's true. But first of all, the gains of the Poles' and Lithuanians' victory at Orsha were quite modest: according to the treaty of 1522, Smolensk and the territory around it remained part of Moscow, although Gomel, Chernigov and Bryansk were given to Poland. [106] Secondly, the scale of this victory and its significance were immediately blown up to enormous proportions for the sake of propaganda. The Poles began to compare their local victory over the Russians at Orsha with the famous Battle of Vienna that stopped the Turks' invasion of Europe. Later, based on the fact that they had proven victorious, and seeking to gain support from neighboring states, the Poles began to depict the Muscovites in a negative light. In Poland there is even a special term "Orsha propaganda".

It went something like this: the Muscovites are savage and cruel, said the Poles and Lithuanians. The Muscovites wanted to conquer all of the lands around them. If they seized them, they would plunder them and burn them, like they did to the towns in the Smolensk territory. But the Muscovites are no knights in shining armor, they cannot wage war as effectively as the people of Europe. The Muscovites wanted to bring their savage and cruel way of live to all of Europe. The people of Europe are very fortunate that the Poles and Lithuanians heroically stopped the Muscovites and did not let them into Europe.

If Europe did not want to be invaded by the Muscovites, it should support the Poles and Lithuanians. Only they could stop the Muscovites because their soldiers are brave knights, defenders of Europe.

As a result, the Holy Roman Empire and the Livonian Order began to fear the rise of Moscow. Faced with this "Orsha propaganda", the Holy Roman Emperor Maximilian cancelled the creation of a military alliance with Vasily III. The Livonian Order also began to recognize the primacy of the Grand Duchy of Lithuania and ended its trading pact with Muscovy.

Thus, in spite of its rather modest military victory, Poland won the PR war.

Such "Orsha propaganda" is actively used even today by some politicians in Belarus, Lithuania, and Poland. A number of historians and politicians in Belarus call the soldiers of the Grand Duchy of Lithuania "Belorussians", identifying the Grand Duchy of Lithuania with modern Belarus. Some even refuse to admit that the Poles took part in the battle, saying that they, the Belorussians, did everything.

However, "Orsha propaganda" never had a Europe-wide significance. It was only a collection of regional myths that existed only in Eastern Europe and not even in all of it.

The territorial context of the myth: the Livonian War

The Livonian War of 1558–1583 can be considered aggressive by all sides. Muscovy began this war with an attack on the Livonian Order, which had by then attacked Russian lands many times. The Livonian Order collapsed instantly, and Sweden, Poland, the Grand Duchy of Lithuania, and Denmark sought to take as much land on the Baltic as possible. Russia had an even more "historical" basis for such an acquisition, as it had long sought an outlet to the sea and tried to annex the lands of Novgorod.

But the Livonian War only gave rise to new slanderous myths about Russia. The Muscovites were accused of great atrocities and of not following the laws of war (however, all sides displayed unbelievable cruelty in war by 21st-century standards). And of course, the Muscovites were blamed for attacking Livonian Order and later the Grand Duchy of Lithuania.

There is a great difference between the propaganda efforts of the two players who sought the most to grab territory from Russia: the Polish-Lithuanian Commonwealth and Sweden.

The Poles attached great importance to political propaganda in this war. In the end, the union of the Kingdom of Poland and the Grand Duchy of Lithuania in 1569 meant that a significant part of Rus' became part of a Polish state. Original Russian lands were taken away. Who was the aggressor here?! However, Poland wanted to look good to the other countries of Europe. Polish propaganda worked in several languages and in a number of areas throughout Europe. One must note that this propaganda was effective.

In 1579 the first mobile printing works in Polish history was used in the army of Stephen Báthory. The manager of the printing works, a commoner by the name of Lapka, was later granted a noble title, whence the aristocrat name Lapchinksky. [107]

Stephen Báthory's court writers and his mobile chancellery continued the tradition of "Orsha propaganda", justifying the aggression of Poland and accusing Russia of "anti-European" designs.

In Europe, at the end of the Livonian War and as a result of the Time of Troubles, the first plans arose to conquer and divide up Russia.

One such plan came from the German adventurer Staden, and he proposed this to the powerful princes of Germany. The plan involved the conquest of Russia, the capture of Ivan the Terrible and then his exile to Europe, and the establishment of an occupation force throughout the country. All of this was presented as a sorely needed "pre-emptive strike" against the Muscovites.

Swedish propaganda was much more restrained. It accused the Russians not of being aggressors, but victims of their own backwardness and savagery.

The Swedish aristocrat Jacob De la Gardie visited Russia as head of a military detachment which Sweden had sent under a treaty with the government of tsar Vasili IV for war against Poland. Here he came up with a plan to restore the principality of Novgorod as a Swedish protectorate.

To De la Gardie's credit, he was completely polite to the Russians, and he explained his intention to divide Russia not as a battle against Russian aggression, but as a result of northwest Russia's "historical ties" to Sweden. "Sorry, guys, you have such a mess here. It's not personal, it's just business." De la Gardie, an educated aristocrat, even pointed to the story of Rurik, but he said nothing about some perennial desire of Russians to conquer others. How could he point to Russian aggression while he was with his troops in Novgorod.

And who would have believed him during the Time of Troubles, when Russia became a land of opportunity for every European adventurer?

In general, it is those who attacked Russia the most who cried loudest about Russian aggression, and those who were most afraid of Russia.

The Romanovs of Muscovy — along with the rest of Europe

In the 16th and 17th centuries the myth of Russian aggression was only a regional Polish and Lithuanian myth. Poland imposed this myth on Europe, but it didn't work out very well.

In the first half of the 17th century, Muscovy fought against the Polish–Lithuanian Commonwealth for control of the western Russian lands, and it proved successful in annexing the territory around Smolensk. But in the rest of Europe, this was treated as a war between two states for disputed territory. "Orsha propaganda" did not set Europe against Moscow, as Europe was indifferent when it came to Smolensk and the territories east of it.

> In the Polish-Lithuanian Commonwealth, the southern Russian lands of the future Ukraine were part of the Kingdom of Poland. The Orthodox population of Russia was treated cruelly by the Catholic Poles, who called these Orthodox peasants simply *bydło* 'cattle'. From 1600 to 1640 up to a hundred uprisings broke out among the Orthodox population in Ukraine. After 1648 individual centers of rebellion came

together in one single movement under the leadership of Bogdan Khmelnitsky.

We won't portray this complex man as an advocate of the people and supporter of a united Russian state. He started the war with Poland for money and out of personal grievances: the low-born Khmelnitsky came to blows with influential wealthy people, the Vishnevetsky princes. It became a personal war with armed troops attacking the estates of rival families. During one such attack, the enemy not only looted and burned the estate of Bogdan Khmelnitsky, but they even beat his 10 year-old son to death.

This is of course a terrible story, and one can feel nothing but pity for the poor child. But this was very much in the spirit of the time, and in the spirit of the feudal freemen, who savagely fought one another.

Bogdan took advantage of the fact that the Polish crown had not included in its "registry" all the Cossacks who wanted to be listed. Registered Cossacks were considered servants of the Polish crown and received a salary and weapons from the state. People who weren't on the list naturally wanted to get their names on there. The war between the Cossacks and Poland broke out precisely to get as many Cossacks registered as possible, or in other words, the soldiers who were not registered and did not receive benefits declared war against the state.

And this is where Khmelnitsky's personal ambitions come in. He wanted to found his own state, whether as a Russian principality within the Polish-Lithuanian Commonwealth, or Duchy of Chigirin independent of everyone.

But in the stress of waging war alone with Poland, Khmelnitsy declared his wish to "bring Ukraine under the sovereign hand of the tsar of Muscovy" (for that reason, contemporary Ukrainian historians consider him a "traitor to the interests of his country"). Moscow hesitated for a long time, dragged its feet, and fidgeted, but eventually it got involved in the war. We note right away that in that time there was no conception of such a people as the Ukrainians. According to Europe, Rus', Muscovy, the Polish-Lithuanian Commonwealth, the territory of the Austrian Hapsburgs, and the Carpathians there were only Russians, one people.

CHAPTER 6

In October 1653 the Zemsky Sobor, after long debate, agreed to consider the Russians/Rusyns in the Polish-Lithuanian Commonwealth subjects of Moscow and to protect them by force of arms. In January 1654 in Pereslavl, the assembly proclaimed an "eternal union" of the Ukrainians and Great Russians.

The new subjects of the tsar totalled 700,000 people. This particular figure is an unusually secure one for history: an oath was sworn by "the entire Russian population of Little Russia", 127,000 men. If one includes their households, one reaches 700,000 people. Incidentally, the members of the Zemsky Sobor understood that now war with Poland would be inevitable, and they would have to fight and fund the war campaign on their own (in Moscow the representatives of trading guilds gathered as well).

At the end of the 17th century, Europe needed Muscovy as a valuable ally in the war with the Ottoman Empire. Turks formed a serious threat to Europe. Their plans included capturing Poland, Germany, parts of the Austrian Empire such as the Czech lands, Slovakia, and Hungary, and also Russia.

Part of the Turkish campaign was a brutal, bloody war between Russia and the Ottoman Empire's vassal the Crimean Khanate in 1676–1681. The cause of the war was the Ottoman Empire's attempt to get involved in the Russian-Polish dispute and seize control of Ukraine west of the Dnieper. This war also went down in history as the "Chigirin campaigns", as the major victories and defeats of both armies were linked to this town.

At the end of July 1677 the army of Ibrahim Pasha, consisting of a hundred thousand men, reached Chigirin, a town which proved the political and strategic military center of the whole of southern Ukraine. On August 3 the Turks and an allied Tatar army consisting of 40,000 swords came up to its walls.

Chigirin repelled several assaults, its defenders even staged diversionary attacks on the Turkish camp. The approaching Russian-Ukrainian army under the command of general Grigori

Romodanovsky [108] and the hetman Petro Konashevych-Sahaidachny routed the Turks after a pitched battle. Ibrahim-Pasha suffered a truly catastrophic and shameful loss of his army. It was easier for the Tatars, they simply rode off toward the steppe, easily evading pursuit. But in short time the Turkish army of the vizier of the sultan Kara Mustafa was again at the walls of Chigirin and began a new siege.

Thus a great battle was fought, in which the armies repeatedly came right up to one another and then separated. There was a moment when Romodanovsky, in the opinion of other commanders, missed his chance (by literally just a few hours) to completely encircle the Turkish army. In the end, the Russian army left the smouldering ruins of Chigirin and retreated. The Turkish army however had no strength left to take advantage of this possible victory. The Turks followed after them for some time, but as is typical of them, they didn't even try to attack, for the Muscovite army was not fleeing, it wasn't even defeated outright.

The Russian forces marched away in complete formation to the beat of a drum and under flying banners, and when the enemy appeared, the Russians pointed their cannons at them.

The Turks not only didn't attack the army of Grigory Grigoryevich Romodanovsky any further, after Chigirin they never attacked Muscovy at all! If is Chigirin was a loss, it wasn't any bigger than Borodino. The Russian army also left from Borodino, opening for Napoleon a path to Moscow.

The Chigirin campaigns were an important part of the war that the Ottoman Empire waged against all of the European powers: the Polish-Lithuanian Commonwealth, the Austrian Empire, and the German principalities. The Christian world rallied against a common and terrible foe. Europe followed the battle between Russia and the Ottoman Empire with enormous interest. The success of Russian weaponry was a guarantee that the Turkish authorities would not be able to wage war against its European neighbours — Poland, Venice, and the Holy Roman Empire.

The European press reported extensively on the Russian army's Chigirin campaigns. In German and Dutch newspapers there were hundreds of articles on this theme. Thus no one accused Russia of being an aggressor, and no one accused it of seeking to crush Turkey, seize the Crimean peninsula and take over the Black Sea region. So from Europe's point of view, this was a highly sensible and understandable goal. The Crimea was a stronghold of slave traders. To this day no one knows how many people, went through the Isthmus of Perekop under the whips of slave raiders. Historians talk about 500,000 or 5 million people. No one can tell now what the exact figure was. The Black Sea region became deserted, because no one could settle it under the danger from the Crimean Tatars.

Turkey was an enemy of civilization, an outpost of the Muslim world, and any Christian state would only approve of battling against it.

The revival of the myth

> You hate us
> What for? Answer: it is because
> On the ruins of burned Moscow
> We did not acknowledge the insolent will
> Of the man that you trembled at.
>
> —*Alexander Pushkin, "To the Slanderers of Russia"*

The new accusation that the Muscovites had been aggressive, this time seized upon by the whole of Europe, arose during the Northern War of 1700–1721 in the time of Peter the Great. The essence of this accusation has been clearly stated by Ignatius Christophorus von Guarient, a former Austrian envoy to Russia, who published in 1698–1699 a book titled *Notes of the Embassy Secretary Johann Georg Korb*. It was published so covertly that for a long time people thought that this was the ambassador's own book, as it was called *The Diary of Ignatius Christophorus von Guarient's Journey to Moscow as Ambassador of the Emperor Leopold I to the Tsar and Great Prince Peter Alexeevich in 1698, Drawn Up by the Embassy Secretary Johann Georg Korb*. That is,, the real author was the secretary Korb, but putting the ambassador there as the supposed coauthor increased readers' confidence in the book. Korb was the first foreign author to really describe Russia under Peter the Great. During his time at the court in Moscow, Korb often met with people close to Sophia and Peter such as Lev Naryshkin, Boris Alekseyevich Golitsyn, Yemelyan Ukraintsev, and Aleksandr Danilovich Menshikov. Korb often saw the tsar and dined with him at the same table. Among Korb's informants was the famous Russian general of Scottish origin, Patrick Gordon.

The testimony of this eyewitness, which tells something of the personality of the young tsar, the life and customs of the Muscovite court, the pace of reforms and how Russian society viewed them, is of great significance. Korb had the opportunity to witness one of the most dramatic events of Peter the Great's reign, the Streltsy Uprising of 1698. What is exceptionally valuable for historians is Korb's description of the terrible Streltsy Uprising; it is confirmed in its details by Russian sources.

However, Korb's notes contain the same features that distinguish the majority of foreign reports of Russia. His text is undermined by a multitude of errors, caused by his ignorance of Russia's language and history, and also connected to the fact that he used only oral sources.

Korb admired Peter the Great; he was drawn by the Russian's ruler interest in the culture of Western Europe. But he little believed that the tsar's transformative policies would succeed, as his subjects were mere barbarians. For example, why did Peter begin the Northern War? Because he was a barbarian greedy for conquest, like all Russians. If you gave him an opportunity, he would seize the whole of Europe.

Korb's book quickly won great fame. It was translated into English, French, and German. The Russian authorities reacted to its appearance very negatively. The resident Prince Golitsyn, who thought that the ambassador Guarient was the author of the book, did not want to let him visit Russia. Golitsyn wrote to the

CHAPTER 6

foreign minister Fyodor Alexeyevich Golovin (in August 1701), "The king wishes to send to Moscow an embassy that include Guarient, a former envoy to Moscow. He has published a book on the state of affairs in Muscovy. Do not let him be sent to us: truly, as I have heard, there have never been such heathen claims and curses directed against Muscovy. Since his arrival here, they think us barbarians..."

Guarient tried to exonerate himself and wrote to Golovin (on December 24, 1701): "I beg you not to blame me for what someone else has done. I did not participate in that business in either word or deed. This is the work of my secretary, who could not refrain from writing something because he is not from these parts but from another region." [109]

Nonetheless, Peter the Great's diplomats insisted that Guarient be dismissed from his appointment as ambassador to Russia. In addition, they banned the book and destroyed the copies that remained unsold, which made it a bibliographical rarity — and naturally only increased Europe's interest in it.

Such a pained reaction from the Russian diplomats was caused by the fact that Korb's book appeared at the same time as the Russian army's default at Narva in 1700 at the hands of Charles XII. This defeat dealt a significant blow to Russia's international prestige. And there is an accusation of aggression here too. We must note that Korb's book had no connection with "Orsha propaganda". The accusation of being aggressive and desiring to seize foreign lands arose and disappeared without a trace. Korb's book was not immediately taken up by someone else.

Such an accusation arose neither during the Russian Empire's annexation of northern Persia in 1722–1723 during Peter the Great's Persian campaign, nor during and after the Seven Years' War of 1756–1763. The latter, an inherently colonialist war, which involved the interests of Great Britain, France, and Spain, did not spare Russia. However, Russia came out of this war as a full-fledged player in great Europcan politics.

The Seven Years' War grew out of England and France's wars for colonies. The forerunner of this war was the clash between the French and English in Canada in 1754–1756. The hostilities within Europe itself between the French and English were mainly important for protecting their backs. After its Glorious Revolution of 1688, Britain called the House of Hanover to take the throne. Hanover was a very important territory on the continent for Britain. Britain ought to have entered into an alliance with Prussia, so that Prussia could watch over the ancestral home of the British royalty.

France wanted to take Hanover, and Austria wanted to get back the territory of Silesia that Prussia had seized from it. Naturally, they became allies. Sweden wanted to occupy Pomerania and became another ally of France and Austria.

Napoleon would have envied Prussia's plans. Prussia relied on an alliance with England and wanted to conquer Saxony, giving the Saxon king Bohemia to rule instead, but it had still not managed to conquer Bohemia. In addition, Prussia wanted to annex the Duchy of Courland, surround its territory at Poland's expense, and make the rest of Poland its vassal.

The Russian Empire wanted to annex the Duchy of Courland itself and make Poland its vassal. That would have happened, had it not been for a peculiar aspect of Russian politics.

In April of 1757, Friedrich left a force of thirty thousand men in East Prussia as a barrier against the Russians, while he moved with his main army into Bohemia, aim to defeat the Austrians before the arrival of their allies. He did not succeed in this, however, and the allies – the French, Austrians, and Swedes – came at him with several armies and forced him to retreat.

Against the backdrop of these events, the Russia army with seventy thousand men came into Eastern Prussia, seized Memel, and then crushed the Prussians at Gross-Jägersdorf.

Prussia had essentially already lost the war, and the Duchy of Courland and Eastern Prussia were left to Russia. However, a Prussian surrender and division of the country into several parts did not happen because the Russian Empire simply suddenly withdrew from the war.

It was amazing luck for the Germans: Elizabeth of Russia had

CHAPTER 6

fallen unconscious as she was walking out of church. She lay in this state for some two hours, with others afraid to touch her, because the science of medicine in that time forbade touching people who had fainted.

When Elizabeth died, the throne should go to her nephew Karl Peter Ulrich, who had been baptised Orthodox as Peter Fedorovich, the future Peter III and a great supporter of Friedrich of Prussia. Everyone knew that as soon as he ascended to the throne, there would be an alliance with Prussia.

So Elizabeth was lying on the ground. It should be noted that in the 18th century, long-distance communications were more complicated than in our day: there were no mobile phones, not even a simple telegraph for communicating with the army. Thus a messenger was immediately dispatched to the army with word that Elizabeth might die. Right after he received this news, the commander of the forces serving in Eastern Prussia, Stefan Stepan Fyodorovich Apraksin, immediately turned back towards Saint Petersburg.

To this day historians debate what kind of person Apraksin was. Was he a traitor? Was he a cowardly courtier, more afraid of the emperor's anger than losing the war? Or was he a member of great conspiracy against Peter III? In the event that the empress died, conspirators would not want the throne to go to Peter III, and they had in mind to proclaim the underaged (born 1754) Pavel Petrovich emperor instead, and then make Peter III's wife Catherine regent until the new emperor came of age. Apraksin led his troops into Saint Petersburg, where they would be needed in the event of a civil war. Whether that would have happened or not is hard to say, because Elizabeth soon got up from where she had fallen.

Elizabeth made a full recovery. Apraksin died while being interrogated by the ruler's secret functionaries. But history had already been made. If such a sudden end hadn't come to Russia's involvement, the Seven Years' War would have gone on for another two years and ended only in 1758. Russian would have got at least all of Eastern Prussia.

However, the war did eventually go on. Now under the command of William Fermor, the Russian army reached Königsberg on January 11,

1758. The Prussians across all of Eastern Prussia swore allegiance to the empress Elizabeth. Until the end of the Seven Years' War, or rather until it left the Russian Empire in 1762, East Prussia spent four years as part of the Russian Empire. The Prussians paid taxes and were utterly loyal to the *Kaiserin Elisabeth* and the Russian Empire.

By the end of 1761, Prussia had been drained and no longer had the strength to keep fighting the war. It could only debate what the terms of surrender would be and whether there would even be a state called Prussia on the map.

However, here internal developments in Russia again intervened. On December 25, 1761 Elizabeth died. Peter III, sympathetic to the Germans, came to power. The first thing that the new emperor did is end the hostilities and, what's more, he returned to Friedrich all the Prussian territory that Russia had conquered, including Eastern Prussia.

On April 24, 1762 Peter III even signed an official alliance with Friedrich, which finally saved the already devastated Prussia. Once again, events throughout Europe depended on what was happening internally in Russia.

After just over a month, Catherine the Great overthrew Peter III and took the throne for herself. One of her first decisions was to end the alliance with Friedrich.

The partition of Poland

Even the partition of Poland did not lead to this myth arising. The Russian Empire, as one of the great European powers, was able to accomplish something that Muscovy had never been capable of doing: defeating its eternal rival, the Polish-Lithuanian Commonwealth.

In the 1770s the Russian Empire proved so much stronger than the Polish-Lithuanian Commonwealth that it could assert its territorial claims even against the two strongest states in the German-speaking world, the Austrian Empire and Prussia.

Russia initially sought to reject Prussia's plan to partition Poland, as Russia wanted to keep Poland within its sphere of influence.

CHAPTER 6

There was yet another Russian-Turkish War in 1768–1774. It proved to be a long and drawn out affair and demanded a great deal of Russia's effort. Prussia actively campaigned for partition a state that supposedly had no future, the Polish-Lithuanian Commonwealth. Under these circumstances, there was a real threat of a military alliance between Prussia and Austria against Russia if Russia refused to open a second front. War with Austria and Prussia was something that Russia could have done without at that time, because it urgently wanted to improve its relationships with the two German states and Russia was forced to make a pact peace with them… at Poland's expense, that is, I must emphasis, according to the Russian plan Poland should remain a united and substantial European state. In the long term there could have been a sort of union with the Russian Empire, as a "younger brother and ally" of course, but the international situation was not conducive to these plans. Gently nudge the Polish-Lithuanian Commonwealth into a union with Russia required peace and stability, but the stability of Europe at the time — as usual — was not sufficient.

In 1772 the three states met in Saint Petersburg and concluded an agreement that the Polish-Lithuanian Commonwealth would be partitioned and the armies of each of the three states would take up "their" territories, what we would not call their zones of occupation. In 1773 the Polish assembly called the Sejm recognized the partitioning of the country.

On May 3, 1791 the Sejm Polish-Lithuanian Commonwealth adopted a constitution that was a victory of the so-called "patriotic" party bringing together supporters of public reforms. This constitution was meant to overcome the country's longterm political instability and create a solid political system which would strengthen a weakened state and defend it from the claims of its powerful neighbors, Prussia, Russia, and Austria. For these states, as well as for those Polish aristocrats who had been able to benefit from the weakness of their own state, the new constitution was disadvantageous. Three powerful Poles met in the small town of Targowica, near Uman in what is now Ukraine, and proclaimed an Act of Conferedation. Their names are very well known in Poland today and cause much wailing and gnashing of teeth: Franciszek Ksawery Branicki, Seweryn Rzewuski, and Stanisław Szczęsny Potocki. In 1792, on the very day that the Act of Confederation was proclaimed, the Russian army crossed the border of the Polish-Lithuanian Commonwealth. Soon Prussia began its own intervention to meet this. In fact, Poland was dealing with a civil war, and the occupying powers supported one of the sides.

The Polish-Lithuanian Commonwealth was quickly occupied and Austria, Prussia, and the Russian Empire signed in Saint Petersburg the Convention on the Second Partition of the Polish-Lithuanian Commonwealth.

The winter of 1793–1794 passed uneventfully, but in March the famous Polish uprising of 1794 broke out under the leadership of the legendary Tadeusz Kosciuszko.

The Polish uprising began under the slogan of Polish national unity, freeing the Polish lands from the Russian, Austrian, and Prussian empires and bringing them together into one country, but they wanted all of Ukraine and Belarus "back" too. On March 24, 1794 in Krakow Kosciuszko made his proclamation giving him command over the armed forces.

After recovering from the initial blow, Prussia and Russia brought their regular forces into battle. By September, according to Suvorov's account, all of Lithuania and Galicia had been "cleansed of rebels". The Ukrainian and Belorussian lands were ablaze. On October 10, six months after the uprising had begun, Kosciuszko was seriously wounded and taken prisoner. On November 10, the Polish capital Warsaw surrendered and thus the rebellion ended.

According to the Third Partition of Poland in 1795, the Russian Empire took all lands inhabited by Russians, that is, the lands that are now known as western Ukraine and western

Belarus. Also ceded to Russia were Lithuania with Vilnius, Trakai and Siauliai, and the Latvian region of Courland.

Austria took the Galicia and Volyn regions of what is now Ukraine with its cities of Lvov and Halych, as well as the Greater Poland region with Krakow, the historical heart of the country, which it would rule until the collapse of the Austro-Hungarian Empire in 1918.

Prussia took the west and north of ethnic Poland. On January 26, 1797 Catherine the Great confirmed the partition of Poland, the liquidation of the Polish government, the abolition of Polish citizenship, and any mention of Poland in noble titles.

Here could have been a perfect opportunity to blame Russia for all sins intended and unintended, but this didn't happen. Russia shared responsibility for events in Europe with Austria and Prussia.

Napoleon's political PR

The dubious honor of stirring up a myth of Russian aggression in books and newspapers belongs to Napoleon Bonaparte. He — like any politician — needed a justification for his actions. To fight against a country, defeat them, and annex them to one's territory is one thing, but stopping an aggressor and restoring justice is something different.

Apparently a deeply hidden complex was at work too: after proclaiming himself emperor, receiving his crown from the Pope, and even marrying the daughter of the Austrian emperor, Napoleon knew perfectly well that according to his birth he in no way belonged to royalty. This low-born aristocrat from Corsica needed a way to legitimize his imperial pretensions. In June 1813 he said in a conversation with Klemens von Metternich, "Your princes, who were born on the throne, cannot understand the feelings that inspire me. They return to their capital cities defeated and for them it's all the same. I however am a soldier, I need honor and glory, and I cannot be seen as humiliated in front of my people. I need to become great, glorified, and commanding admiration." Only support from the French people could legitimize his rule, and the French greatly depended on military victories.

Napoleon was initially successful with his "PR campaign": his aggressive military actions directly continued the French Revolution of 1792–1796. In the view of most French, Napoleon was bringing liberty to the peoples of Europe and a more just social order.

It is no wonder that two statues were carried in Napoleon's baggage train on the way through Russia to Moscow itself: white stone sculptures of Napoleon himself in a toga with a laurel wreath. Napoleon was depicted with a scroll of laws in his hand, as the spiritual successor of the Roman emperors — though he did not risk freeing the serfs and introducing the Napoleon Code into Russia. The core of his military campaign was nonetheless the idea of a battle for "justice".

Napoleon grasped much earlier and more profoundly than many rulers the meaning of agitprop. As soon as he took command of the Italian Army he issued a famous proclamation on March 26, 1796 which stated:

Men! You have no boots, uniforms, or shirts. You don't have enough bread, and your storehouses are empty. Meanwhile, the enemy has everything in abundance. It depends only on you to get hold of everything. You want to do this and can do it. So, forward march!

At the time Napoleon had not yet crowned himself emperor, but was only a mere general of the Directory. In this role he regularly sent bulletins to the members of the Directory with short briefings on battles and campaigns.

On October 7, 1796 the first bulletin was published as a printed flyer, intended not for members of the government but for the people. The bulletin was adorned with a picture of Napoleon in profile, crowned with a laurel wreath, and an imperial eagle that held a lightning bolt and a bundle of rods in its talons. The bulletin consisted of only eleven points. He

CHAPTER 6

briefly described the crossing of the Rhine, the encircling of the Austrian forces, and the names of the cities that he had taken. The simple format and short text with pictures helped his soldiers understand what glorious historical events they had just taken part in. The everyday folk saw what great things the army had done under Napoleon's command.

This is all of the following proclamations were of course widely distributed among the soldiers. Napoleon quickly understood how important the support of the French masses was, so he made every effort to ensure that his proclamations were distributed among the civilian population. He achieved this through publishing newspapers, putting up posters, and issuing leaflets that could be passed from hand to hand.

Initially Napoleon planned to issue his bulletins regularly, once every eight days. Soon he decided that he would be better to do so less often, so that the larger battles and the capture of cities would command greater attention. Soon there was a whole series of bulletins on the Grand Army. In subsequent campaigns a whole mobile printing words marched with the army. The bulletins were sent to French directly from the battlefield. The venture proved invaluable. Bulletins were issued also for the campaigns that Napoleon led as emperor in 1805, 1806–1807, 1809, 1812 and even 1813.

Napoleon always dictated the text of his bulletins, and his secretary or chief of staff edited them. The first copies were printed on the field printing press or through printing works in nearby towns. Often the bulletins came in different editions with different typefaces. Then the bulletins were distributed among the troops, and junior officers or sergeants read them aloud. Handing out these leaflets widely was not the best way since there were so few of them.

The most successful bulletins were reprinted as posters, which were put up on the walls in towns and nailed to trees in villages. From the very start Napoleon issued an edict that the bulletins be reprinted by state printing works and official newspapers, and not just in Paris or across the whole of France, but in all conquered or dependant countries.

In 1811 Napoleon tasked Alexander Berthier with collecting all of the bulletins from the previous campaigns and issuing them in book form. Here already it was not a matter of keeping the French informed of the Grand Army's victories, but about reinforcing the legend of these victories and Napoleon's exceptional personality.

These bulletins treated historical events in so peculiar as fashion that a saying was soon coined among the troops, "He's lying like a bulletin." But to be mentioned in them was a great honor even for a general or field marshal. The soldiers were proud when a bulletin mentioned their division or corps.

By the end of the Italian campaign, on July 20, 1797, Napoleon even found a "corporate" newspaper *Le Courrier de l'Arme d'Italie*. From that time on, in the army under Napoleon's command, and then across the whole French army, the field printing presses printed not only the emperor's proclamations and bulletins, but even real military journalism.

So Napoleon had a powerful propaganda tool in his hands, a toll that he thought up himself, and which made a living legend out of him and the soldiers and offices faithful to him. This propaganda strengthen the ties between the commander-in-chief and the army, and it made everyone involved part of the same legend.

Napoleon paid as much attention to denouncing his enemies as to promoting his own greatness, the strength of his army, and the righteousness of the ongoing wars. The French press depicted all of his opponents inside the country and outside as completely worthless, miserable, unworthy. Napoleon saw to the fact that newspapers throughout France would reprint editorials and all articles about the war, domestic politics, and international affairs from the major Parisian newspaper *Le Moniteur*. He left altogether a handful of newspapers: *Journal de Paris*, *Gazette de France*, *Journal de l'Empire*, *Le Moniteur*, *Mercure Galant*, and *Mercure de France*.

CHAPTER 6

In all occupied territories, every newspaper had to do the same. At the slightest attempt to print their own editorial line, they were shut down. It was the first government-controlled press in the world.

Napoleon's approach to propaganda was simple:
- constantly belittle one's enemies;
- delay the reporting of bad news or don't report it at all;
- release information in careful doses.

We can tell how well-behaved the French press was from the following well-known affair. On February 26, 1815 Napoleon escaped from his exile in Elba and soon landed in France with a force of a thousand men. His triumphant march through Paris quickly changed the tone of newspaper writing about his return. At first there were such headlines as "The Corsican monster has landed in the bay of Antibes". Two days later, it was "General Bonaparte has reached Lyon", and in another two days "Yesterday His Majesty the Emperor arrived at his palace in Tuileries".

Napoleon's ideological campaign inspired the French with the idea of a special mission for their country and the invincibility of their army, led by the emperor. The fact that this propaganda had a powerful effect on the masses and endowed them with a fantastical view of the world can be seen from the following: even after the defeat of France by England's allies, the English were stunned to find out that the French had not even heard of the Battle of Trafalgar, where Admiral Nelson had defeated the French navy. No one had reported on this battle to them.

Within Napoleon's policies a special role in the creation of political myths was played by Russia.

The revival of the myth of a Russian threat under Napoleon

In the whirlwind of European appears in the late 18th and early 19th centuries, the Russian Empire had participated in several anti-France coalitions. Napoleon dealt constant and bitter defeats on the Austrian and Prussian armies. Of all the allies in the Second Coalition (Britain, Austria, Turkey, the Russian Empire, and the Kingdom of Naples), only two European powers could defeat him: Britain and Russia.

Britain crushed, scattered and set fire to the French fleet that had intended to land on the shores of England. After the Battle of Trafalgar (in 1806), Napoleon had to give up his hopes of a quick victory over the British Isles.

The Russian army was an important obstacle to Napoleon on the continent, both in the Russian-Prussian-French wars of 1804–1807 and during the Russian-Austrian-French war of 1805. Russia pursued an independent policy, moving closer to Britain and supporting allied forces on their territory. It was this that allowed Napoleon to accuse Russia of aggression.

"You see?" said his journalists and commentators. "Look at how the Russians have own again. Soon they will take over all of Europe."

Napoleon's rhetoric was directory against a strong and dangerous enemy, and it was essentially no different than the "Orsha propaganda" of the Poles from the time of the Muscovite-Polish wars in the Smolensk region. Had the Russian Empire stayed the same as Muscovy in the 16th century, no one would be interested in it now.

And then the Testament of Peter the Great was taken out of mothballs. In 1797 a Polish emigrant named Mikhail Sokolnicky wrote to Europe of the Testament and Russia's hostile intentions. At the time few had noticed his pamphlet, but in 1807–1811, as he prepared to invade Russia, Napoleon began to mold a general public opinion in Europe favorable to his campaign. He reprinted Sokolnicky's pamphlet in an enormous print run for those times.

Then, under direct orders from Napoleon, the French official Michel Lesur, trained as an historian, wrote a book on Russia's growing power up to the 19th century.

Among other things, this book claims, "They say that in the private archives of the Russian emperor a secret memoir is

CHAPTER 6

preserved, written by Peter the Great with his own hand, which openly states the plans of this state." [110]

Lesur did not publish any text of this supposed Testament, relying instead on rumor, innuendo, and speculation. His main goal was to convince the European public of Russia's aggressive ambitions, its willingness and readiness to conquer the whole of Europe.

In preparing for his attack on Russia, Napoleon was not just leading another military campaign, but the final stage in the creation of a "universal empire", France's full control over Europe. Essentially, he was after world domination.

On the eve of 1812 Napoleon pronounced, "In three years I will be the ruler of the world. Only Russia remains and I will crush her." These words were perfectly familiar to the soldiers in his army. They were the last independent country in continental Europe. There was still Britain, but it would be attacked by another force, the navy. Russia was the last recalcitrant country that the French had to march into. Napoleon would make the Russian Empire a vassal of France, and would relax after the incessant wars and campaigning that had lasted since 1792.

The soldiers of the Grand Army knew well that they were marching into a barbaric, half-civilized country and bearing with them the greatest culture in the world, the French culture; that they were led by the greatest general of all time, whom it would be pure savagery, uncivilized behavior, and even a crime to oppose.

"In order to win," Napoleon said and explained to his generals, "it is not enough for a soldier to hate the enemy, but he must truly despise them."

Ordinary soldiers despised Russia and the Russians. They were brought up with this contempt. They knew that Russians were dangerous savages, the servants of their masters, and hostile to Europe, constantly threatening Europe. If the Russian freaks won, they would bring their horrible customs to them too.

Napoleon's Grand Army had regiments and battalions from twenty countries. The French made up only a quarter of the Grand Army, and it was mainly based on Germans and Poles, as well as Italians, Spaniards, Portuguese, Croatians, Danes, and Mamlukes.

The Grand Army had over 600,000 men with 1420 guns. In terms of economical, military, and human resources, this empire of the West surpassed Russia by several times. It was led, so it was thought, by the best general in the world.

In spite of his feigned temper, Napoleon never went into something without thinking it over. He spent at least two years preparing for his Russian campaign, and he did so seriously. He worked through public opinion and diplomat channels.

By the summer of 1812 Napoleon had forced all European countries except Britain and Sweden to take part in his upcoming campaign. Napoleon even brought the USA into the war against the Russian Empire, as it was an ally of Britain. On May 18, 1812, nearly a month before the attack on Russia, the United States declared war on Great Britain, something which was important to limited British sea power.

At the moment that Napoleon was to attack Russia, she was also engaged in a war with the Ottoman Empire. Only thanks to the military and diplomatic talents of Mikhail Kutuzov did Russia managed to make peace with Turkey on the eve of Napoleon's invasion. But even with a peace concluded the Russian command had to keep a large portion of the country's forces in the south: as many as thirty thousand men were not able to assist in the fight against Napoleon.

Due to the slowness of vehicle of that time, the Danube army could reach the theatre of operations only in autumn of 1812, when the main events had already happened and Napoleon had already entered Moscow. On all fronts it was a brilliant success of diplomacy for Napoleon. Only Kutuzov was able to deprive Napoleon of the chance to drag Russia into a war on two fronts.

The fiercely fought war of 1812 is known as the Battle of Borodino in Russia. Its outcome is seen as a draw and it was a moral victory of Kutuzov. Among the French it is known as the Battle of Moscow and seen as a crushing defeat of the Russian forces. But even Napoleon recognized, according to the account of the French general Pelet who was present at the battle, "The battle was the most marvellous and most terrible, the French showed themselves worthy of victory and the Russians deserved to be unbeaten." [111]

The Battle of Borodino was followed by the surrender of Moscow to Napoleon's forces, the destruction and burning of the city, and the hasty retreat of the French army. The army of Napoleon initially maneuvered to reach winter quarters in an area that had not been ravaged by the war, but then they retreated to the Russian border, pursued by the Russian army and suffered from hunger and cold. The war ended with the almost complete annihilation of Napoleon's army, the liberation of Russian territory, and the movement of the action to the Duchy of Warsaw and Germany in 1813. Among the reasons for the defeat of Napoleon's invading force, historians point to the wide participation of the Russian population in the fighting and the heroism of the soldiers, the unpreparedness of the French to fight a war over such a large territory and in Russia's harsh climate, and the leadership of the Russian commander-in-chief Mikhail Kutuzov and other generals.

Russia played a central and crucial role in the final defeat of Napoleon. But neither this nor the Russian army's foreign campaigns in 1813–1814 made Russia any more population in Europe. It was already large and intimidating. As in 1799, the Russian army was active in the heart of Europe, but at that time Suvorov had been prepared to go to Paris and was unable due to the treachery of the Austrians. Now the Russians were entering Paris without the Austrians. [112]

At the Congress of Vienna in 1814–1815, which defined the political structure of Europe, the Russian Empire was the most important participant and guaranteed its implementation.

Until 1818 France had an occupying force of thirty thousand Russian soldiers. According to the decision of the Congress of Vienna, the Russian Empire annexed the Duchy of Warsaw, a territory with three million people. Russia has never been forgiven for this! Under Catherine the Great, Poland had been divided up among three predatory actors, and none of them could get around the other two. Now however Russia annexed a huge piece of the indigenous territory of Poland without asking anyone. Russia overtook its allies and proved first among equals and the strongest among the victors. Perhaps their common enemy Napoleon had launched the campaign anti-Russian propaganda, but it was enthusiastically taken up among Russia's former allies. In 1815 Russia seemed too powerful.

Here's the paradox. Even after Napoleon had been defeated, one of his favorite myths, that Russia was aggressive and dangerous, lived on without him. Europe too, after Napoleon, played the same political card: Poland.

Bonapartism and its influence on Russia

It is thought that Napoleon hoped his propaganda would influence the Russians too, especially the aristocracy and educated officials, who were brought up among French culture and often knew French better than Russian.

Many scholars suggest that Napoleon bore the worldview and values of the West. For example, Karl Marx wrote, "Bonapartism is a true religion of the bourgeois today. For it has become more and more clear that the bourgeoisie is incapable of ruling itself directly, and therefore wherever there is no oligarchy that could take over the direction of the state and the interests of the bourgeoisie for a good reward (as is done here in England), you'll find a Bonapartist semi-dictatorship as the normal way of doing things."

The most informed person of Europe in those days, the minister of police Joseph Fouché wrote in his memoirs of 1824 that, in 1812, Napoleon seriously counted on the support of the "Saint Petersburg's French party". In Saint Petersburg and Moscow plans were made for a coup d'etat in Napoleon's favor and the assassination of Alexander I. Napoleon supposedly had strong support among the Russian opposition. Perhaps the idea of Bonapartism, a man who towered over history and strode across entire nations, found deep roots in Russia.

But all of that changed when Napoleon's forces invaded Russia. In writing about Bonapartist ideas among Russian society,

CHAPTER 6

Leo Tolstoy showed that interest in Napoleon as a person did not hinder the Russian battle against him. In 1812 Russia saw the birth of a Romantic idea of national unity. Russia did not want to become a French colony. The looting, arson, and desecration of Russian Orthodox churches and monasteries carried out by Napoleon's soldiers, their use of the local population as draft animals "without distinction to sex, condition, or age", [113] caused mass resistance among the Russian people. Napoleon's popularity in Russia waned rapidly.

Much later Mikahil Banunin would write about Bonapartism, "A gang of criminals simply took over France and held power for twenty years. Three vices in France worked in their favor: the cowardice of the bourgeoisie, the disorganized state of the working masses, and the ignorance of the peasantry." The idea of the predatory conduct of the Grand Army was underlined by the historian Yevgeny Tarle, "The ruin that the passing army inflicted on the peasantry, the countless examples of looting and outright robbery by French deserters was so great that hatred of the enemy grew daily." [114]

In the Winter Palace, the Russian emperor Nicholas I kept an enormous and colorful painting titled *Parade of the Old Guard at Tuileries*. This was a typical product of Napoleon-era political and military propaganda. The painting depicts Napoleon surrounded by his field-marshals watching his grenadiers on parade. However, Nicholas I did not worship Napoleon or his "military genius". He occasionally explained why he needed to have this painting: "I want to look everyday at what a strong and dangerous foe we routed with God's help."

The Poland card, or the russophobic campaign of the 1830s

The Napoleonic Wars ended with the Congress of Vienna in 1815, which set new borders for the European states. Poland was again partitioned. Prussia took the northwest part of Poland, the Grand Duchy of Posen. It also got the "free city" of

Danzig, today known as Gdansk. Austria received the Wieliczka region, while Krakow with its surrounding lands was turned into a Krakow Republic under the joint authority of Russia, Austria, and Prussia. These lands saw a campaign of foreign germanization, and there was no level of self-government beyond city magistrates.

The remaining part of the Duchy of Warsaw returned to the Polish Kingdom (*Królestwo Polskie* in Polish), a state that was in union with Russia. It was set up as a constitutional monarchy, headed by the king, who had a viceroy in Warsaw. The Kingdom had its own army, consisting mainly of veterans of the Polish legends that had fought in the Napoleonic Wars on the side of France. Alexander I had great sympathy of the Polish nationalist movement and gave Poland a liberal constitution, which he however began to violate when the Poles exercised their rights and opposed him. The constitution made everyone equal before the law, guaranteed personal and property rights, and recognized freedom of speech and religion. The Poles had their own parliament, the Sejm, with two chambers. The upper chamber, the Senate, brought the aristocracy together. The chamber of deputies was elected from among the general population of the Kingdom of Poland. Over 30% of the population had the right to vote. In France in 1820 no more than 18% did, and in Britain around 15%. There wasn't anything like serfdom in Poland.

In 1816 Warsaw University opened with teaching in Russian, German, Polish, and Latin. High schools operated with teaching in Polish.

In general, except for the viceroys, even the most dramatic desires of the progressive Polish society were realized. Napoleon had given Poland nothing like this.

Nor in Russia itself with its serfdom and lack of a constitution was there anything like it. Under Russian rule, the Polish national economy made enormous advances, and from 1815 to 1830 there was rapid development of industry.

CHAPTER 6

It would seem that Poland had opened a wide field of cooperation with Russia and economic and cultural growth. It had such freedom, essentially there was no interference of the mother country in its "colony".

But Poland prepared almost immediately to leave the Russian Empire. The violations of the constitution were not the sole or even major cause for discontent among the Poles, especially as the Poles in the other parts of the former Polish-Lithuanian Commonwealth were not subject to it. The main motive was patriotism, a protest against foreign rule over Poland. Besides this, there was also a desire for a Greater Poland. The "patriotic society" in Warsaw made connections with conspirators among the Russian aristocracy, the so-called Decembrists. These "patriots" proclaimed the slogan "For your freedom and ours!", which meant supporting all forces that sought to overthrow the lawful government of the Russian Empire. This society prepared an armed uprising against Russia, and plotted an attempt on the life of Nicholas I when he was crowned head of Poland.

The Polish uprising of 1830–1831 is known in Poland as the Polish-Russian War and considered an uprising of national liberation against the Russian Empire. The way Poles see it, it was not Russian subjects rising up against a lawful government, but a national government fighting for its independence under the slogan of restoring the historical commonwealth in its borders of 1772, i.e. not just the territories with a majority Polish population, but also the territories inhabited by Belorussians and Ukrainians, and also Lithuanians and Jews. In Europe this uprising was met with great sympathy. Right after hearing of it, the French poet Casimir Delavigne wrote his poem "La Varsovienne" (The Woman of Warsaw), which was quickly translated in Poland, set to music, and became one of the most famous Polish patriotic anthems. In Russia, a large part of society stood against the Poles, especially because of the ambitions for a Greater Poland among the uprising's leaders and the Polish aristocracy. On June 1, 1831 Alexander Pushkin wrote a personal letter to Pyotr Vyazemsky in which he said:

For us the Polish affair is a family affair, an old, hereditary feud. We cannot judge it according to European views, whatever they are, but according to our own thoughts. Europe however, both the people and the governments, need something general to hold its attention. Of course, it would be in the interest of all governments to avoid an unpleasant hangover, but the people are clawing and barking for it. So look at what Europe is forcing on us. [115]

The press all over Europe, especially in France and Bavaria, published articles that strongly condemned the Russian Empire. They reported complete fantasies of "atrocities committed by the Russian troops against the peaceful local population" and reinforced the image of the Poles as the vanguard of Europe, heroic fighters against Russian barbarity.

What happened? Throughout the 16th and 17th centuries, Europeans consistently viewed the wars between Muscovy and the Polish-Lithuanian Commonwealth as an internal affair of the Slavs. Not long before, already in the 18th century, hadn't the European powers together with Russia had partitioned Poland and recognized its right to fight? Only fifteen years before, had they not agreed that Russia would annex the Duchy of Warsaw? Had they put the crown of the Kingdom of Poland on the head of the Russian emperor? It's easy to understand: after 1812–1815 Russia had become a strong country — not one of the strongest, but *the* strongest. It was not a helper, a "little brother" but a formidable competitor, which later would be called — not in jest but out of fear — the "policeman of Europe". The European powers quickly changed their outlook. Proclaiming Russia an aggressor that strangled sovereign Poland help in a propaganda war. Alas, the Russian government, ten months after losing the real war, lost in that propaganda war. Russian official propaganda did not use the strongest arguments; it did not write, for example, about the fact that under the supposedly feudal oppression of the Russian tsars, more people in Poland had the right to vote than in France of the time.

CHAPTER 6

The great European powers did nothing to help Poland, they did not sacrifice the lives of a single one of their soldiers or waste a single bullet. In fact, they were completely indifferent to Poland's fate. There are many examples of how Poland served as a political bargaining chip for the Europeans. One of the reasons this bargaining chip was valuable is that it served as everlasting proof of Russia's aggressive foreign policy.

The era of colonialism

> Russia has no allies... Everyone fears our might.
>
> —*Alexander III, Emperor of Russia*

The growth of colonial empires

The myth of Russian aggression that had arisen under Napoleon was used against it throughout the 19th and 20th centuries. After 1812 it became customary to blame Russia for any expansion of its territory. In the Europeans' view, the Russian Empire was constantly, throughout its history, waging wars of aggression. This accusation was flung by countries that had built their own prosperity on expanding their borders at the expense of conquered territories.

That is because the 19th century was the age of colonial empires. It was a time when all European powers were building empires, a process that involved considerable brutality and was concerned exclusively with material gains.

> European history in the 19th and 20th centuries is a continual series of wars for new territory. The European states fought over nations that had already been conquered or fought for the right to conquer them. Take, for example, the numerous wars between England and Spain and the English–Dutch wars of the 17th and 18th centuries.
>
> Throughout the 18th and 19th centuries Britain fought a series of wars to conquer India. In the 19th and 20th centuries the war for India was "logically" followed by the Anglo-Afghan, Anglo-Burmese and Anglo-Tibetan wars.

The Anglo-Chinese War of 1839–1842 is still referred to as the Opium War. The result was that the English were given back their right to sell the opium they grew in Bengal on the Chinese market. Britain also tore off from southern China a small, rocky island, unremarkable except for the fact that it was located in a strategic place, a sort of key to all of Southeast Asia and southern China, and it had one of the best natural bays in this region. This small island, which became one of the jewels in the British Empire crown, was called Hong Kong.

Soon a new English-French-Chinese war broke out in 1856–1860. In America, Britain fought with France over Canada in 1754–1756. It then fought with essentially the same people for the independence of the United States in the American revolution of 1777–1783. Later there was another, less remembered Anglo-American war in 1812–1814.

After taking Canada, the English launched a massive campaign against the Iroquois and Mohawk Indians.

In 1852 the British navy bombarded Lagos, the chief city of the Yoruba people. Britain then seized the coast of Nigeria. In the 19th century Britain colonized Abyssinia, Bechuanaland, it founded the colonies of North and South Rhodesia, and occupied Kenya, Uganda, Egypt and Eastern Sudan.

In 1806 Britain seized the Cape Colony in South Africa. By that time there was already a small population of Boers, the descendants of settlers from Holland, Germany, and France. Frankly speaking, the Boers were no less colonizers than the British. They founded their own republics of the Transvaal and Orange State, which put into place the most terrible slave-owning regime. In the war of 1899–1902 that followed, the British annulled the Boers' independent republics and founded their own protectorate, the Union of South Africa.

The conquest of Australia in 1788–1815 was accompanied by the destruction of local tribes. In 1840–1872 England fought against the Maori tribes in New Zealand. On top of that, several islands in the Pacific, Indian, and Atlantic Oceans were taken.

Britain was of course the largest of the colonial powers, but France waged no fewer wars, fighting for Canada, vying with Britain for colonies in India, and in 1826–1849 it was in a nearly constant state of war with the Serer and Wolof tribes of West Africa and took Gabon.

CHAPTER 6

In 1857 France completed its conquest of Senegal by annihilating the state of the Fula people.

Still in the 19th century, France occupied Algeria, and quashed an uprising of the Berber tribes with unspeakable cruelty. It took nearly all of the islands of Oceania and occupied Somalia and Madagascar. During the war for Madagascar, the population of the island fell by a third. Then France took Tunisia, and in Central Africa it vied with Belgium for possession of the Congo river basin. In Southeast Asia France fought without stopping for the whole 19th century. In Asia during that time the French-Chinese War of 1884–1885 broke out, which was essentially for control of Indochina.

And these were just the most important of these wars.

France conquered Africa, Indochina, and it gained possession of islands in the Pacific and Indian Oceans. Britain divided Africa almost equally with the French, it took possession of India, fight a series of wars for Afghanistan, conquered Burma, and colonized Australia and New Zealand. Even the tiny country of Belgium managed to seize an enormous territory in Africa along the Congo River, and the northern country of Sweden grabbed a few Caribbean islands.

What is especially interesting is that in Central Europe and Scandinavia, there were no negative feelings in these various countries' dealings with these empires. The military adventures of colonial officers were romanticized. Colonial myths were treated as fascinating aspect of history, not as a tragedy. One cannot deny that Russia was working for its own interests on the European continent like other European states. It's simply that Russian colonization was never the enactment of the tsar's aggressive and paranoid inclinations by subservient Russians, as some historians like to portray it. The east, the south, and in the north were mainly settled by "free players", Cossacks, merchants, and farmers, who were free to search a better life or their own benefit. The Russian Empire continued to expand naturally under the same principles that Muscovy had grown in the 14th through the 17th centuries and the Russian Empire in the 18th century. The story of the Russian-Turkish Wars is especially illustrative in this regard.

The Russian-Turkish Wars: The Crimean War

The cities of southern Russia were originally founded as forts to protect against the constant raids of steppe peoples. These cities finally cease to function as fortresses in the 18th century, after the annexation of the Crimean, which had been preceded by eight wars between Russia and Turkey.

The pretext, partially one of the main reasons for Russia's actions against Turkey in the 19th century, was the Turks' regular persecution of Christians in the Near East and in the Balkans. Russia traditionally played the role of protector of Christians.

> After the Mongolian invasion, Rus' lost its southern steppe lands. The Slavic population left the steppes for the forests in the north, a colder, more forested region, but a much safer one. The steppes became deserted and were used only as a pastoral area. The Russian lands, which had never been especially fertile, returned to wild fields.
>
> Annexing these lands was of strategic and ideological importance. It was not only important to end the "Crimean nightmare". Russians had always considered the steppes of the Black Sea coast their territory. They had every moral basis for claiming that these lands were theirs and had been unfairly taken away from Russia.
>
> In 1771 the Russian army went into Crimea, and these time the Crimean khans could not repel it. The might supporter of the Crimea Tatars, the Ottoman Empire, was already not in the right shape to beat Russia. Under the Treaty of Küçük Kaynarca, the Crimean Khanate ceased to be a vassal of Turkey and was declared independent.
>
> In 1783 the last Crimean khan Şahin Giray abdicated in favor of Russia. A stream of settlers poured into the limitless southern steppes. Already in the 19th century, Novorossiya was the breadbasket of Russia, and not just Russia. Through the port of Odessa, the grain harvested in southern Russia fed Europe too.

CHAPTER 6

Cities buzzed on the Black Sea: Kherson, Mariupol, Nikolaev, Odessa, and in the Crimean peninsula Sevastopol and Simferopol grew. Through Russia's efforts, this outpost of civilization and wild steppe zone turned into part of the civilized world.

Nonetheless, Russians got no peace. Through the 19th century the Russian south had to keep its powder dry, for across the Black Sea that anyone could sail lay Turkey, which had not been pacified and would not put down its arms. That Muslim country, which wanted revenge for the loss of Crimea forced on it, would not allow Russia to leave the Black Sea.

Turkey was a powerful empire, much stronger than the old Crimean Khanate, as everyone remembered well — until the Russian victory at the end of the 18th century, the Black Sea was a sort of Turkish lake. Turkey was a military threat to Russia's new province of Novorossiya.

The Russian south remained an outpost of Christian civilization. Russia had to maintain its Black Sea fleet there, so the southern cities became mighty fortresses.

In 1787 the Ottoman Empire, which was not resigned to the loss of Crimea, again declared war on the Russian Empire. After the storming of Izmail (in 1790), the defeat of the Turks at Machin (1791), and the victories against the Turkish fleet in the battles of Tendra (1790) and Cape Kaliakria (1791) the Ottoman Empire formally recognized Russia's annexation of the Crimean Khanate. Only in 1812, however, after its defeat in another war, would Turkey again and permanently confirm Russia's permanent authority over Crimea. The Russians settled the Black Sea coast, moved into the warm Kuban territory, and plowed the rich soil of the Northern Caucasus.

This bothered the powerful colonial empires. Russia could not be allowed to grow stronger — and it was bound to grow stronger if the waning Ottoman Empire recognized its claims.

But if the Ottomans dared to fight, then the Russian Empire was fully capable of defeating Turkey, which had colonies throughout the Middle East and North Africa. If the Russian Empire defeated Turkey, it would sail through the Dardanelles and Bosphorus, and then its navy could easily enter the

Mediterranean. This gave Russia too great an advantage. How could Britain and the whole of Europe stand by in the Crimean War of 1853–1855?

Here Nicholas I acted in a very naïve fashion. Still, he was an officer by training and in his approach to politics. Nicholas I completely lacked the Byzantine views that so distinguished his older brother. He negotiated for the neutrality of the European states like his grandmother Catherine the Great might have negotiated with Prussia and Austria for the partition of Poland.

But during the partition of Poland, the European states who came together were of the same stature, understood each other, and were not especially afraid of one another. In the course of seventy years the world had changed beyond recognition. Russia had beat Napoleon, the Russian army had marched into Paris, and a large part of Poland had become part of the Russian Empire. The Caucasus had been annexed, and Turkey and Persia had been defeated in several wars. Russian ships rounded the globe, and it was Russian sailors who had first caught sight of Antarctica.

Basically, since the name of Catherine the Great, Russia had grown so strong that it could no longer be considered just one of the European powers.

Nicholas I sincerely believed that he could start negotiations on some kind of "First Partition of Turkey": Let Britain take Egypt and let it have a much-needed naval base on Cyprus; let France strengthen its position in North Africa; Russia would receive what it needed, an outlet from the Black Sea through the Bosphorus and Dardanelles; and let the Western powers not interfere with Russia's concern for the Orthodox Christians who were subjects of the Ottoman Empire.

Essentially this would be a realization of the great dream of all Russian and Slavic patriots since the time of Oleg and the conception of Moscow as the "Third Rome". The Russian shield would be at the gates of Constantinople. Russia in Constantinople, the second eternal city, would stand as a symbol

CHAPTER 6

for Orthodoxy. The Russians would unite under its protectorate (and perhaps within its borders) all Slavs and Orthodox Christians from the Adriatic to the Mediterranean, and from the Black Sea to the Baltic Sea.

There was one more "moral" argument that Nicholas I foolishly thought would help him control potential allies. Had no Russia helped the Austrian Empire survive through its terrible revolution of 1848? The Austrian Empire could have collapsed, and the Hungarians had really left it. Austria was saved by a force of a hundred thousand men that Nicholas I had sent under the command of Ivan Paskevich. Instead of detailed instructions, Nicholas I gave his faithful servant just three historic words: "Show no mercy!" Indeed, Paskevich spared no one. The Hungarian revolutionaries were smashed to smithereens. The Austrian Empire had been saved, not now Nicholas I expected the Austrian emperor Franz Josef to do something in return, or to at least show gratitude.

Such incredible naivete is inappropriate for foreign policy! Nicholas I seems to have forgotten the message of the gospel: expect no gratitude.

Nicholas I supposed that if Austria (known since 1848 as Austro-Hungary) gave its support, Russia could win any war in Europe, and then it would finally establish itself in the Balkans. However, Austria was afraid that Russia would be too interested in the Slavic subjects of its own empire. Franz Josef shrugged his shoulders, "Politics is decided by one's interests, not out of a show gratitude."

In February 1853 Nicholas I send an emergency embassy to Constantinople, headed by prince Alexander Menshikov, to demand that the sultan recognize Russia's protection of the Orthodox Christians in the Ottoman Empire. In that month France and England sealed a secret treaty that if the Russian Empire started a war with Turkey, these countries would act on the side of Turkey. The British ambassador Stratford hinted at this to the Turkish sultan, but his advisors told him directly:

Britain was ready to understand Turkey's desire to have Crimea back. Menshikov left Istanbul in May 1853 without having accomplished anything. British and French forces had already been placed on alert.

In June 1854 Nicholas I ordered his troops to enter the Danubian principalities of Moldavia and Wallachia (now part of Romania). The sultan felt that he had the support of Britain and France and declared war.

Russia's first actions confirmed Europe's worst fears: Russia had indeed become very strong. Admiral Nakhimov in the Battle of Sinope annihilated the Turkish navy. In December 1853 the detachment of general Vasiliy Bebutov defeated near Bashkadyklar (in Armenia) the Turkish army that had invaded the Caucasus. On the Danube, the Russian army repelled the Turks that had threatened Bucharest, entered Bulgaria, and in March 1854 besieged Silistra. The Bulgarians gladly welcomed the Russian troops, and in Greece the Christians staged an uprising.

Here's where the masks came off! In November in 1853, the British prime minister Lord Aberdeen announced Britain's readiness to stand up for "Turkish independence" and stop the aggression of the "Russian bear". The French emperor Napoleon III spoke out in the same fashion.

Britain's war minister Lord Palmerston still had not finished drawing up his strategy for the war. It involved bringing a small contingent into the south of the Russian Empire, either Odessa or Crimea, attacking Russia's navy from the north in Saint Petersburg, and separating the Far East, Alaska, and Kamchatka from Russia. It was supposed that after the war, the Russian Empire would be deprived of Bessarabia, Finland, Poland, the Caucasus, Crimea, and the Baltics. In general, the Russian Empire was to be reduced to the border of the Grand Duchy of Moscow in the 15th century.

Napoleon had launched this ideological campaign with his cry of "Russian aggression" and "the Russian threat". After the defeat of Napoleon in 1814, all of Europe began the exact

CHAPTER 6

same anti-Russian campaign. It intensified with every Russian achievement, no matter what it consisted in.

Now, in 1853, Europe moved from theory to action, that is, it showed extreme aggression and attacked the Russian Empire at that same time that it was shouting about Russian aggression.

The war ended with the signing of a peace treaty in Paris on March 18, 1856. This treaty declared the Black Sea was neutral, the Russian navy was to be limited only to a necessary minimum, and the fortresses there were torn down. In addition, Russia lost the mouth of the Danube, the southern part of Bessarabia, the fortress of Kars that it had captured in the war and the right to protect Serbia, Moldavia, and Wallachia. Palmerston's plans were not fulfilled, however.

Within Russia, one consequence of the war was a series of legal and socioeconomic reforms in the 1860s. After the military defeat, the government of Alexander II rapidly forced reforms through, but this haste led to certain distortions in Russia's social structure. These distortion were brought about by ideological trends that came from the West.

Clashes in the Pacific

In the mid 19th century the battle intensified for influence in the Pacific Ocean. At the end of the 18th century, when Russia made it to Alaska, no one cared, nor did anyone care in the beginning of the 19th century when Russia built Fort Ross and other fortified settlements in California and along the Pacific coast of what would become part of the USA.

A lot had changed since then, however. Britain had tried to get its hands on China. France had taken a large number of islands in the Pacific. The United States expanded westward to the Pacific, and took California from the Spanish. In 1853 the Americans forced Japan to abandon its policy of isolation and open up to trade with the USA.

During the Crimean War, when the "great powers" of Europe not only stood up for Turkic but gave Russia a crushing defeat and landed in Crimea, the United States remained on the sidelines. American ships were sailing along the Pacific coast, but did not participate in the fighting. General McClellan, the future commander of the US army, was at the time with Britain in the Crimea, learning best practices.

But in August 1854 a joint British-French force under the command of rear admirals Price and Fevrier de Point reached Petropavlovsk, Russia's main outpost on the Pacific Ocean.

The Petropavlovsk garrison had 920 people (41 officers, 825 soldiers and sailors, 18 Russian volunteers, and 36 Kamchadal volunteers. The Russians had 40 guns on 6 coastal batteries and 27 on their ships, the frigate *Aurora* and the transport vessel *Dvina*. Each had about 30–40 rounds of ammunition.

Such an insignificant force cannot compare to the mighty armies that had clashed in Crimea, but this miserable garrison defended itself, while the small allied force tried to take hold of a huge and almost unpopulated territory, an area of three million square kilometers with vast natural resources. The "peaceful" British-French force, which had saved poor Turkey from the Russian onslaught, were now thousands of kilometers from Turkey and Crimea, trying to get their hands on the untold wealth of Russia.

One would think that these opposing sides were not equally matched. In August 1854, firing on the port and suppressing fire from the two coastal batteries, the British-French team landed 600 men with the goal of seizing Petropavlovsk. The Russian force of 230 men supported by the guns of the *Aurora* and *Dvina*, counterattacked and threw them into the sea.

A second landing party of 970 men on August 24 were also turned back by the 360 Russian soldiers and seamen. The allied force saw about 450 of its men killed or wounded, including the British commander Price. The Russian losses totalled around a hundred men.

The allied force had to leave to Vancouver and San Francisco. Thanks to the heroism and endurance of just a few hundred

Russian soldiers and soldiers, who not only repelled the attack but also launched a counterattack against a much larger enemy, the plan to take an enormous territory from Russia — Kamchatka and the Far East — failed.

The Russo-Turkish War of 1877–1878

In many respects the Russo-Turkish War of 1877–1878 was part two of the Crimean War. Russia sought to defend their blood brothers, the South Slavs, and their brothers in faith, the Orthodox Christians, in their quest for independence from the Ottoman Empire. This war was popular across all of Russian society. Thousands of volunteers left Russia to fight in the Serbo-Montenegrin-Turkish War of 1876.

Russia wanted to resolve the matter of the Black Sea straits, ensuring its free passage through the Dardanelles and Bosphorus. It wanted to strengthen its influence in the Balkans and restore its international sway after the Crimean War.

This time Western diplomats tried to convince Turkey to wage war, but the Turks were in no hurry to do so. In December 1877 and January 1878 the Russian army was close a victorious end to the war. It made an unprecedented winter crossing of the Balkan mountains, and surrounded and engaged the Turkish forces of Veisel Pasha. Pursuing their fleeing opponents, the Russian army took control of Sofia on January 8, followed by Adrianople (now Edirne), and approached Constantinople (Istanbul). Turkey had no remaining combat forces.

It seemed that Russian forces would shortly enter the former capital of the Ottoman Empire. The popular slogan of that time was "We'll set a cross atop Hagia Sophia!" The entire Orthodox world, all Slavic peoples were ready to greet the Russian army's occupation of Constantinople.

And then a British force entered the Sea of Marmara. British diplomacy "strongly advised" Alexander II against taking Constantinople. The tsar was given to believe that Britain was prepared to declare all-out war if the Russian Empire did not follow this advice.

The tsar wavered — the memory of the Crimean War was still fresh — and he ordered his army to stop, to not enter the Turkish capital. Negotiations began and a truce was declared.

A storming of Istanbul, naming the city back to Constantinople and turning Hagia Sophia back into an Orthodox church, did not happen. Later, after World War I, the Ottoman Empire quietly and without any remorse was divided up among the European countries, but now without Russia's participation.

Cold War myths

What does one's historical memory say?

National epics arose at practically a single era in history: the German *Nibelungenlied*, the Spanish *Cantar de Mio Cid*, the French *Chanson de Roland*, the Scandinavian sagas, and the Russian *byliny*. Wars, conquests, battles against enemies — these are basic themes of the stories made by various peoples in the early Middle Ages. They fully reflect the ideology and psychology of Europe's peoples of the time.

In the German *Nibelungenlied* warriors exhibit truly barbaric cruelty. Generosity, a distaste for death and danger are found together with men who fight like savage beasts. They calmly describe how knights on the battlefield quench their thirst with the blood of fallen enemies. Rivers of blood flow, practically every stanza offers the reader details of bloody fighting. Not only men but women too were involved in bloody massacres that spared no one young or old.

In these stories it is described in detail with what weapons men fought, how exactly they killed their enemies, and what they took from the bodies of the slain, or the camps of the vanquished.

CHAPTER 6

> Then the good knight Hagen smote the child Ortlieb,
> so that the blood spurted up the sword towards his
> hand and the head fell into the lap of the queen...
> He dealt the queen a grievous sword-blow, which did
> cut the high-born dame in twain.
> —*The Nibelungenlied*

In the *Cantar de Mio Cid* we find, "Attack boldly, plunder deftly / Don't shy away from goods or money"

Chivalry, a knight's adoration of a beautiful lady, is one theme of the epic. It is found also in the French *Chanson de Roland* and in the stories of King Arthur. But parallel with this we find descriptions of rape of peasant women as well as domestic violence. The *Nibelungenleid* tells of a woman's bones being broken.

Of course, Ilya Muromets and his comrades-in-arms were not distinguished by an especial humanity when fighting against the "pagans", but there are no examples of such cruelty in the Russian poems called *byliny*. The heroes of these tales do not kiss the hand of ladies and their lady's scented glove across the Cuman steppes. There are no love scenes at all in these poems, as Russian epics are more chaste, more discreet. There are also no scenes of rape, or beatings of women.

The Russian *byliny* were written, or rather composed by singers, in the 12th and 13th centuries. The Russian national epic served as an unwritten chronicle handed down from generation to generation for centuries.

According to the *byliny*, heroes would rise up as the first sign of danger to defend the Russian land. All the "brave band of men". The prince of Kiev calls upon the heroes, i.e. the people, to defend the Russian land. These heroes were not a feudal class of hereditary warriors.

These are not Japanese samurai or European knights. Ilya Muromets was a commoner. From his surname, one knows that Alesha Popovich came from a line of priests. The heroes did not work to make themselves or the prince rich. The Russian epics do not describe plundering or even the transfer of loot.

Ilya Muromets is depicted as grabbing an enemy by the legs and spinning him around, or by creating a street with the wave of his hand. The tales deal with the pathos of battling the enemy, the mortal danger of laboring for the defense of one's homeland. There is not a single description of how much money these heroes made, what swords and armor they took from their slain foes, how many horses they plundered, or what riches they received. The Russian epic is not interested in any of that. These heroes had a special role as the true defenders of the Russian land.

In Western European epics the reader won't find any heroes from the common folk, because the epic was formed by the general principle of Western history at the time: in the West during the Middle Ages it was not the people who made history but the feudal class of hereditary professional soldiers.

Russian heroes are not vassals, servants, or bodyguards of the prince. The Russian epics strongly emphasize their independence. The wide fields of Russian epics are nothing more than an epic symbol of freedom.

Russian epics also describe battles differently. There are over a hundred *byliny* plots, but none of them have awful scenes of violence, let alone rivers of blood and rape. Even the image of the enemy in *byliny* is collective: either the "Tatar horde" or the mythical Slavic Dragon, or the dragon Tugarin Zmeyevich.

Russian epics do not describe how the heroes split the skulls or chest of the enemy. No one flays people alive, cuts off their nose or ears, or drinks human blood.

For a contrary tendency, look at the descriptions of the Crusades! In medieval European epics and in later times, the 12th through the 15th centuries, the goal of a Crusade was to baptise whoever was not killed in battle. That was the goal, and religious conflict could easily replace older tribal rivalries.

Themes of religious warfare are completely absent from Russian epics, as are themes of religious or racial enmity. The

CHAPTER 6

main goal was to depend the land of Russia, and not to make oneself rich or plunder others. Only in Rus' could the people call themselves Christians in their way of thinking. The Russian words for "Christian" (*khristianin*) and "peasant" or "ordinary person" (*krestyannin*) are related and was the most widely held class identification in the country.

There is an amazing legend linked with the image of a Holy Rus' populated by Christians, namely the City of Kitezh epic. According to this legend, the people living in the city of Kitezh did not want to surrender their city during a Mongol siege, and through their prayers Lake Svetloyar opened up and swallowed Kitezh. That is, the city itself mysteriously disappeared into the lake and was hid from the invaders by the waters of Svetloyar. The righteous cannot be hurt by a flood. Through some miracle they passed through the water into and perhaps into a better world.

Today if one sits on the shore or rows a boat on a sunny day, you can supposedly see the submerged houses and towers, and on holidays hear bells ringing from beneath the waters. The city of Kitezh will live on under the waters until the end of the world. Only on Judgement Day will it rise up again. Then the unvanquished army of prince Yury Vsevolodovich will issue forth from the city and his warriors together with all other souls will be judged by God.

Is this a mere legend or myth? Absolutely! But it is so full of self-respect, so beautiful and poetic. It is one of the pearls of Slavic epic storytelling. It is a myth about a fearless Russian people who don't give in to conquerors. It is a myth of a motherland that saves her children, the people living there. This myth, or rather a national bearing based on it, has had an enormous influence on Russia.

It is interesting to compare the myth of the city of Kitezh with its corresponding European legends that tell of a city that is now underground or underwater. In the south of Europe they spoke of cities that had been cursed by God because of the wickedness of their inhabitants, and thus fell underground.

Sometimes these cities again appear on the surface of the earth, whether on a full moon, on Halloween, or on the first of May, when all kinds of evil spirits go forth to trouble people. On these days a person can enter the city of the damned and find treasure in its streets and houses. Here is a skeleton whose rotting pockets are full of gold coins. There are the bones of a great beauty, whose jewels still lie atop her skull. While the moon has not yet set and the first rays of the sun have not yet shone, one has to snatch whatever one can and leave. Only knowledgeable people say that found treasure doesn't bring happiness, but perhaps some people can get lucky.

There is an old Germanic myth about a city that went under the waters because of its greed. Its citizens did business at such high prices that no one could buy anything at all from them all day. Once in a hundred years this city rises from the depths of the sea, and for the course of a whole day its market is open for business. If a person bought the smallest little thing in this city, then the curse would be lifted.

Do I have to explain that the myth of the city of Kitezh reflects a completely different worldview? It tells of a great feat of self-sacrifice in the name of salvation!

If we take a careful look at the wars which Russia waged during the time of the Russian Empire, one can see that a significant part of these were defensive wars. Russia was always an enticing conquest for invaders, it was too great and rich. Even as far back as Ancient Rus', it was the target of aggression from nomadic steppe-dwellers, Varangians, and Catholic crusaders.

Muscovy and the Russian Empire could have never given up their independence and give in to Western powers that wanted to bite off some part of the country or another. If Staden's plan had been realized, then there would be no Russia. If Lord Palmerston's plan had been released, then Russia would have lost an enormous part of her territory.

One can look to the most well-known wars that the Russian Empire fought in its last years: World War I was a war declared on Russia, which dragged the Russians into a conflict they didn't need; as for the Russo-Japanese War, the Japanese attacked the Russian navy without even declaring war; when it comes to the Russo-Turkic War of 1877–1878 Russia had spent two years asking the Turks to cease their violence against the Slavs and Christians in the Balkans, to introduce reforms, and only the refuse of the Sublime Porte to live up to its earlier commitments made a war necessary. In the Crimean War, the Turks declared war on Russia, as they knew they had support from Britain and France. If Russia had really been aggressive, considering all of its military capabilities, which have at times been greater than anything in Europe (during the wars against Napoleon and Hitler), its possessions in Europe would have been much bigger. The myth of Russian aggression has been actively put forth in the former Soviet republics. Since the end of the 1980s (the time of perestroika), there has been a hysteria about the introduction of "Soviet (Russian) occupation". This propaganda can have a strong effect on people without a knowledge of the situation, and there are ever more of them due to the decline in the quality of education in the republics of the former USSR.

But if we look closely at the historical facts, it becomes clear that find yet another slander. Can one call it occupation (from Latin *occupatio* 'seizing, hold') if parts of Georgia voluntarily joined the Russian state in 1801 after an appeal from George XII, king of Kakhetia and Kartli? Furthermore, the first requests to join Russia were made as far back as the 16th century: in 1586 Georgian envoys begged the Russian tsar Fedor Ivanovich to "take this people as his subjects and save their lives and souls". According to the calculations of Russian historians, when the Russian Empire won the Georgian lands of the Persians and Turks and defended them from attacks by Caucasian highlanders, it lost a total of around 130,000 men.

In Georgia the matter of calling this an occupation has gone so far that there are not only museums to the supposed occupation, but they have destroyed memorials raised to the heroes of World War II such as the Glory Memorial in the city of Kutaisi. Essentially the Georgian authorities have struck a blow on the historical consciousness of the Georgian people, who played their part along with other peoples in the fall of the Third Reich and the Nazi order. The Georgian government has set a course for total russophobia, and young people view the Soviet era as one of the worst periods in Georgian history.

It's a complete mystery who Russia was occupying in Ukraine. There was a process of bringing together all the Russian lands that had been taken away from her. One of the stages in this natural process was the famous Council of Pereyaslav in 1654, when a significant part of Ukraine was united with Russia. Nonetheless, an enormous territory still remained under Polish or Austrian rule. There was no separate "Ukrainian people" then, there were Russians living within the Russian state and Russians living in territories occupied by Poles and Hungarians. "Ukrainians" and "Ukraine" were invented in the Vatican, Vienna, and Krakow; at the end of the 19th and in the 20th century this idea gained support in Berlin, and in the West in general, as they understood the importance of such a thing in splitting the Russian people apart.

There was the very same uncertainty in the matter of the Baltic states who were "occupied" by Russia. Under the terms of the Nystadt peace treaty of 1721 was ceded from Sweden to Russia. The Baltic states were Russian not only according to the right of the victors, but also on the basis of arrangements made at that time, and furthermore Russia also bought them. The actions of these "Russian and Soviet occupiers" were rather strange. These "occupiers" did not carry out large-scale looting of the territories they received, and they did not wipe out most of the natives and force the rest into reservations. Instead, they maintained local autonomy in place, built cities and ports, improved education and the sciences, and helped create a local intelligentsia that strongly benefited these "occupied" territories. The "Russian occupiers" did not destroy the culture and identity of the Georgians, Estonians, and other peoples, rather it strongly supported them and improved their level of culture. How true occupiers behave can be clearly seen from history; we know how the colonizers acted in North, Central, and South America, and in the Caribbean. Russians remember how Hitler's followers and their henchmen acted in the Soviet territories.

This slanderous myth about Russia is an incredible hindrance for Russians, both within the country and outside its borders. Unfortunately, the West has actively taken advantage of this "face of the enemy". It is the face of an evil and cruel enemy, which for centuries has maltreated the smaller peoples neighboring it, and still keeps many of them in captivity. Among American films of the most different types, we recognize this face of the enemy, mostly Russian, North Korean, Iranian, Arab, Serb, Chinese, etc. The most popular depiction is Russians as a "mafia", as "terrorists" or "agents", a Russian "warlord" or a general that trades in "nuclear secrets", and other Russian bogeymen.

Quite often a negative depiction of Russians is woven into the film imperceptibly. Take, for example, Gavin O'Connor's sports drama *Warrior* of 2011. The film as a whole is not bad, it speaks to family values (brotherly and fatherly love, love for one's family), to developing the traits of a winner, fortitude, resilience, and courage. But in passing the film shows a powerful Russian fighter named Koba (very symbolic, as this was Stalin's pseudonyms). This fighter is depicted with clear traces of the negroid type that characterizes the "Russian barbarians" from the East. Naturally, one of the main characters beats the "Russian" fighter.

One must also notice American filmmakers attacking Russians with plots of KGB agents present within the United States. Thus in 2010 a film on this subject came out called *Salt*, where the plot is centered around an operation conducted by Soviet/Russian agents that had infiltrated the American intelligence services. In 2011 this subject again came up in the film *The Double*.

This is a true information war carried out year after year against Russia and the Russian people, which turns Russians into "agents", "terrorists", "criminals", "prostitutes", "insane warriors", "bloodthirsty dictators" and other bogeymen.

Alas, the contemporary russophobic myths about the Russians that are widespread in the West and have had an impact on part of the Russian intelligentsia, arose not recently but a long time ago. These stereotypes blossomed during the time of tsarist and imperial Russia. The myth that Russia is an incredibly aggressive, hostile civilization, that it is a servile and authoritarian country were brought back to life during the Soviet era. They are brought back again today, when the country has became to strengthen its rule of law. Of course, not everything happening in the country can be treated as a simple matter, but there is a huge gap between the making of myths and the living fabric of political and economic events. As we have seen, it is necessary turn from ideological clichés to the historical facts, and many slanderous myths about Russia would vanish in a puff of smoke.

NOTES

To Chapter 2

[1] *Puteshestvie v Moskoviyu Rafaelya Barberini v 1565 godu: syn otechestva* [The Journey of Raphael Barberini to Muscovy in 1565: The Son of the Fatherland], Part III, No. 7.1842.

[2] Siegmund Freiherr von Herberstein, *Rerum Moscoviticarum Commentarii*, Vienna, 1549, translation into Russian.

[3] Heinrich von Staden, *O Moskve Ivana Groznogo: zapiski nemtsa-oprichnika* [On Moscow under Ivan the Terrible: Notes from a German Oprichnik], 1925, Moscow.

[4] E. A. Rydzevskiya, *Rus' i Skandinaviya: IX–XIV vv.* [Rus' and Scandinavia: The 9th–14th centuries], 1978, Moscow: Nauka.

[5] A. Ya. Garkavi, *Skazaniya musul'manskikh pisateley o slavyanakh i russkikh (s poloviny VII v. do kontsa X v. po R. Kh.)* [Accounts by Muslim Writers of Slavs and Russians (from the mid 7th century to the end of the 10th century AD)], 1870, Saint Petersburg: Sytin.

[6] A. N. Ostrovsky *Dokhodnoe mesto* [A Profitable Position], collected works in 16 volumes, 1950, Moscow, Vol. 2.

[7] The Raffelstetten (Linz) customs regulations of 906 contain a mention of Russian traders — editor.

[8] G. E. Kochin (ed.), *Pamyatniki istorii Kievskogo gosudarstva IX-XII vv: sbornik dokumentov* [Monuments of the History of the Kiev State in the 9th 12th Centuries: Collection of Documents], 1936, Leningrad: Izd-vo AN SSSR.

[9] True story: the German architect who built one of Krakow's churches could not repay his debt on time. He did not refuse the debt but only asked for more time. Then by a sentence of the court, the craftsman who had built a marvellous church, was blinded. He was blinded by a executioner in the marketplace with a red-hot

iron rod. Naturally, after this had happened, the creditor certainly didn't get his money back.

[10] Bunin, Ivan. *Zhizn' Arsen'eva* [The Life of Arseniev], 2004, Moscow.

[11] Pskov is a city in northwest Russia. It is one of the oldest Russian cities, being first mentioned in the Primary Chronicle for the year 903. In 1348–1510 it was the capital of the independent Pskov Republic. In 1510 it joined the Grand Duchy of Muscovy

[12] A. M. Burovsky, *Otets gorodov Russkikh* [The Father of Russian Cities], 2007, Moscow.

[13] V. A. Rybakov, *Remeslo Drevney Rusi* [The Craftsmanship of Ancient Rus'], 1948, Moscow.

[14] Turukhansky District was a historical region in Eastern Siberia, today it forms the northern part of Krasnoyarsk Krai. It was annexed to Russia at the end of the 16th century and beginning of the 17th. Between the 18th and 20th centuries it was a place for political exiles.

[15] The coup d'etat of November 25 (December 6), 1741 was one of the major court intrigues in Russia in the 18th century, during which the underaged emperor Ivan VI Antonovich and his parents were overthrown, and the 32 year-old Elizabeth Petrovna was placed on the throne instead. It has been called the most bloodless coup in the history of Russia.

To Chapter 3

[16] Herodotus, *Istorii* [Histories], in 9 volumes, 2001, Moscow.

[17] Fletcher (1548–1611) authored a large description of Russia under the tsar in the 16th century. He was the brother of the bishop of London and the uncle of the poet John Fletcher.

[18] From his *Voyage en Russie* of 1867, which describes the Russian peasantry.

[19] Charles Howard Earl of Carlisle (1629–1685) was a British artistocrat attendant to Charles II and sent by him to Moscow in 1663 to express gratitude to Tsar Alexei Mikhailovich and to ask for restoration of English trading privileges.

[20] *Rossiya — eto sama zhizn': zametki inostrantsev o Rossii s XIV po XX vek* [Russia is Life Itself. Notes on Russia by

Foreigners from the 16th to the 20th centuries] at http://www.pravoslavie.ru/put/041028173051]

[21] James Alexander, *Rossiya glazami inostrantsa* [Russia through the Eyes of a Foreigner], 2008, Moscow.

[22] V. M. Beilis, *Arabskie avtory IX — pervoy poloviny X v. o gosudarstvennosti i plemennom stroe narodov Evropy: Dreveneyshie gosudarstva na territorii SSSR* [Arab Authors of the late 9th and Early 10th Century on the State and Tribal Formations of Europe: The Oldest States on the Territory of the USSR], 1985.

[23] The hills amounted to seven, just like there were for many centuries in Moscow.

[24] Vsevolod Ovchinnikov, *Sakura i dub* [The Cherry Blossom and Oak Tree], 2003, Moscow.

[25] More or less the same happened in post-Soviet Russia after the wave of privatization. Apartments in Soviet housing blocks became private property, but every other part of the building — from the entrance to the roof — belonged to everyone and therefore belonged to no one in particular. As a result, these spaces that no one identified with ended up in terrible condition. As soon as one steps over the threshold of one of the apartments inside a housing block, everything becomes clean and well kept.

[26] E. I. Zabelin, *Istoriya goroda Moskvy* [The History of the City of Moscow], 1905, Moscow.

[27] Klyuchevsky (1841–1911) was a professor at Moscow University and author of a number of books on Russian history, including his series of lectures *A Course in Russian History*.

[28] *Rossiya* [Russia], in two volumes, 1880, Saint Petersburg, vol. 1.

[29] The Russian term for Christmastide, *Svyatki*, is an old Russian word meaning 'holiday'. It lasts 12 days from Christmas to Epiphany. It is a remnant of pre-Christian Slavic culture. The great importance of the holiday is shown by its occurrence on another boundary in the solar year: at this time of the year, the sun moves from the winter back towards summer, the days get longer, the old year departs and the new one begins.

[30] Vidukind Korvetsky, *Deyaniya saksov* [The Deeds of the Saxons], 1975, Moscow: Nauka.

[31] *Novgorodskaya pervaya letopis' starshego i mladshego izvodov* [The First Novgorod Chronicle in its Older and Younger Variants], 1950, Moscow and Leningrad, p. 89

[32] A. B. Goryanin, *Mify o Rossii i dukh natsii* [Myths about Russia and the Soul of the Nation], 2001, Moscow.

[33] See E. F. Grekulov, *Pravoslavnaya inkvizitsiya v Rossii* [The Orthodox Inquisition in Russia], 1964, Moscow.

[34] Samuel Collins, *The Present State of Russia, in a Letter to a Friend in London*, 1846, London.

[35] According to the data of the Centre for Demography and Human Ecology, Russian Academy of Sciences.

[36] According to the article "Russia" in the *Brockhaus and Efron Encyclopedic Dictionary*, Saint Petersburg, 1898.

[37] ibid, 1914, p. 74.

To Chapter 4

[38] The Varangians were inhabitants of ancient Rus' whose ethnic, occupational, and social nature have been the subject of debate. The traditional account identifies the Varangians with natives of the Baltic region, hired warriors or traders in the ancient Russian statelets (9–12th centuries) and Byzantium (11th–13th centuries).

[39] Novgorod is a city in northwestern Russia, one of the oldest and most famous Russian cities, founded in 859. It is the place of the convocation of Rurik and the origin of Russian statehood. In the Middle Ages, it was the center of Novgorod Rus' and later of the Novgorod Land.

[40] This submission, which has come to be called the "Mongol-Tatar yoke", lasted in northwest Rus' until 1480. In other Russian lands it ended in the 14th century when they joined the Grand Duchy of Lithuania.

[41] Suzdal, Vladimir, and Yaroslavl are ancient Russian cities that together form the so-called "Golden Ring" of Russia.

[42] M. M. Bogoslovsky, *Zemskoe samoupravlenie na Russkom Severe v XVII veke* [Local Autonomy in the Russian North in the 17th Century], in two volumes, 1909–1912, Moscow.

[43] The Sobornoye Ulozheniye of 1649 was a series of laws enacted by Muscovy that regulated various spheres of life. It is a testament to 17th-century law.

[44] Alexander Goryanin, *Kogda na Rusi bylo zhit' khorosho* [When It was Good to Live in Rus'], *Ekspert* No. 1 (590), December 31, 2007.

[45] The Cossack Hetmanate was the semi-official name of a part of what is now Ukraine in the 17th century.

[46] Mikhail Lomonosov (1711–1765) was the first Russian natural scientist of world importance, a lexicographer, chemist, and physicist. He went down in the history of science as the first chemist to give a definition of physical chemistry close to the modern one, and he pursued an extensive program of physical and chemical research. His molecular kinetic theory of heat in many ways anticipated the modern idea of the structure of matter and many fundamental laws, including one of the principles of thermodynamics. He laid the foundations of the science of glass. He was an astronomer, a designer of new instruments, a geographer, metallurgist, geologist, a poet who worked in founding the modern Russian literary language, an artist, historian, an advocate for state education and the development of science and the economy. He worked on a plan for a Moscow University, which was later named in his honor. He discovered that the planet Venus has an atmosphere.

[47] Andrei Mikhailovich Burovsky (born 1955) is a Russian writer of popular science works, an archaeologist, historian, and philosopher.

[48] The Boyar Duma did not play an independent role and was rather equivalent to a state advisory council. It always acted together with the tsar and together they formed the highest state authority. This unity between them is especially evident in matters of legislation and foreign affairs. In all business decisions were announced with the words, "The ruler has ordered and the boyars decreed".

[49] S. G. Pushkarev, *Obzor russkoy istorii* [An Overview of Russian History], 2000, Saint Petersburg.

[50] In DHI Moscow: *Vorträge zum 18. Jahrhundert* No. 6, 2010.

[51] The State Privy Council was a senior advisory body of the Russian Empire in 1726–1730 which consisted of seven or eight people. Though it was founded by the empress Catherine I as an advisory body, it in fact decided the most important matters of state.

[52] When Peter wed Catherine in 1712, their daughters Anna (who later married the Duke of Holstein) and Elizabeth

(the future empress Elizabeth Petrovna) were then 4 and 2 years old respectively, and even attended at their parents' wedding.

[53] D. A. Korsakov, *Botsarenie imperatritsy Anny Ivanovny* [The Ascension of Empress Anna Ivanovna], 1880, Kazan.

[54] Yakov Gordin, *Mezh rabstvom i svobodoy* [Between Slavery and Freedom], 1994, Saint Petersburg: Lenizdat.

[55] The Prussian envoy Mardefeld reported to his government that all of Russia (by which meant, of course, the aristocracy gathered in Moscow) wanted to limit absolute monarchy, but they could not agree on how to do so. "There is a countless multitude of factions, and although everything is peaceful now, things might explode," the Spanish ambassador De Liria wrote from Moscow in January. "Here in the streets and homes one hears only talk of the English constitution and the rights of the English parliament," wrote a secretary at the French embassy secretary. Ambassadors reported that some in Moscow wanted a constitution like Holland's, while others wanted a parliament like England's, a third faction wanted a republic governed by the aristocracy like in Poland, and still others took Sweden as their example (see A. M. Burovsky, *Nesostoyavshaya Rossiya* [Russia Frustrated], 2003, Moscow.)

[56] The Manifesto on Freedom of the Nobility, the short name of Peter III's decree of February 18 (March 1), 1762 "On granting liberty and freedom to the Russian nobility", marked the first time in the history of Russia that noblemen were exempt from mandatory 25-year civil and military service, and they could retire and travel abroad freely. However, at the request of the government they had to serve in the armed forces during wartime, which meant they had to return to Russia to avoid the threat of their land being confiscated.

[57] In the first half of Catherine the Great's reign, Count Panin was Russia's head of foreign affairs.

[58] M. A. Fonvizin, *Politicheskaya zhizn' v Rossii* [Political Life in Russia], 4th edition, 1907.

[59] From D. I. Fonvizin's collected works in two volumes, 1974, Moscow and Leningrad.

[60] The synod (from Greek *synodos* 'assembly, council') was the highest directing authority in the Russian Orthodox Church for several centuries.

[61] The deputies came from an incredibly wide array of backgrounds. Laws were to be

debated by generals from Saint Petersburg and Maris from Kazan, peasants and merchants, Orthodox priests and Muslims. At one of the meetings, Dmitri Sechenov, a member of the Holy Synod and metropolitan of Novgorod, sat next to Anyuk Ishelin, the representative of the unchristianized Kazan Chuvash, who had a poor command or Russian — editor.

[62] On January 17, 1895 Nicholas II received representatives of the *zemstvo* assemblies and the cities in order to ascertain their mood. The tsar and *zemstvo* assemblies did not see eye to eye. — editor

To Chapter 5

[63] George F. Kennan, *The Marquis. de Custine and his "Russia in 1839"*, 1971, Princeton: Princeton University Press.

[64] Richard Pipes, "Rossia pri starom rezhime" [Russia Under the Old Regime] in *Nezavisimaya Gazeta*, 1993, Moscow.

[65] A. Alekseeva, *Istoriya inakomysliya v SSSR: Noveyshiy period* [The History of Dissidents in the USSR: Recent Times], 1984, Vermont: Khronika

[66] A. Avtorkhanov, *Imperiya Kremlya: Sovetsky tip knolonializma* [The Kremlin's Empire: The Soviet Form of Colonialism], 1988, Franfurt: Posev.

[67] O. Subtel'ny, "Rozpad imperii ta utvorennya natsional'nyx derzhav: vypadok Ukrainy" [The Fall of the Empire and the Creation of National States: The Case of Ukraine] in *Suchasnist'* No. 12, 1994.

[68] Hélène Carrère d'Encausse, *L'empire eclate* [The Shattered Empire], 1978, Paris: Flammarion.

[69] Anton Ivanovich Denikin (1872–1947) was a Russian military commander, a prominent political and social figure, a writer and war reporter. He was one of the most successful generals in the Russian Empire's army during World War I, and one of the major leaders of the White Army during the Russian Civil War.

[70] *Ekspert* No. 1, 2008.

[71] More precisely, they wanted to restore Russia to what it was in February 1917, with a Constituent Assembly and a democratic republic, but they also wanted a "united and indivisible Russia", i.e. within the borders of 1913.

[72] Baron Carl Gustaf Emil Mannerheim (1867–1951) was a Finnish military and political

figure, lieutenant-general in the Russian Empire army (April 25, 1917), calvary general in the Finnish army (March 7, 1918), field marshal (May 19, 1933), and honorary marshal of Finland (June 4, 1942), regent of the Kingdom of Finland from December 12, 1918 to June 26, 1919, and president of Finland from August 4, 1944 to March 11, 1946.

[73] Alexander Vasilyevich Kolchak (1874–1920) was a Russian scientist and oceanographer, one of the foremost Arctic researchers of the late 19th and early 20th centuries, a military and political figure, fleet commander, member of the Imperial Russian Geographical Society (1906), admiral, (1918), commander-in-chief of the White Army, and self-declared supreme leader of Russia (1918–1920).

[74] A. I. Denikin, *Kto spas sovetskuyu vlast' ot gibeli* [Who Saved Soviet Rule from Destruction?], 1991, Moscow: Studiya TRITE and Russian Archives, p. 7.

[75] From the anthology *Rossiya mezhdu Evropoy i Aziey: evraziysky soblazn* [Russia Between Europe and Asia: The Attraction to Eurasianism], 1993, Moscow: Nauka.

[76] Apparently these instructions were only for mountain men serving in the tsar's personal guard. And who was this warrant officer Tuganov?

[77] Karamzin (1766–1826) was an eminent historian and literary figure in the period of sentimentalism, sometimes called the Russian Sterne. He was responsible for a 12-volume history of Russia, one of the first such works.

[78] Interview with the magazine *Ekspert* No. 1, 2008.

[79] ibid.

[80] It is generally believed that Russians today are quite different in terms of their physiognomy from the way that the Slavs of the early Kiev state looked. They have been affected by an admixture of Tatar, Cuman, and especially Finno-Ugrian blood. This paleness that is uncharacteristic for "classic" Slavs of the times of Vladimir the Red Sun, along with wider cheekbones and light-coloured eyes, came from the native inhabitants of what would become Muscovy.

[81] *Istoricheskie pesni* [Songs from History], 1955, Moscow: Khudlitizdat, p. 7.

[82] A. A. Kizevetter, "Evraziistvo" [Eurasianism], *Filosofskie nauki* [Philosophical Studies], 1991 (No. 12), p. 34.

NOTES

[83] G. V. Bernadsky, *Nachertanie russkoy istorii* [Traces of Russian History], 2000, Saint Petersburg, p. 170–171.

[84] The kurultai was a political and military council of ancient Mongol and Turkic chiefs and khans.

[85] S. Snezhko, "Moskva-Kazan': tisyacheletie spustya" [Moscow and Kazan: A Millennium Later], www.pravaya.ru, August 22, 2005.

[86] ibid.

[87] This era is depicted in the classic historical film *Braveheart*. Bruce leads the combined forces of the Scots against the English after the suppression of the uprising led by Mel Gibson, sorry, by William Wallace.

[88] "Gordon" in *Bol'shaya sovetskaya entsiklopediya* [Great Soviet Encyclopedia], 3rd edition, 1972, Moscow, Vol. 7, p. 79.

[89] Their descendants include barons Wrangel, Kotzebue, Krusenstern, Middendorf, Meyndorf and many, many others. — editor.

[90] Vladimir Kabuzan, *Emigratsiya i reemigratsiya v Rossii v XVIII — nachale XX veka* [Emigration and Re-Immigration in Russia from the 18th to the early 20th centuries], 1998, Moscow.

[91] It's their choice, no one has to love us. But just consider that the number of Buryats has grown by twelve times since the 17th century, while the number of Mongols has grown by only five.

[92] In 1608 the embassy of the taisha, as their ruler was known, was received by the Russian tsar Vasili IV. His government accepted the Kalmyks into the Russia state. The process of their entry into Russia was complete in 1657. Initially the migratory Kalmyks were given land along the Irysh. Gradually they settled along the lower Volga in the area in which they live today. From 1664 to 1771 there was a Kalmyk Khanate head by a khan, and later by a representative of the tsar. According to a rough estimate, the number of Kalmyks who chose to become Russian subjects was 270 thousand.

[93] The Uyghurs founded several states of their own. For several centuries the Eastern Turkestan was ruled by the Uyghurs, but in 1760 they were conquered by the Manchu rulers of China. — editor.

[94] Numbers as high as 100,000 or 120,000 are also claimed, but these are less believable. — editor

[95] *Sbornik dogovorov s drugimi gosudarstvami, 1856–1917* [Collection of Treaties with Other States, 1856–1917], 1952, p. 168–169.

[96] E. K. Meyendorff, *Putshestvie iz Orenburga v Bukharu* [Journey from Orenburg to Bukhara], 1975, Moscow, p. 145.

[97] ibid.

[98] According to various sources, the total number of North Caucasian peoples who fled from their homelands range from 500,000 to 1.5 million. Today 80% of Circassians live outside of Russia. The Russian Circassians call this event the Exodus and mark its anniversary every year. It is seen as a deeply tragic event. Turkey "assisted" its coreligionists and allies by sending old boats, a third of which sank. Turkey settled the Circassians on barren land and in an unfamiliar climate, and many died trying to return to Russian. — editor

[99] In practice, of course, people sometimes treated those first-generation converts with suspicion. An old Russian proverb says "A baptized Jew is like a pardoned thief." But let me emphasize, officially once a Jew converted to Orthodox Christianity, he received full rights as a citizen of the Russian Empire. From the second generation no one remembered any Jewish past.

[100] Many Jews returned to Russia after the end of tsarist rule. Figures vary around 100,000 to 300,000 people. — editor

[101] A. V. Yastrebov, *Repressii narodov SSSR: posledstviya tragedii* [Repression of Peoples in the USSR: The Consequences of the Tragedy], 2007, Samara: GUSO DDN.

To Chapter 6

[102] Richard Henning. *Terrae Incognitae*, Vols. 1–4, 1944, Leiden: Brill.

[103] M. V. Lomonosov, *Drevnyaya rossiyskaya istoriya ot nachala russkogo naroda do konchiny velikogo knyazya Yaroslava Pervogo ili do 1054 goda* [Ancient Russian History from the Beginnings of the Russian People to the Death of the Great Prince Yaroslav I or 1054], Saint Petersburg, 1766.

[104] B. A. Rybakov, *Gerodotova Skifiya* [Cynthia in Herodotus], 1975, Moscow: Nauka.

[105] The main subject of this tale is the unsuccessful campaign in 1185 of the Russian princes led by Igor Svyatoslavich, price of Novgorod-Seversk, against the Cumans. The tale was written at the end of the 12th century, soon after the events it describes (which is usually dated to 1185,

occasionally one or two years later). It is imbued with motifs of Slavic folk poetry and pagan mythology, and in its artistic language and literary significance it is among the greatest achievements of Russian medieval epic.

[106] I. Gralya. «Motivy «Orshanskogo triumfa» v Yagellonskoy propaganda» [Motifs of the "Triumph at Orsha" in Jagiellonian Propaganda] in *Problemy otechestvennoy istorii i kul'tury perioda feodaliszma: chteniya pamyati* [Issues of National History and Culture of the Feudal Period: A Reading of the Sources] ed. V. B. Korbina, 1992, Moscow, p. 46–50.

[107] "Pervaya voyna Rossii i Evropy: Materialy kruglogo stola" [The First War of Russia and Europe: Materials from the Round Table] in *Rodina* [Motherland] No. 12, 2004.

[108] The position of general of the Russian (Muscovite) army had existed since 1617

[109] Ya. G. Ustryalov, collected works in 3 volumes, 1997, Moscow, Vol. 1, pp. 328–329.

[110] Michel Lesur, *Des progrès de la puissance russe, depuis son origine jusqu'au commencement du XIXe siècle*, 1812, Paris.

[111] Extract from General Pelet's notes in *Chtenia imperatorskogo obshchestva istorii drevnostey* [Readings of the Imperial Society of Ancient History], 1872.

[112] Incidentally, Kutuzov begged Alexander I not to enter Europe, but the Russian army under the emperor's command to fulfill "the faithful duty of an ally" went into Europe to finish Napoleon off. The result of the Paris campaign and the drastic weakening of France was not simply an enormous debt for the Russian officers' corps, but geopolitically also the unification of Germany. Thus there was now a strong new player on the European scene, plus Britain gained a great deal more power.

[113] *Napoleon v Rossii glazami russkikh* [Napoleon in Russia through the Eyes of Russians], 2004, Moscow: Zakharov, p. 161.

[114] E. N. Tarle, *Napoleon*, 1956, Moscow.

[115] A. S. Pushkin, Letter to P. A. Vyazemsky of June 1, 1831 in his collected works in 10 volumes, 1949, Moscow and Leningrad, Vol. 10.

Dear Reader,

Thank you for purchasing this book.

We at Glagoslav Publications are glad to welcome you, and hope that you find our books to be a source of knowledge and inspiration.

We want to show the beauty and depth of the Slavic region to everyone looking to expand their horizon and learn something new about different cultures, different people, and we believe that with this book we have managed to do just that.

Now that you've got to know us, we want to get to know you. We value communication with our readers and want to hear from you! We offer several options:

- Join our Book Club on Goodreads, Library Thing and Shelfari, and receive special offers and information about our giveaways;
- Share your opinion about our books on Amazon, Barnes & Noble, Waterstones and other bookstores;
- Join us on Facebook and Twitter for updates on our publications and news about our authors;
- Visit our site www.glagoslav.com to check out our Catalogue and subscribe to our Newsletter.

Glagoslav Publications is getting ready to release a new collection and planning some interesting surprises — stay with us to find out!

Glagoslav Publications
Office 36, 88-90 Hatton Garden
EC1N 8PN London, UK
Tel: + 44 (0) 20 32 86 99 82
Email: contact@glagoslav.com

Glagoslav Publications Catalogue

- *The Time of Women* by Elena Chizhova
- *Sin* by Zakhar Prilepin
- *Hardly Ever Otherwise* by Maria Matios
- *The Lost Button* by Irene Rozdobudko
- *Khatyn* by Ales Adamovich
- *Christened with Crosses* by Eduard Kochergin
- *The Vital Needs of the Dead* by Igor Sakhnovsky
- *METRO 2033* (Dutch Edition) by Dmitry Glukhovsky
- *METRO 2034* (Dutch Edition) by Dmitry Glukhovsky
- *A Poet and Bin Laden* by Hamid Ismailov
- *Asystole* by Oleg Pavlov
- *Kobzar* by Taras Shevchenko
- *White Shanghai* by Elvira Baryakina
- *The Stone Bridge* by Alexander Terekhov
- *King Stakh's Wild Hunt* by Uladzimir Karatkevich
- *Depeche Mode* by Serhii Zhadan
- *Saraband Sarah's Band* by Larysa Denysenko
- *Herstories*, An Anthology of New Ukrainian Women Prose Writers
- *Watching The Russians* (Dutch Edition) by Maria Konyukova
- *The Hawks of Peace* by Dmitry Rogozin
- *The Grand Slam and Other Stories* (Dutch Edition) by Leonid Andreev

More coming soon…

www.ingramcontent.com/pod-product-compliance
Lightning Source LLC
LaVergne TN
LVHW041954060526
838200LV00002B/11